In our times

Prentice-Hall, Inc., *Englewood Cliffs, New Jersey*

NORMAN L. ROSENBERG
Macalester College

EMILY S. ROSENBERG
Macalester College

JAMES R. MOORE
Hofstra University

In our times
America Since World War II

Library of Congress Cataloging in Publication Data

ROSENBERG, NORMAN L (date)
  In our times.

  1. United States—History—1945– I. Rosenberg,
Emily S., (date) joint author. II. Moore, James R.,
joint author. III. Title.
E741.R667   973.92   75-35533
ISBN 0-13-453613-4

Prentice-Hall International, Inc., *London*
Prentice-Hall of Australia Pty. Limited, *Sydney*
Prentice-Hall of Canada, Ltd., *Toronto*
Prentice-Hall of India Private Limited, *New Delhi*
Prentice-Hall of Japan, Inc., *Tokyo*
Prentice-Hall of Southeast Asia Pte. Ltd., *Singapore*

To our parents

Joe and Dorothea Rosenberg
Albert and Helen Schlaht
Ray and Wilma Moore

Contents

For several decades, American history teachers and texts have used the Civil War to mark the midpoint of the American experience. Courses in "modern America" have concentrated on the twentieth century or, perhaps, on the period since World War I. As America passes its bicentennial year, however, our historical calendar—and our curriculums—are already undergoing considerable revision. To educate students of the future (increasing numbers of whom will have been born after 1960), the period since World War II must be accorded greater emphasis than it has received in the past. Indeed, to most college students of the 1970s, the cold war may appear as distant as the Civil War; Joseph and Eugene McCarthy, Henry and George Wallace may seem devilish inventions of the writers of multiple-choice exams rather than important demarcations of our political spectrum. This book results, in large measure, from our experiments with courses in America since 1945 and from our recognition of the unique problems arising from this area of study.

In Our Times is designed to meet the need for a textual account of postwar America. Its length makes it ideally suited for use either as the final book in a survey course or as a core text in a class on America since 1945. Although any attempt to interpret a period so recently passed into history invariably contains hazards—as well as delights—the task must be begun. Naturally, not everyone will agree with our selection of subjects, much less with every interpretive judgment. But differences of perspective should not be a drawback to the teaching of recent history. We hope that the book can stimulate classroom debate, not end it; it is a tentative view of the last quarter century, not a definitive account. Emily and Norman Rosenberg have prepared a selection of primary readings, *Postwar America: Readings and Reminiscences*, which provides students with additional perspectives on the complex issues of the era.

In Our Times contains an unusually broad coverage of issues, a diversification of subject matter which we believe will enhance its appeal to students. Going beyond a conventional chronology of politics and diplomacy, it explores socioeconomic developments which have often had a more formative influence on our age. The baby boom, developments in popular culture, the rise of conglomerates, and patterns of land use are examples of subjects often neglected in other texts which are discussed in this book. We have tried to be thorough without being

Preface

encyclopedic; we have sought to be colorful and illustrative without being simply anecdotal; and, above all, we have tried to tie these years together in interpretive themes rather than simply to relate events in chronological order. Despite the multiple authorship of the book (Emily and Norman Rosenberg collaborated on chapters 1, 2, 3, 5, 7, and 8; James Moore contributed chapters 4, 6, and 9), we have closely coordinated themes and writing styles to produce a cohesive volume.

We would like to thank Guadalupe Lara and Maria Williams for their help as typists; special thanks should go to Albert Schlaht for his editorial assistance. Our editors at Prentice-Hall, Brian Walker and Carolyn Davidson, have always been cooperative and helpful while maintaining a critical eye.

The war was over! Japan had surrendered! At seven in the evening on September 6, 1945, President Harry S. Truman made the official announcement. Across the country people began to celebrate the end of World War II. Outside the White House, a crowd that had been waiting all day struck up the chant, "We want Harry, we want Harry." The President appeared, said a few words, and left, only to be called back twice more by repeated shouts. Finally, he sank into a chair and expressed the universal sentiment: "I'm glad that it's over."

Pressing problems and hard decisions did not end with the war. Postwar reconstruction and the development of a cold war between the United States and the Soviet Union kept international affairs in a state of perpetual crisis.

A War-shattered World

Before World War II Europeans believed that they occupied the center of progress, civilization, and world power. London and Paris set the trends in world culture, held the reins of government for colonial peoples throughout the globe, and provided financial institutions for the business of far-flung empires. But World War II, coming only two decades after the tremendous financial strain of World War I, dramatically altered Europe's position. The extravagant costs of the long struggle left the nations of Europe—both victor and vanquished—exhausted and bankrupt. As Europeans spent their military and economic strength in what some historians have called a European civil war, their grasp

1

The world's superpower

over colonized areas weakened. Worldwide fighting strengthened local nationalist movements and whetted tastes for independence and self-determination. Revolution, a child of political and economic instability, threatened to dismember the great European empires and to create a host of new and unstable nations in Asia and Africa.

As the old order of European dominance and colonialism disintegrated, few dared to predict what would happen after the war. Cordell Hull, Franklin D. Roosevelt's Secretary of State, warned that "the people of many countries will be starving . . . homeless . . . their factories and mines destroyed; their roads and transport wrecked. . . . Disease will lurk everywhere. In some countries confusion and chaos will follow the cessation of hostilities." Hull advised that "victory must be followed by swift and effective action to meet these pressing human needs."

It fell to America to supply the blueprint for a postwar order and to provide the "swift and effective action." Untouched by battle, enriched by wartime profits, and free from scarcity, instability, or serious left-wing challenges, the United States emerged as victor of the victors. With much of the world in its debt, America became the undisputed superpower. And American leaders were ready to use this power in postwar diplomacy. The supposed folly of interwar isolationism and the "lessons" of appeasement had turned many American policymakers into internationalists. Throughout the war, they planned for postwar reconstruction.

An architect of American policy, Undersecretary of State Dean Acheson (later Truman's Secretary of State), entitled his memoirs of this period *Present at the Creation*. The title was revealing. It reflected Americans' belief that they would have to construct a new world order. It also displayed confidence—even arrogance—in their ability to shape events. To policymakers like Acheson, forming a postwar settlement would involve little give-and-take diplomacy; it would be primarily an act of creation, a monumental American-directed effort affecting the well-being of future generations.

The American Vision

How did American policymakers envision the postwar world? Drawing upon tradition, they focused on two articles of faith deeply rooted in the American past: free trade and federalism.

A trading nation with a dynamic, expanding economy, America had always opposed barriers which restricted the free flow of its trade and investment. During the depression decade of the 1930s, Americans uneasily watched as economic restrictions threatened to close large parts of the world to their businessmen: Great Britain moved toward an "imperial preference" system that placed nations outside of the British empire at a commercial disadvantage; Japan's expansionist leaders threatened to create a closed economic sphere in Asia; German fascism reached out to encompass new sources of raw materials. Americans hoped to reverse such trends in the postwar world. They believed that unhampered commerce brought peace, while economic restriction—such as excessive tariffs, preferential commercial arrangements, and currency inconvertibility—bred jealousy and war. "If we could get a freer flow of trade," Cordell Hull wrote, "the living standards of all countries might rise, thereby eliminating the economic dissatisfaction that breeds war." While ushering in prosperity and peace, free trade would, not incidentally, also enhance United States influence worldwide because of America's dominant financial position. In planning a postwar world, as in most other endeavors, ideology and self-interest dovetailed.

Since the time of Woodrow Wilson, Americans had also periodically sought to apply principles of representative federalism to international relations. Many Americans felt that their country's refusal to join the League of Nations after World War I had contributed to the breakdown of peace in 1939, and during World War II Roosevelt revived that Wilsonian dream. This time, the idea commanded more domestic support. The creation of a world body, such as the United Nations, became one cornerstone of America's plan for lasting peace.

Why did Americans place so much hope in a multinational body? The notion that a free exchange of ideas promoted understanding, compromise, and consensus had been a persistent American belief. Americans believed that under their constitution representative bodies forged the diverse interests of individual states into a unified national policy, and except for the Civil War, this federal system had functioned fairly successfully. Americans understandably felt that a similar federal arrangement, with modification, might also work on a grander scale. Influential Americans became convinced that internationalism would serve, not undermine, national interests. Behind this conviction lay certain assumptions: that international conflicts often stemmed from breakdowns in communication, that free debate would produce a consensus behind the most convincing argument, and that the American point of view would invariably triumph in an open forum. A representative world assembly, policymakers believed, would provide a means of moderating tensions and building a world community under the aegis of the United States, Britain, France, and the Soviet Union. Working through an international body, these powers would become the collective guarantors of postwar peace.

American postwar plans sounded selfless and impartial. Free trade and an open forum for debate appeared to give everyone an equal chance and to set aside narrow nationalism. But critics of American policy claimed that free trade and international assemblies were, in fact, instruments to advance American hegemony; that Americans used internationalist rhetoric only to camouflage self-interest and desire for world domination.

Did American policy serve the world or itself? Could it do both? These questions have formed the basis for many of the postwar dilemmas in American foreign policy. They have also been central to interpreting the cold war which developed between America and the Soviet Union. In the immediate postwar period, few American observers doubted that their country's policy was righteous and benign, but a newer generation of analysts, writing mostly after the debacle of Vietnam, severely criticized an America which tended to identify the world's well-being with its own. America's role in the postwar world—benevolent giant or avaricious colossus—promises to remain a great problem of historical interpretation.

Reconstructing an International Economic System

Secretary of State Cordell Hull made America's economic position clear: it expected equal access to trade and raw materials in the postwar world. As a condition for receiving lend-lease assistance from the United States, Allied nations had to promise to work toward the "elimination of all forms of discriminatory treatment in international commerce." And in July 1944, representatives from forty-four countries gathered at Bretton Woods to work out a postwar economic settlement. While they did not adopt every American proposal, the Bretton Woods delegates put together a system generally reflective of American goals.

Stable monetary exchange rates and unrestricted convertibility among the world's currencies were essential to free-flowing trade and investment. The delegates consequently created the International Monetary Fund (IMF) and charged it with maintaining a stable international system of exchange with each national currency convertible into any other at a fixed rate. A country could alter its exchange rate (that is, adjust the value of its money in relation to other currencies) only by agreement with the IMF. The architects of the IMF hoped that the system would combat the economic nationalism of the 1930s and believed that it would forge an interdependent world economy which would contribute to peace. The system of exchange rates did provide the foundation for unparalleled growth and prosperity in the developed nations of the world.

The delegates to Bretton Woods also set up an International Bank for Reconstruction and Development, now called the World Bank. This institution was to encourage loans for postwar economic recovery. Loans would help restore war-ruined economies and bring resumption of normal trading patterns; financial stabilization would also help curb radical political movements which fed on economic discontent. Since its creation, the World Bank has been dominated by American capital and headed by an American director. It gained its most prestigious head when Robert McNamara, former Secretary of Defense under Presidents John F. Kennedy and Lyndon B. Johnson, assumed command in 1967.

United States support for the World Bank stemmed not only from a desire to stabilize and assist needy nations, but also from the pragmatic realization that America's trade would suffer unless other countries possessed the money to buy its products. In addition, the World Bank advanced American interests by promising to foster private investment. The bank would participate in or guarantee private American loans made in foreign nations. America was by far the richest nation in the postwar world, and the bank helped many Americans invest their excess capital around the globe. The outflow of American investment reduced the pressures toward runaway inflation at home and greatly increased America's financial holdings abroad. Americans believed that the World Bank served world reconstruction and America's domestic well-being equally well.

The Bretton Woods agreements stabilized the international economy and helped revive trade and investment. They helped sustain America's postwar economic predominance, and the dollar became the kingpin of international finance. Although by the early 1970s strains began to appear in the postwar system, for a quarter of a century the Bretton Woods agreements had provided the foundation for a dynamic and comparatively well-functioning international economy.

Creation of the United Nations

During the second world war, American officials revived Woodrow Wilson's idea of a League of Nations. Americans proposed an international body which would mediate disputes and create a multinational force to deter potential aggressors. They hoped to substitute collective security for old-style balance-of-power diplomacy.

At Dumbarton Oaks in August 1944 and at San Francisco in April 1945, the wartime allies hammered out the structural details of the United Nations (UN). They established a General Assembly, in which all member nations had one vote; a Security Council composed of five permanent members (the United States, Great Britain, France, the Soviet Union, and Nationalist China) and six rotating temporary members; a Secretariat to handle day-to-day business; and an Economic and Social Council comprised of committees for worldwide social rehabilitation and economic development.

The Security Council, which according to the charter had the "primary responsibility for the maintenance of international peace and security," consisted of the major victors in World War II. The inclusion of China, at American insistence, always seemed incongruous. At the time of the UN charter, China possessed an unpopular and corrupt government led by Chiang Kai-shek. Many observers doubted that Chiang could maintain control at home, much less play an active role in international affairs. But the inclusion of Nationalist China represented the Roosevelt administration's desire to turn China into a friendly Pacific power which would fill the vacuum left by Japan's defeat. In 1949, however, the Nationalist government fled to the small island of Formosa, and an unfriendly communist regime headed by Mao Tse-tung came to power. Under Mao, China did become a major power, but Nationalists continued to sit on the Security Council. This discrepancy between the realities of world power and Security Council membership contributed to the weakness of the United Nations.

The provision for veto power within the Security Council also undermined the UN's effectiveness. The charter provided that each permanent member of the Security Council could exercise an absolute veto over UN decisions. None of the great powers would have joined the UN without this means of safeguarding their national interests. But the veto provision meant that the United Nations could act only when all five permanent members agreed, and unanimity was rare in the postwar world. The UN's strongest action, sponsoring a military force to assist South Korea in 1950, was approved during the absence of the Soviet Union's delegate.

If the Security Council did not always fulfill the peace-keeping role that its founders envisioned, other UN bodies did serve useful functions. The General Assembly provided a forum for articulating national positions on various issues; it was a barometer of international tensions and a gauge of shifting positions on various issues. It also provided a platform for smaller nations whose viewpoints might not otherwise be heard. In some respects the most successful parts of the UN structure were the social and economic agencies, such as the World Health Organization (WHO) and the United Nations Educational, Scientific, and Cultural Organization (UNESCO). These organizations boosted UN prestige through their humanitarian programs. The UN did not fulfill the hopes of American internationalists during the 1940s, but neither was it a failure.

THE ONSET OF THE COLD WAR

The Allies Fall Out

The political and economic order American leaders had planned depended upon cooperation among the great powers. But divisions within the wartime Grand Alliance eventually undermined the strength of the United Nations and the liberal, open world which American policymakers had envisioned.

Throughout the war, tensions had existed between the Soviet Union and the other allies. The greatest disputes centered around the issue of wartime strategy. British planners, eventually supported by the United States, favored peripheral campaigns against Germany, first into French North Africa and then up through Sicily and Italy. Soviet Premier Joseph Stalin denounced these Anglo-American offensives because they delayed the opening of a second front to the west of Germany and forced the Soviet Union to bear the main thrust of German power. Stalin came to believe that his allies were carving spheres of influence in Northern Africa, Italy, and the Middle East, while allowing Germany and the Soviet Union to exhaust each other. The long delay in opening a second front, Stalin reasoned, indicated that capitalist hostility toward Soviet communism was more important than the wartime alliance against Nazism.

The fierce fighting on the eastern front and the Soviet army's tremendous casualties helped shape Stalin's postwar policies. The Soviet leader wanted to eliminate the German menace that had repeatedly threatened his country and to create a buffer zone of friendly governments in Eastern Europe. While the Americans talked of eliminating spheres of influence (except in their own sphere, Latin America), Stalin viewed a pro-Soviet zone in neighboring Eastern Europe as vital to his country's national interest. In this he had at least some support from Great Britain. At a meeting in 1944, Winston Churchill and Stalin reached an informal agreement: Churchill would grant Soviet predominance in Rumania and Bulgaria in return for British preeminence in Greece. Roosevelt refused to endorse this arrangement, but the incident reflected the allies' disparate feelings regarding spheres of influence.

In the end, the course of battle determined the postwar power situation in Europe. Soviet troops marched into Berlin from the East as

American forces advanced through Germany from the West, and the separate zones of occupation eventually hardened into a divided Germany. In 1949 military areas administered by France, England, and the United States became the Federal Republic of West Germany and the Soviet zone became the Democratic Republic of East Germany. The nationality of the occupation forces likewise determined the destiny of the countries surrounding Germany. Anglo-American influence was strong in France, Italy, Greece, and the Middle East; Soviet authority predominated in Eastern Europe.

Stalin largely ignored his pledge at the Yalta Conference of early 1945 to hold free elections in Eastern Europe. Pro-Soviet governments came to power in Rumania, Hungary, Bulgaria, Albania, Poland, and eventually Czechoslovakia. In Poland, Stalin reneged on specific assurances to include an Anglo-American–sponsored group in the new government, and communists took control. Despite British and American cries of betrayal, however, Polish communists, who had remained in their country and organized underground resistance to the Nazi occupiers, may well have had more popular support than the Anglo-American supporters who sat out the war in London as a government-in-exile.

To Stalin, a Soviet-dominated zone in Eastern Europe represented a minimal guarantee of future security. It seemed a just reward for having borne the brunt of Germany's force and for having suffered staggering casualties. (The Soviet Union lost more than ten times as many soldiers as the United States.) Stalin also recalled that Anglo-American commanders had not allowed Soviet participation in governments under their military influence. In Italy after Benito Mussolini's overthrow, for example, England and the United States had installed a rightist regime committed to purging any leftist or pro-Soviet sentiment.

Stalin may have regarded his Eastern European policy as defensive, but to the United States it appeared aggressive. The new Soviet satellite zone struck American policymakers as the same sort of closed sphere they had fought during the war. Republicans especially blamed President Roosevelt for failing to obtain stronger guarantees for Eastern Europe at the Yalta Conference and felt that he had betrayed the cause of democracy. Americans of Eastern European descent and others who had expected the war to open all of Europe to American trade and ideas began to view the Soviet Union as a new threat to peace. And Stalin's brutal, iron-handed repression of domestic dissent made him a convincing villain. Accustomed to thinking in terms of an evil and aggressive enemy, a growing number of Americans substituted the Soviets for the Germans as the new arch enemies. A former State Department official, William C. Bullitt, expressed this attitude: "The Soviet Union's assault upon the West is at about the stage of Hitler's maneuvering into Czechoslovakia." This analysis could have only one conclusion—that there should be no appeasement, no compromise with Soviet power.

Mounting Distrust

American–Soviet relations degenerated from an atmosphere of cooperation at Yalta in early 1945 to one of deep distrust by the end of the same year. Stalin's Eastern European policies provided the backdrop to this cooling of relations, but events in the United States also contributed to a hardening of attitudes.

Several months into his fourth term as president, Franklin D. Roosevelt died, and Americans discovered that a relatively unknown and inexperienced Missourian, Harry S. Truman, was their new leader. Truman lacked the cool self-confidence, the easy affability, the cosmopolitan world-view of his predecessor. He had not been close to the president and knew little of Roosevelt's policies or intentions. In attempting to form guidelines for his new administration, Truman quickly sided with those advisers who advocated a harder line against the Soviet Union. Setting a style for his successors, he began to talk tough to the Russians.

Truman and his advisers had two potent weapons in bargaining with Stalin. The first was atomic power. Even before Roosevelt's death, some advisers had suggested that the bomb might be an effective diplomatic lever. After demonstrating the horrible power of this weapon at Hiroshima and Nagasaki to bring Japan's rapid surrender, some officials believed that Stalin could no longer ignore American demands to open Eastern Europe. Truman also hoped that the Soviet's need for postwar economic assistance would bring Stalin into line. After the termination of Lend-Lease, Stalin requested additional aid to help rebuild Russia's war-damaged economy. But Truman's tough tone indicated that assistance would be contingent upon a change of Eastern European policy. Possessing overwhelming nuclear and economic power, Americans were in no mood to compromise.

Rather than forcing Stalin into accommodation, Truman's policy reinforced Stalin's apprehensions about Soviet security. Fearful of the strings America might attach to any economic aid package, he eased his country's difficulties in other ways: a new Five Year Plan to rebuild Soviet industry, and an expropriation of materials from occupied territories, particularly East Germany. Just as the United States had removed thousands of tons of military materials and scientific documents from West Germany, so the Soviet Union carried away whatever it could use—in some cases whole factories. More and more, Stalin closed the Soviet zone to Anglo-American influence.

Some Americans believed that Truman's hard line was at least partially responsible for Stalin's growing hostility. Secretary of Commerce Henry A. Wallace, for example, advocated a more cooperative attitude toward the Soviet Union and warned that the United States had everything to lose by "beating the tom-toms against Russia." In a speech in 1946 he pleaded that the United States "should recognize that we have no more business in the political affairs of Eastern Europe than Russia has in the political affairs of Latin America." Wallace argued that a secure and prosperous Russia would be more accommodating than a frightened and hungry one. But this view ran counter to Truman's foreign policy. Embarrassed by the public display of disunity within his administration, the president asked for Wallace's resignation.

From allies in a hot war, the United States and the Soviet Union had become enemies in a "cold war." In 1946 Stalin publicly expressed distrust of his capitalist allies. Their objections to Soviet policy in Eastern Europe, he believed, indicated their intention to crush socialism and isolate the Soviet regime. On the other side, Winston Churchill denounced Soviet policies, charging that Stalin had dropped an "iron curtain" across Europe. With the collapse of the wartime alliance, the world plunged into a period of bipolar politics in which America and the Soviet Union vied for influence worldwide.

Cold War Aid Programs

By 1947 the American government faced a dilemma. It had almost completed a period of rapid demobilization, and the public longed for the "normalcy" of peace. At the same time, government policymakers perceived Russia as a new aggressor and decided to adopt a hard line. Would the American Congress and public approve the appropriations which a strong anticommunist policy required?

By early 1947 the issue could no longer be postponed. A communist-backed revolution threatened the conservative regime in Greece, and Great Britain, which had previously considered Greece within its sphere of responsibility, announced that it could no longer provide economic and military assistance. The State Department wanted to grant extensive military aid to Greece, a move which would have established a precedent for America's entry into other areas as a replacement for European power. But the chances for such a commitment seemed slim. Senator Arthur Vandenberg correctly assessed the situation: "If Truman wants it he will have to go and scare hell out of the country."

Truman was equal to the task, and he set out to sell Congress and the public on the aid program and the cold-war viewpoint. A revolution in Greece, he explained, would lead to communist take-overs in other parts of Europe. Before a joint session of Congress in March 1947, the president advanced the Truman Doctrine. He explained that the struggle in Greece represented a conflict between two ways of life, one "distinguished by free institutions, representative government, free elections, guaranties of individual liberty, freedom of speech and religion, and freedom from political oppression." The other system relied upon "terror and oppression, a controlled press and radio, fixed elections, and the suppression of personal freedoms." By failing to act, Truman concluded, "we may endanger the peace of the world—and we shall surely endanger the welfare of our own Nation." These arguments helped bring a $400 million authorization to extend assistance, primarily military aid, to Greece and neighboring Turkey.

The rationale for the Truman Doctrine set the terms of international analysis for years to come and formed the core of a policy later called *containment*. The classic and most sophisticated statement of containment came in a 1947 article in *Foreign Affairs* written by George Kennan, a respected foreign service officer. Writing under the pseudonym "X," Kennan analyzed the Soviet Union's "expansive tendencies" and advocated a "firm and vigilant" application of counter-force to meet Soviet maneuvers until internal change in Russia moderated rivalries with the West.

In December 1947, the president again requested a strong commitment of economic aid—this time to European nations. Again Congress balked, but a pro-communist coup in neutralist Czechoslovakia convinced congressmen that Soviet aggression threatened Europe and that containment must be implemented. The new aid program—the Marshall Plan—passed by an overwhelming margin.

The Marshall Plan sprang not only from a genuine desire to alleviate human suffering but also from a very practical assessment of America's national interests. The entire economic and political system which American policymakers had arduously constructed in postwar conferences depended upon the economic revival of European nations. But European economies were faltering, and West Germany remained a weak and defeated nation. American leaders recognized that their own country's prosperity ultimately required a prosperous and stable Europe. In addition, as hostility toward the Soviet Union mounted, it seemed increasingly necessary to counter Soviet power with a strong, industrialized West Germany. Germany, the Nazi enemy which had once united capitalists and communists, now became the focal point of the cold war, ominously divided between the two competing camps. As Russia changed from ally to enemy, West Germany changed from enemy to ally. Germany would later provide the first real showdown in the cold war.

From the enunciation of the Truman Doctrine through the most troubled years of the cold war, the United States would continue to employ economic and military aid as a major weapon against instability. The money often brought needed assistance to poverty-ridden areas and contributed to boosting America's trade and investment abroad. American aid helped revitalize Europe. But if the policy was sometimes successful, it also frequently led to expensive or impossible commitments. While the Soviet Union took advantage of global postwar disruption by backing revolutionary and anticolonial movements, the United States tried to "contain" instability. Threats to the status quo became suspect, and nationalist movements in the "third world" were too often viewed solely as part of an international communist conspiracy. At a time when Europe's empires were breaking down, the United States moved into these power vacuums and often continued to back unpopular regimes. (Vietnam was the most tragic example.) Once the champion of social justice and the right of revolution, the United States increasingly pitted its might against any change which it did not control.

COLD WAR CRISES

The cold war grew more menacing during Truman's second term, and Dean Acheson, who became Secretary of State in 1949, tried to bring order to a disorderly world. He reorganized and enlarged the State Department, hoping to make it more efficient and productive. He called for a new approach to foreign affairs: broader perspectives, bolder actions, more centralization in planning and direction. Acheson, who liked to quote his predecessor General George C. Marshall's advice: "Don't fight the problem. Decide it!," never doubted the accuracy of his assessments or the morality of his decisions. He hoped that later generations would recognize the "truly heroic mold" of the Truman administration's reactions to cold war crises or, as the less polished chief of state put it, that Americans would realize that Harry Truman "done his damnedest."

The Berlin Crisis

By 1947 American policymakers had accepted the need to contain Soviet aggression by stabilizing Europe through economic assistance. The reestablishment of Germany as an industrial power and its reintegration into Europe's economy seemed essential for the continent's full recovery. Consequently, the United States, Great Britain, and France decided to merge their zones of occupation into one federal republic and to institute a program of economic rehabilitation. On June 18, 1948, the three powers announced a currency reform for West Germany.

The Soviet Union saw the strengthening of West Germany as a provocation. Stalin wanted Germany to remain weak and divided; he desired German reparations for war damage; and he sought to dismantle the country's industrial capacity, not to rebuild it. In retaliation for the West's actions, he closed off West Berlin, an Anglo-American–controlled sector of the capital city which was wholly within the Soviet zone.

Only one way remained into the blockaded city—by airplane. American planes began flying around the clock to deliver food, fuel, and medicine to the two and one-half million people in West Berlin. In Montana pilots practiced landings at a flight training center with an air corridor, runways, and navigational aids exactly duplicating those in Berlin. Assisted by the latest radar techniques, Operation Vittles, as the pilots dubbed the airlift, landed almost 13,000 tons of provisions during

United Press International

American C-47 transport planes discharge their vital food cargos at Templehof Airdrome in Berlin, after the Russians blockaded the city, refusing to allow land transport to bring supplies into the German capital.

its peak day. By the spring of 1949 the airlift was bringing as much into Berlin as water and rail had provided before the blockade. To underscore how seriously Americans viewed the crisis, Truman also reinstated the draft and sent two squadrons of B-29s to Great Britain. In the face of this commitment, the Soviet Union backed off. In May 1949 Stalin once again opened certain corridors of surface travel into West Berlin, and the city returned to its uneasy equilibrium. The divided city would remain a symbol and point of tension throughout the cold war.

During the year-long Berlin crisis, which had closely followed the communist coup in Czechoslovakia, the nations of Western Europe grew increasingly anxious about Soviet expansionism. With United States encouragement, Britain, France, Belgium, the Netherlands, and Luxembourg signed the Brussels Pact, pledging cooperation in economic and military matters. They also appealed for a stronger United States commitment to their security. Finally, in the spring of 1949, twelve nations, including the United States and the Brussels Pact countries, established the North Atlantic Treaty Organization (NATO). This collective-security pact provided that an attack against one of the signatories would be considered an attack against all and promised to encourage economic ties among the contracting nations. NATO laid the groundwork for America's long-lasting military presence in Western Europe and formed a pattern for later collective-security pacts, CENTO and SEATO, in other parts of the world. NATO, together with the Marshall Plan, brought Western Europe under America's economic and military umbrella.

The Chinese Revolution

Throughout World War II, civil war plagued China. The United States consistently supported the Nationalist government of Chiang Kai-shek, providing it with arms, money, advisers, and a prestigious position on the United Nations Security Council. Yet most American diplomats in Asia believed that Chiang's government could not last. Joseph Stilwell, who went to China in 1942 to organize its military effort against the Japanese, reported that Chiang was too corrupt and incompetent to gain wide support among the Chinese people. The communist forces under Mao Tse-tung were both more effective in fighting the Japanese and more popular with the peasants.

Statistical comparisons made Chiang's victory over the communists seem a sure thing: by 1947 he had twice the number of men under arms and three or four times the number of rifles. From V-J Day through 1948 the United States extended him a billion dollars in military aid and another billion in economic assistance. Yet these figures only measured his incompetence and lack of support. Despite American help, Chiang's armies rapidly lost ground; Chinese peasants flocked to the communist side, which promised land reform and popular government.

Realizing Chiang's limitations, American officials attempted to mediate between the opposing sides after World War II, but the effort failed. The United States government was left uncomfortably supporting Chiang at the very time that most officials came to believe his downfall inevitable. By the end of 1948 the director of the American military advisory group in China, Major-General David Barr, reported that "the military situation has deteriorated to the point where only the active participation of United States troops could effect a remedy." And this adviser "certainly [did] not recommend" allying with what he termed "the world's worst leadership" to attempt the impossible: regaining the enormous expanse of Chinese territory which Chiang had lost to the communists.

Early in 1949 the Nationalist government withdrew to the island of Formosa, leaving Mao Tse-tung in complete control of the mainland. To Secretary Acheson the turn of events was disturbing, but in a White Paper presented to the president he wrote that the situation in China was "beyond the control of the government of the United States." America's containment policy as yet applied principally to Europe, and policymakers recognized some realistic limits to their ability to shape world events. But the United States government was now trapped by its previous attempt to strengthen Chiang. Not wishing to harm the Nationalist cause, American officials had concealed the full extent of Chaing's unpopularity and ineptness. What seemed inevitable to officials knowledgeable about China looked like a sell-out to communism by Americans who viewed Chiang as the strong and respected leader of "free" China. By the time Chiang retreated, it was too late to reeducate the public. The news of China's "fall" hit America like a bombshell, and following swiftly upon this news came word that the Soviet Union had exploded a nuclear device. America had "lost" China and no longer had sole possession of the ultimate weapon.

The Anticommunist Crusade

The constant crises of 1949—Czechoslovakia, Berlin, China, and Russia's new bomb—were more than many Americans could rationally understand. The communist threat appeared to be everywhere; American power seemed in retreat. Many Republicans and some Democrats sought the source of America's problems not in the world at large but in traitors in their midst. The charge gained credibility when a former State

Department officer, Alger Hiss, was accused of passing government papers to the Soviet Union. The search for Soviet spy rings became the order of the day; Republican Senator William E. Jenner of Indiana charged that the Truman administration consisted of a "crazy assortment of collectivist cutthroat crackpots and Communist fellow-traveling appeasers." Acheson's assessment regarding China—that America could not control all world events—sounded to some like a new doctrine of appeasement, and many Republicans demanded Acheson's resignation. The cry for an all-out crusade against communism, including suppression of dissent at home and of revolution abroad, would affect American life and policy for years to come.

The international shocks of 1949 and the fire from Republican congressmen prompted senior officials in the State and Defense Departments to draw up a paper outlining foreign-policy assumptions and future strategy. The paper, called N.S.C. 68, was approved by the National Security Council and the president. In 1950 Acheson traveled throughout the country trying to regain his credibility as a tough anticommunist and preaching the assumptions upon which N.S.C. 68 was based. The report's logic eventually became the conventional wisdom of the cold war. According to N.S.C. 68, the Soviet Union was determined to stamp out freedom and dominate the world. Negotiation with the communists was futile, for they did not bargain in good faith. And there could be no valid distinction between national and world security. The United States could not, as Acheson put it, "pull down the blinds and sit in the parlor with a loaded shotgun, waiting." The country had to embark upon a massive military buildup at home and create "situations of strength" abroad, regardless of cost.

In his cold-war speeches, Acheson argued that freedom meant simply anticommunism. Those people who wanted to go from ally to ally "with political litmus paper testing them for true-blue democracy" were "escapists." Furthermore, domestic consensus served freedom while differences of opinion aided the enemy. The "fomenters of disunity" who advocated negotiation with the Soviets, Acheson explained, contributed to American weakness. Later observers, noting how often "freedom" was invoked to support dictators abroad and to suppress dissent at home, have suggested that language, and therefore communication, was one of the first serious casualties of the cold war.

Korea

In June 1950 the assumptions and fears articulated in N.S.C. 68 seemed to come alive: communist North Korea attacked South Korea. There was no evidence that Stalin had ordered the attack across the

Thirty-eighth Parallel or that he knew of it in advance, yet Americans still viewed the Korean conflict as a showdown with the Soviets and their "satellites." Using the same logic he had outlined in his Truman Doctrine for Greece and Turkey, the president announced that "if aggression is successful in Korea, we can expect it to spread through Asia and Europe to this hemisphere." One weak spot in the "free world" defense would start the "dominoes" falling.

In line with the new worldwide containment policy, Truman responded immediately. He gained United Nations support for an American-controlled defense of Syngman Rhee's South Korean regime (the Soviet delegation was boycotting the United Nations and could not exercise its veto); he also announced protection for Chiang Kai-shek's exiled regime in Formosa and ordered support of the French in maintaining their hold against communist-led nationalists in Vietnam. Assistance extended even to the Philippines to suppress leftist Huk rebels. In Europe more troops went to NATO, and a program for rearming West Germany was announced. The front line against communism lay everywhere, and America committed its power, prestige, and treasure as though they had no limits.

Americans were torn between two goals during the Korean war: simple containment (which would leave Korea divided), and roll-back (which would unite it totally under American influence). As long as South Korean and American troops were retreating southward early in the war, restoration of the Thirty-eighth Parallel boundary seemed victory enough. But when a regrouped force under General Douglas MacArthur landed at Inchon behind enemy lines and drove the North Koreans back from the Thirty-eighth Parallel, decisions became more complicated. Could MacArthur "liberate" North Korea, and would Russia and China intervene if he did? The president gave MacArthur authority to pursue the war in the north as long as it did not bring a wider war with China, but the general underestimated Chinese reaction. After crossing the Thirty-eighth Parallel American soldiers began to encounter Chinese "volunteers." Then, as American forces penetrated farther into North Korea and approached the border of China, the dam broke. Chinese troops streamed into Korea and sent MacArthur's armies reeling backward across the Thirty-eighth Parallel once again. This time, when MacArthur regrouped and began pushing northward, Truman ordered him to seek a negotiated settlement.

Truman's order provoked a dramatic clash between civilian and military authority. The general publicly opposed Truman's "limited war" and balked at his instructions. He pressed for a full-scale commitment to victory over North Korea, even over China, and claimed that this was America's chance to roll back communism in Asia. Truman, however, held to his position that a lengthy conflict in Korea would weaken America's defense posture in other, more vital areas. He viewed the Soviet Union as the real enemy, and believed a costly Asian land war would only play into Stalin's hands. In the face of MacArthur's challenge to presidential authority, Truman had only one choice: he removed the general from his command.

Those "Asia-firsters" who had excoriated Truman following Chiang Kai-shek's fall in China now had new ammunition and a popular martyr. They condemned the "no-win policy" against communism, and MacArthur returned home a hero. Telegrams demanding Truman's impeachment flooded the White House. Huge crowds greeted the general in San Francisco, Washington, and New York. A parade in New York on the general's behalf attracted seven and a half million people (compared to four million for Eisenhower at the end of World War II) and produced over three thousand tons of litter. George Gallup reported that only 29 percent of those polled supported President Truman's action against MacArthur.

The outpouring in favor of MacArthur, including a MacArthur-for-president boomlet, subsided quickly. Senate hearings on the general's dismissal convinced the public that most military strategists opposed a wider conflict in Asia, and few Americans wanted full-scale war. Admiration for MacArthur's military achievements remained, but Americans welcomed negotiation. When the next Republican nominee for president, General Dwight D. Eisenhower, promised to go to Korea and end the struggle, he received applause and votes. As Truman's presidency ended, the war in Korea had grown less intense and both sides had gathered around a conference table. Hammering out the details of a negotiated settlement (which eventually reestablished the Thirty-eighth Parallel division) would fall to the new Republican administration.

LONG-TERM TRENDS IN CONDUCTING FOREIGN POLICY: A LOOK TOWARD THE FUTURE

World War II vastly changed the United States government bureaucracy. Before the war the federal government employed about 800,000 civilians, 10 percent of whom were involved with national security; by the end of the war the figure had risen to nearly four million, with 75 percent working for national security agencies. Although the new government bureaus were designed to increase the efficiency of wartime operations, their sheer size and complexity often complicated decision-making. New photocopying techniques brought additional problems.

The "paper revolution," designed to assist interdepartmental communication, often beleaguered policymakers, burying both the important and the trivial under a mountain of duplicate copies.

The State Department, the agency traditionally responsible for creating and executing foreign policy, was transformed during the war. The department and its related agencies outgrew old quarters and, during the 1950s, expanded into twenty-nine buildings throughout Washington, D.C. In 1961, when all of these offices were finally brought together, it took eight stories covering a four-block area to house them. Before the war, a few men would meet in the secretary of state's office, discuss world problems, and set policy. By the end of the war, the cozy familiarity and easy communication had given way to faceless bureaucratic routine. Truman's secretary of state, Dean Acheson, once asked Cordell Hull, Franklin Roosevelt's secretary of state, to come by the department and meet the assistant secretaries. Hull declined, wryly commenting that he had never done well in crowds.

The cold war also helped swell the State Department's staff. In its new role as global superpower, the United States seemed to need a resident expert on every conceivable topic so that it could react quickly to a wide variety of situations. In this era of confrontation, the most casual decision could suddenly mushroom into a matter of major importance. In 1961, when a Far Eastern correspondent was pressing Robert Kennedy with the urgency of the situation in Vietnam, the president's brother shrugged him off, saying, "Vietnam . . . We have thirty Vietnams a day here." The remark underscored how rapidly a minor issue could take on major proportions. Contingency plans and position papers on seemingly obscure subjects had to be ready at all times.

The climate of the cold war delivered even stronger blows to the State Department's effectiveness. Mao's victory in China in 1949 outraged those Americans who believed that communism could never triumph on its own merits. A number of influential people were convinced that State Department officials must have sold out China, and pressure mounted to purge the "old China hands" who had advised against an open-ended commitment to Chiang Kai-shek. Throughout the 1950s, many seasoned diplomats lost influence to newer men who took a harder anticommunist line. The immediate suspicion which turned against anyone who questioned cold-war verities submerged healthy differences of opinion. The State Department became less involved in forming policies according to world realities and more caught up in interpreting the world according to a preestablished cold-war viewpoint. The consensus of the early and mid-1950s, in addition to attacks upon experienced diplomats, damaged the effectiveness, and ultimately the prestige and power, of the State Department.

19

Other agencies challenged the State Department's preeminence in international concerns. Before the war, nearly all foreign policy functions were centralized at State; after the war, other departments—especially Agriculture, Treasury, and Commerce, as well as independent agencies like the CIA—assumed responsibilities in foreign nations. Policymaking became a complex process involving many different bureaucracies, each with its experts and points of view.

Sometimes the plethora of agencies meant delay. In 1961, when President John Kennedy, facing what he viewed as a potential crisis, requested an immediate policy paper on British Guiana, he was told that "it would have to be drafted, and then it would have to move up through the various levels of the office of Inter-American Affairs. Then there would be clearances and concurrences—European Affairs, International Organization Affairs, Intelligence Research, Political Affairs. Then when it got up near the Secretary's level, there would be interagency clearances—the Pentagon, the Central Intelligence Agency, maybe Treasury or Commerce." The process would take a week or two. Little wonder that Kennedy tried to bypass conventional channels by placing McGeorge Bundy in a new position right in the White House, as special assistant on foreign affairs.

Overlapping jurisdictions sometimes even produced conflicting policies, particularly between the Central Intelligence Agency (CIA) and the State Department. The CIA grew out of the Office of Strategic Services (OSS), a wartime intelligence-gathering agency. After the war, the State Department, the armed services, and the FBI all sought to assume the functions of the OSS. As a compromise, the CIA was created as an independent agency under the new National Security Council. Although the CIA's finances and operations were kept secret, scholars have estimated that the agency rapidly surpassed the State Department both in number of employees and in budget. And personnel of the two departments frequently worked at cross-purposes. In Indonesia, Burma, and Costa Rica, to name just a few examples, CIA agents helped movements attempting to overthrow governments with which the State Department was dealing. American ambassadors in foreign lands often complained that their ignorance of their own country's clandestine activities undermined their prestige.

The Pentagon also became a powerful rival in handling foreign affairs. During the war, Roosevelt increasingly turned to the military for advice, and the Joint Chiefs of Staff, created in 1941, eroded the secretary of state's position as preeminent foreign policy expert. In the 1960s this trend continued. Secretary of Defense Robert McNamara, mastermind of Ford Motor Company's postwar reorganization, easily outmaneuvered Secretary of State Dean Rusk in bureaucratic power plays. Armed with ironclad self-confidence, detailed statistics, and convincing analyses, McNamara solidified the Pentagon's position, and the views of generals, rather than of civilians, tended to shape decisions regarding Vietnam.

The outflow of power from the postwar State Department stemmed from other causes as well. The Treasury Department's handling of international monetary policy impinged upon State Department territory. When President Richard Nixon, for example, sent Secretary of Treasury John Connally to negotiate with foreign nations in the wake of America's decision to devalue the dollar, many State Department regulars felt that Connally had neither the expertise in foreign matters nor the finesse which such delicate negotiations required. Nixon's reliance during his first term on his special assistant, Henry A. Kissinger, to shape America's major foreign policies also caused resentment in Foggy Bottom (the State Department's nickname). Building on a trend begun under Kennedy and Bundy, Kissinger and his staff often ignored State Department officials and circumvented traditional channels. The office of special assistant did facilitate the conduct of foreign policy by cutting through red tape, but the creation of yet another authority and staff could, in the end, contribute only to duplication and inefficiency.

Some elements of foreign policy even flowed out of the government altogether. Although private businessmen in foreign lands had always influenced international relations, the giant United States–based multinational corporations which mushroomed in the postwar era exerted an unparalleled impact. The turbulent international monetary situation of the late 1960s, for example, was exacerbated by gold speculation of large companies interested more in their profits than in the stability of the American dollar. In addition, price negotiations between the consortium of oil companies and representatives of oil-producing nations had long-range consequences which surpassed most official State Department dealings. Some companies even conducted their own foreign policies. International Telephone and Telegraph carried out an unsuccessful campaign of pressure to prevent leftist Dr. Salvador Allende from becoming president of Chile and then joined nationalized copper companies to work for his ouster. Noting the financial strength of multinational companies, some scholars have begun to wonder whether these essentially unregulated entities might not be a wholly new force in international relations, ultimately rivaling nation-states in their power and developing company interests which could surpass national loyalties.

BIBLIOGRAPHY

Two primary sources which provide a good beginning for understanding the development of the cold war are George F. Kennan, "Sources of Soviet Conduct," *Foreign Affairs* 25 (July 1947), pp. 566–82 (published under the pseudonym "Mr. X"); and Dean Acheson's memoirs, *Present at the Creation* (1969). An example of the standard view which blamed the Soviet Union for the cold war is Herbert Feis, *From Trust to Terror: The Onset of the Cold War, 1945–1950* (1970). Revisionist historians, who place at least equal or preeminent responsibility on the United States, include Walter LaFeber, *America, Russia, and the Cold War, 1945–1971* (1972); Gabriel Kolko, *The Politics of War: The World and United States Foreign Policy, 1943–1945* (1968); Gabriel Kolko and Joyce Kolko, *The Limits of Power* (1973); Gar Alperovitz, *Atomic Diplomacy: Hiroshima and Potsdam* (1965); David Horowitz, *The Free World Colossus* (1971); Thomas G. Paterson, *Soviet-American Confrontation: Postwar Reconstruction and the Origins of the Cold War* (1973); Diane Shaver Clemens, *Yalta* (1973); and Lloyd C. Gardner, *Architects of Illusion: Men and Ideas in American Foreign Policy, 1941–1949* (1970). The evidence and interpretations of many of these revisionist historians have been sharply criticized by Robert James Maddox in *The New Left and the Origins of the Cold War* (1973). Two balanced and readable treatments are Stephen E. Ambrose, *Rise to Globalism* (1971); and John Lewis Gaddis, *The United States and the Origins of the Cold War, 1941–1947* (1972). For the impact of the cold war upon domestic elections, see Robert A. Divine, *Foreign Policy and United States Presidential Elections 1940–1948* (1974).

Richard J. Barnet, *Roots of War: The Men and Institutions Behind U.S. Foreign Policy* (1972), contains an important analysis of the forces which shaped postwar foreign policy. See also John C. Donovan, *The Cold Warriors: A Policy-Making Elite* (1974), and David P. Calleo and Benjamin M. Rowland, *America and the World Political Economy* (1973).

Reconversion

President Truman and his close advisers had awaited the end of the war with both hope and fear. The return of peace, they hoped, would allow the Democratic party to retrieve the fallen standard of domestic reform, to revive the New Deal spirit. But the end of war also brought the possibility of economic stagnation. Economists recognized that it was not New Deal programs but World War II, with its huge government outlays for weaponry, that had finally ended the Great Depression of the 1930s. Remembering the sharp economic downturn which had followed the first Great War—and the bitter social conflicts which the depression of 1919 had brought—many people dreaded the transition from war to peace. What would happen when wartime production slowed? Only a few weeks after the final victory in 1945, almost 100,000 defense workers in Detroit alone lost their jobs. Could production for civilian consumption take up the slack and put people back to work?

Liberal economists and Democratic politicians argued that the national government should continue the social and economic programs—and also the political gains—of the Roosevelt era. Government welfare measures should not be limited to times of acute depression, liberal economists contended, but must become a permanent part of the postwar economic system. Increased spending for social welfare

2

Postwar readjustments, 1946 - 1953

programs would pump money into the economy, easing the problem of reconversion and providing a cushion against social conflict. Unless the national administration took decisive action, some forecasters claimed, postwar unemployment might reach 11 million workers.

Only three weeks after the Japanese surrender President Truman sent Congress a message proposing twenty-one domestic spending programs. These included an increased minimum wage, money for hospital construction, funds for small businesses, permanent government price supports for farmers, and legislation to ensure full employment. The Truman administration faced congressional opposition from a coalition of anti–New Deal Republicans and southern Democrats, but the seventy-ninth Congress did pass a number of Truman's proposals, including the Hospital Construction Act, the Veterans Emergency Housing Act, funds for power and soil conservation projects, and a bill to encourage full employment.

The Full Employment Bill

Truman's most controversial proposal was the Full Employment Bill, the brainchild of the president's liberal economists. The bill's drafters announced that it would "establish a national policy and program for assuring continuing full employment," largely through continual planning, direction, and spending by the national government. Washington would take responsibility for ensuring that the "free enterprise" system would produce full employment. The specter of massive government planning and spending in peacetime alarmed many conservatives; to them the Full Employment Bill seemed another giant leap toward socialism.

The employment bill and similar economic proposals drew their inspiration not from socialism but from the theories of British economist John Maynard Keynes. A complex capitalist economy, Keynesians argued, required centralized planning and, in times of lagging consumer demand, high government expenditures. Whenever consumer spending declined, increased spending by government could take up the slack, maintain full employment, and prevent recession. Funds for public housing, hospitals, schools, and social welfare would provide assistance for the poor while maintaining a high level of economic growth. In addition, government planners could use controls over taxation as an economic tool: in times of slow growth, they could lower personal and business taxes to stimulate buying power and output; when inflationary pressures developed, they could raise taxes as one means of reducing the amount of spending. His American disciples did not follow all of Keynes's ideas—political pressures, for example, made it difficult to

24

raise taxes or reduce government expenditures—but the "new economics" became orthodoxy to most Democratic liberals after World War II.

Even many conservatives and businessmen saw the need for some type of continuing economic role for the federal government, and a modified version of the Full Employment Bill became law in 1946. Economic planning and extensive government spending became prominent features of the postwar welfare state. The modern "free enterprise" system was too fragile to be left to the mechanisms of the marketplace.

Although it did not entirely satisfy the liberals, the Employment Act established an important precedent and provided the institutional framework for more extensive government action. Congress created a new executive body, the Council of Economic Advisers, charged with the responsibilities of advising the president and establishing policies to "promote free competitive enterprise, to avoid economic fluctuations . . . and to maintain employment, production, and purchasing power." Since 1946 the Council has gained more and more influence over economic policy. Citizens have come to expect that the national government, especially the presidency, will deal firmly with economic problems. Any administration which fails to develop effective programs, to maintain high levels of employment, or to curb inflation invites political disaster. In retrospect, the Employment Act of 1946 was more than a legislative pronouncement. With its mandate for positive action by the national government, the measure assumed almost the status of a constitutional amendment.

Inflation, Black Markets, and Strikes

Despite all the analysis and planning, a variety of economic problems beset the nation in the immediate postwar period. Most liberal economists had feared that peacetime consumer spending would not maintain wartime levels of production and employment, but the gloomy forecasters were proved wrong. Consumers took the money in their savings accounts—funds which they had been unable to spend because of wartime rationing and production controls—and went on a spending spree. They wanted all the items which had been scarce or out of production during the war: refrigerators, new-model cars, nylon stockings, cameras and film, rubber-centered golf balls, and even wire coat-hangers. Toy manufacturers promised to fill the demand for electric trains. Taking advantage of greater supplies of gasoline, Americans began to travel again, and hotel and cabin owners (plastic-coated, chain motels were still in the future) complained that they could not handle the crowds of tourists.

In all areas of the economy supply could not equal demand, and a steep inflationary spiral began. Even as prices continued upward, supplies dwindled. Producers could not provide enough meat, cars, and new homes. In June 1946 a delivery man in Denver lost his entire truckload of bread to a crowd of women who overpowered him outside a grocery store; rumors of a shipment of meat produced an angry, shoving crowd of over two thousand in front of a Brooklyn store; and outside a Detroit supermarket, employees served coffee and donuts to placate angry shoppers who were waiting in line. A thriving black market soon developed. If people wanted a new car or a juicy steak, they often had to tip the automobile salesman or the butcher. When one woman walked into a Detroit meat market, the butcher asked his boss if she was a regular customer. "No," the boss replied; "starve the bitch." Some butchers tried a barter system: a meatcutter in Atlanta offered steaks and roasts in exchange for nails, flooring, and plumbing fixtures for his new home.

President Truman received much of the blame for postwar economic problems. While Republicans berated him for rising prices and black market conditions, he also faced opposition from labor unions, groups which had been firm supporters of the Democratic party and Roosevelt's New Deal. A series of labor strikes in 1946, including walkouts in the coal and auto industries, tried the president's patience. When a nationwide rail shutdown threatened to disrupt the transportation system, Truman proposed drafting striking workers into the army. This threat won him the enmity of many labor leaders and the title of the nation's foremost strikebreaker. A number of pro-Democratic labor leaders questioned Truman's capacity for leadership; many liberal Democrats also became disenchanted, dismissing Truman as a country politician with a weak social conscience.

Throughout his first year in office, Truman did appear scarcely able to handle his responsibilities. Seeking political popularity by promising rapid discharges for service personnel, he mishandled demobilization of the armed forces. At one point, the navy found it lacked the ships to transport the large number of soldiers scheduled to return to the States. By Truman's admission the process soon "was no longer demobilization . . . it was disintegration." Although he did face extremely difficult economic decisions, Truman made things even worse by failing to develop clear and consistent policies. He wavered in support of the Office of Price Administration (OPA), an executive agency which regulated wages and prices, and listened instead to people who favored a quick end to economic controls after the war. In June 1945 Truman vetoed a bill which would have renewed OPA's authority while limiting its powers; but after a short period with no controls at all, he signed a second bill which differed very little from the first. (Finally, in November 1946, Truman proclaimed an end to virtually all controls.) In all of these matters, Truman projected the image of an indecisive leader, a person who leaned too heavily upon old political cronies and representatives of special-interest groups. Even most of Truman's supporters could find few examples of effective leadership during his first year in the White House.

A Republican Victory: 1946

Republicans hardly lacked campaign issues in 1946: soaring prices, black market conditions, labor strikes, an unpopular president. By October the Gallup polling organization reported that only 32 percent of their sample approved of Truman's performance, compared to a figure of 87 percent a little over a year earlier. One pro-Republican columnist suggested that the Democrats nominate W. C. Fields for president. "If we're going to have a comedian in the White House, let's have a good one." Other Democrats were the targets for similar jibes, and after nearly fifteen years as the minority party, Republicans found themselves almost back in control. Summing up all the Democratic sins, Republican posters asked, "Had enough?" In the November 1946 elections Republicans gained control of the new eightieth Congress and captured twenty-five governorships. Jersey City's political boss, Frank Hague, was philosophical. "The Republicans would have won even had they put up a German," an aide quoted Hague. And 1948 promised to be an even better year for Republicans.

Truman made little effort to work with the new Republican-controlled eightieth Congress (1947–49) in domestic policy. He challenged Republicans to pass legislation which he knew they opposed, and refused to seek any common ground on measures such as a higher minimum wage and labor legislation. At the same time, the president infrequently consulted congressional Democrats, failing to give them any clear indication of the White House's domestic priorities. At one point, Democratic Senator Alben Barkley grumbled that working with Truman was like playing a night baseball game in the dark. "I'm supposed to be the catcher and I should get the signals. I not only am not getting the signals, but someone actually turns out the light when the ball is thrown." Thus, while Truman proposed expensive social welfare programs, he also urged reductions in federal expenditures. Such doubletalk provided little executive leadership, but it helped Truman build a record upon which to run in 1948.

In reality, Truman could point to few domestic innovations and could not cite many instances of Republicans trying to tear down popular programs begun by Roosevelt's New Deal. By the late 1940s many Republican politicians were coming to recognize that outright opposition to liberal Democratic measures such as Social Security offered little hope for increasing the GOP's vote totals. This pragmatic attitude gained most support from younger Republicans, particularly those who came from larger Northern cities or held state offices. Increasingly, they battled older, more tradition-bound Republicans in Congress for influence within the party.

Ridiculed by Democrats as a do-nothing body, the eightieth Congress actually passed several significant pieces of legislation. The National Security Act of 1947 reorganized the armed forces and the entire defense establishment. In recognition of the new importance of air power, the air force became a separate branch of the military; a new Department of Defense, under a civilian head, replaced the old Departments of War and Navy; top-ranking uniformed officers from the air force, navy, army, and marines sat on a new coordinating body called the Joint Chiefs of Staff; and the new National Security Council (NSC) and Central Intelligence Agency (CIA) assumed important tasks in planning and executing foreign policy. In a highly popular move, the eightieth Congress also approved and sent to the states the Twenty-second Amendment, which prohibited presidents from serving more than two terms. In addition, the Congress accepted Truman's suggestion that it create a special commission to study reorganization of the federal bureaucracy. Under the chairmanship of former President Herbert Hoover, the commission reported a plan which became the basis of the Reorganization Act of 1949. By clarifying lines of authority and reducing the number of executive agencies, the Hoover Commission hoped to make government administration more efficient.

Robert Taft, Republican majority leader in the Senate, emerged as the dominant figure in the eightieth Congress. Son of President William Howard Taft, the middle-aged Ohioan was a shy, thoughtful man who often seemed uncomfortable in the glare of national politics. Certainly he lacked the charm of Roosevelt or the fire of Truman. But Taft's close attention to detail won him respect from Senate colleagues, and his reputation for honesty and integrity gained him the admiration of older, more conservative Republicans. "Mr. Republican" argued that liberal Democrats were abandoning the New Deal measures of Roosevelt and moving toward socialism. Their programs, he charged, threatened to bankrupt the country and to place individual liberties at the mercy of an overbearing federal bureaucracy. By 1946, however, Taft had moderated some of his more extreme anti–New Deal views; to the consternation of more reactionary Republicans, he supported some federal aid to education, a limited program of public housing, and some social welfare measures. In view of Truman's increasing problems, Taft hoped that his vision of "modern Republicanism" would make him the GOP's nominee in 1948.

Passage of the Taft-Hartley Labor Act of 1947 demonstrated the Ohio senator's economic ideas and legislative skills. The law, aimed at reducing the political and economic power of organized labor, outlawed the "closed shop" (the practice of hiring only union workers), prohibited use of union dues for political activities, and authorized presidential back-to-work orders whenever labor strikes threatened national security. The law, Taft claimed, would not destroy labor unions; it would actually help workers by curbing the abuses of corrupt labor bosses. Taft skillfully managed the bill through the Senate and worked out a compromise with House Republicans who wanted a stronger anti-union statute. Truman vetoed the measure, but Taft collected the votes to override the president's action. Labor leaders denounced the bill as "a slave labor act" and the "Tuff-Heartless Act"; pickets appeared at the wedding of Taft's son carrying placards which read "CONGRATULATIONS TO YOU. _____TO YOUR OLD MAN."

The Election of 1948

Despite his impressive leadership in Congress, Robert Taft lost the 1948 presidential nomination to Governor Thomas E. Dewey of New York, the GOP's standardbearer in 1944. Taft's reputation as a poor vote-getter and a conservative worked against his nomination. After twelve years without a president Republicans wanted a winner, and Dewey and his runningmate, Governor Earl Warren of California, appeared to be shoo-ins. Dewey had run well against FDR in the last presidential contest, had won a smashing victory in the 1946 New York gubernatorial race, and belonged to the more progressive, Eastern wing of the GOP.

But the victor in 1948 was not Tom Dewey: Harry Truman surprised almost all the political "experts," his Democratic critics, and the entire Republican party. "You've got to give the little man credit," admitted Republican Senator Arthur Vandenburg. "Everyone had counted him out, but he came up fighting and won the battle. That's the kind of courage the American people admire." To the extent that the

United Press International

President Harry S. Truman laughs as he holds an early edition of the Chicago *Tribune* for November 4, 1948. The editor had jumped to an erroneous conclusion as early election returns came in.

presidential sweepstakes was a "beauty contest" between competing images, Truman emerged the clear winner. Dewey displayed little of Truman's warmth and personality. "I don't know which is the chillier experience—to have Tom ignore you or shake your hand," claimed one of his detractors. "You have to get to know Dewey to dislike him," another complained. Overconfident and overly cautious, "Thomas Elusive Dewey" made fewer personal appearances than Truman and relied upon well-worn platitudes and bland appeals to national unity.

In contrast, Harry Truman sounded more like a country politician—which he had been—than like the president of the United States. Speaking from notes rather than prepared texts, Truman slashed away at the Republicans' eightieth Congress. With his arms in perpetual motion, Truman denounced Republican representatives as "errand boys of big business" and bragged that he had vetoed more legislation than any other president since Grover Cleveland. During the interval between the Democratic convention and the November election, Truman called the eightieth Congress into special session and presented it with a list of "must" legislation. When the Republican-controlled legislature predictably adjourned after passing only a few minor bills, Truman escalated his attacks upon Dewey and the eightieth Congress: the president's seventeen-car, armor-plated campaign train whistle-stopped across the country to shouts of "Give 'em hell, Harry."

When he was not roasting the Republican "no-account, do-nothing" Congress, Truman emphasized his own liberal proposals. His chief strategists, especially Washington lawyer Clark Clifford, advised that an aggressively liberal stance would keep urban Democrats from supporting Henry Wallace, FDR's former vice-president who was running on the Progressive party ticket, and not seriously hurt Truman's campaign in the South. Truman called for a higher minimum wage, repeal of Taft-Hartley, more public housing, and higher farm prices. During the final week of the campaign he became the first president to appear in Harlem. There he told a crowd of 35,000 blacks that he supported the "goal of equal rights and equal opportunities" for all Americans.

The civil rights question, which would become a more pressing political issue after 1948, did cost Truman some Southern votes. His advisers had hoped that the party convention would adopt a mild statement in support of civil rights, but liberals and big-city bosses, who relied upon black voters, pushed through a stronger proposal. Following the heated floor fight, delegates from Alabama and Mississippi stalked out of the convention, and segregationists eventually formed the States Rights or "Dixiecrat" party. Their platform denounced "totalitarian government" and advocated "segregation of the races." With J. Strom Thurmond of South Carolina as their presidential nominee, the Dixiecrats hoped to gain one hundred electoral votes in the South—enough ballots, they thought, to throw the presidential election into the House of Representatives. Thurmond, however, lacked sufficient financial support to conduct an effective campaign, and the strategy failed. Most Southern Democrats stayed with Truman.

Truman survived another revolt within his party: the Progressive party candidacy of Henry Wallace. Truman had fired Wallace as Secretary of Commerce because Wallace had publicly criticized the administration's hard-line anti-Soviet foreign policy. With the support of a wide range of left-wing groups, including the Communist party, Wallace launched a new party which advocated greater cooperation with the Soviet Union, an end to the military draft, and more money for social and economic justice at home. Wallace's early appearances drew large and enthusiastic crowds. His rallies resembled old-time revival meetings, as folksingers like Peter Seeger and Woody Guthrie campaigned for Wallace and his guitar-playing running mate, Senator Glen Taylor of

Idaho. One of Woody Guthrie's songs, adapted to the tune of "Wabash Cannonball," reflected the class appeal of Wallace's left-wing supporters.

> *There's lumberjacks and teamsters and sailors from the sea,*
> *And there's farming boys from Texas and the hills of Tennessee,*
> *There's miners from Kentucky and there's fishermen from Maine,*
> *Every worker in the country rides that Wallace-Taylor train.*

But the Wallace-Taylor special never reached the White House. Wallace's acceptance of Communist support, bitter opposition from large labor unions, the defection of anticommunist liberals, his forthright stand on civil rights, and the insurmountable problems of any newly formed party all caught up with Wallace. In December 1947 a poll showed that 13 percent of the electorate favored Wallace's candidacy; by election day his campaign had collapsed, and he received less than 3 percent of the popular vote.

Truman's victory demonstrated the strength of the old Roosevelt coalition. Middle Western farmers, urban ethnic voters, organized labor, blacks, and most Southerners continued to support the Democratic party. Many voted Democratic because of family tradition and because of the social and economic programs begun during the New Deal. Truman's energetic campaign, like most political efforts, did not suddenly convince great numbers of voters to support the Democratic party; but it revived many Democrats' party loyalty and raised fears that GOP reactionaries would mount a general assault on New Deal measures. The four-way contest apparently confused some voters. Nineteen forty-eight was what political scientists call a "decline election," and only 54 percent of the electorate turned out. The election maintained the basic political configuration of the late 1930s and provided a mandate for following the outlines of the New Deal.

THE FAIR DEAL

Truman's Domestic Program

After the uphill Democratic victory of 1948, Truman and his advisers planned a new set of domestic proposals which they hoped would move beyond Franklin Roosevelt's New Deal. FDR's programs had been designed to stop the Great Depression and to restore the prosperity of the 1920s; Truman's Fair Deal offered measures aimed at creating an ever-expanding economy.

Truman's liberal economists believed that they had solved the mysteries of economic management. One aide, Charles F. Brannan, championed an ambitious proposal which he claimed would give farmers higher prices while providing consumers with cheaper food. Under Brannan's program, the government would lift New Deal restrictions on the number of acres planted and would maintain farm income through direct price supports.

Another of Truman's economic advisers, Leon Keyserling, predicted that the national government could guarantee full employment, higher wages, and greater profits through well-planned and well-executed spending programs. Americans had no need to take from the rich to care for the poor. Properly managed, America's capitalist economy could outproduce any socialist system in the world. In 1948 nearly two-thirds of all American families lived on incomes of less than $4,000 a year; but by 1958 it would be possible, Keyserling predicted, to generate enough economic growth to make $4,000 the minimum income for *every* family. "The people of America need to be electrified by our limitless possibilities," he proclaimed.

In addition to government measures to stimulate economic growth, the Fair Deal promised a variety of programs to advance social and economic justice. Truman proposed expansion of Social Security, generous federal funding for public housing projects, a national plan for medical insurance, federal aid to education, and civil rights legislation for black Americans. Truman and his liberal advisers believed that the Fair Deal represented the middle way between socialism and fascism. "Between the reactionaries of the extreme left with their talk about revolution and class warfare, and the reactionaries of the extreme right with their hysterical cries of bankruptcy and despair, lies the way of progress," Truman declared. The Democratic historian Arthur Schlesinger, Jr., provided an appropriate title for cold war liberalism—"the vital center."

Following World War II, the Truman administration achieved some of its social programs, and government and business leaders built upon the economic gains of the war years. Congress passed measures which extended Social Security benefits; raised the minimum wage (to seventy-five cents an hour); and appropriated federal funds for soil conservation, flood control, and public power. Despite some fluctuations, the economy performed fairly well during the late 1940s and early 1950s. The United States came nowhere near Leon Keyserling's optimistic predictions, but real income did rise. People who had survived the

Great Depression of the 1930s, with help from the New Deal, continued to do well under the Fair Deal.

The Fair Deal: An Assessment

Sandwiched between the Democratic reforms of Franklin Roosevelt's New Deal and Lyndon Johnson's Great Society, the Fair Deal of Harry Truman has generally suffered by comparison. Many historians have viewed it as an addendum to the New Deal, a grab-bag of programs left over from the 1930s; others have seen it primarily as a prelude to the burst of legislation enacted during Johnson's second term. But the Fair Deal deserves to be evaluated on its own terms. Going beyond the goals of the New Deal, Truman's liberal advisers sought to establish programs and bureaucratic institutions which could ensure continual economic growth and a more adequate, albeit limited, social welfare system. Truman's proposals, more than FDR's, remained the basic aims of the Democratic party for almost two decades. A whole generation of liberal politicians—people such as Hubert Humphrey, John Kennedy, and Eugene McCarthy—began their careers during the Fair Deal. Most never moved beyond it or questioned the essential benevolence of big government.

The Fair Deal, like the whole postwar liberal program, contained significant limitations; the welfare state expanded relatively little after World War II. In 1962 Michael Harrington's *The Other America* reminded affluent liberals that nearly one-fourth of the population still lived in deep poverty, largely unaided by federal programs. The more ambitious portions of the Fair Deal never got through Congress. Determined lobbying by the American Medical Association, which raised the cry of "socialized medicine," helped kill the plan for national health insurance. Opposition from other powerful pressure groups encouraged a coalition of Republicans and conservative Southern Democrats to block repeal of the Taft-Hartley law, a program for general federal aid to state school systems, and the Brannan plan for agricultural subsidies. But the failure of the Fair Deal cannot be blamed solely on the conservative coalition in Congress or on special-interest groups. Preoccupied with foreign affairs and oftentimes inept in his dealings with Congress, Truman failed to provide vigorous domestic leadership. In addition, many of the president's programs lacked broad popular support. Most middle-class Americans, the people who made up the bulk of the electorate, wanted to enjoy the benefits of expanding economic production—a home, household appliances, a second car. Few voters showed much interest in a grand new campaign for social and economic justice.

Civil Rights

The lack of enthusiasm for new crusades was most evident in the fate of civil rights legislation. Revulsion against Nazi racism helped encourage greater rhetorical denunciations of discrimination at home; wartime economic gains produced a desire among blacks for broader attacks on discrimination; and the outbreak of racial violence immediately after the war intensified efforts to calm racial hatreds. Despite these forces for change, however, the Fair Deal meant only small gains for most black Americans.

As part of his broader liberal program, the president pushed for a variety of civil rights measures, including a ban on poll taxes, an anti-lynching law, and legislation to guarantee equal employment opportunities. During the 1948 presidential campaign, he issued executive orders which ended (at least on paper) discrimination in federal employment. Truman took great pride in his civil rights record; he once went so far as to claim that desegregation of the armed forces, which began during his second term, was "the greatest thing that ever happened to America."

The Truman administration also played a role in several important Supreme Court decisions which affirmed the legal rights of black Americans and other minority groups. In *Shelly* v. *Kraemer* (1946) the justices unanimously held that no court could enforce restrictive covenants, agreements which prevented minority groups from acquiring real estate in certain areas. In two other cases—*Seatt* v. *Painter* (1950) and *McLaurin* v. *Oklahoma Board of Regents* (1950)—the Court ruled that a separate law school established for blacks violated the Fourteenth Amendment's requirement of equality in education and that graduate schools could not segregate students according to race. Although these cases did not declare all segregated educational facilities inherently unequal, they did point the way toward the broader school desegregation decision in *Brown* v. *Board of Education* (1954). And in *Henderson* v. *United States* (1950) the Supreme Court outlawed racial segregation in railroad dining cars. In all these cases Truman's Justice Department supported the claims of the black plaintiffs.

Despite these positive marks on Truman's record, civil rights provided another example of the gap between liberal promise and performance. Some civil rights activists blamed Truman for the lack of new legislative initiatives; they claimed that the president gave their cause a low priority and too often deferred to the feelings of Southern Democrats. Truman tried to avoid a direct stand on civil rights; the threat of black voters defecting to Henry Wallace, for example, prompted his executive orders in 1948. But Truman was not entirely to blame for the failure to achieve more during his administration. The conservative coalition in Congress effectively bottled up legislation which would have aided black Americans, and some military officials did their best to delay desegregation of the armed forces. Similarly, the president's initiatives in ending job discrimination ultimately depended upon the attitude of other officials in the federal bureaucracy.

There was also a good deal of popular opposition to even limited moves toward racial equality. In the Southern states the Confederate flag became the symbol of resistance: one flag company estimated that Virginians owned more Confederate banners in 1951 than during the Civil War, and a New York City firm reported that the demand for rebel flags exceeded orders for the Stars and Stripes. Throughout the nation, racists violently opposed the drive for integration. When a black couple attempted to move into an apartment in Cicero, Illinois, a mob of about 5,000 angry whites broke through National Guard lines and set the building ablaze. In the same year, 1951, a black school principal and civil rights leader died when explosives destroyed his Miami home on Christmas Day. Decrying the increased use of explosives, Walter White of the National Association for the Advancement of Colored People observed that "the bomb has replaced the lynchers' rope" as the main weapon of racist resistance.

The upsurge in white violence was one more brake on the pace of national action against racial discrimination. White America's long-delayed commitment to concede legal equality to blacks barely began during the Truman years. Still, Truman's record looked better than that of any previous twentieth century president. He was the first chief executive to make civil rights a national political issue, and his administration at least proposed a comprehensive legislative program.

ANTICOMMUNISM AT HOME

The Communist Problem

Although the Truman administration moved cautiously on civil rights, it acted decisively against the alleged threat of communist subversion in the United States. In 1947 Truman established a comprehensive "internal security" program designed to uncover "subversives" in the federal bureaucracy. Employing flimsy procedural safeguards and broad definitions of "disloyalty," agencies purged a number of supposed "security risks." The president did oppose suggestions for more Draconian measures—such as abolition of the Fifth Amendment in national security cases—but the White House often failed to restrain the

Department of Justice. J. Edgar Hoover's FBI (Federal Bureau of Investigation), with the administration's consent, pried into the private lives and political beliefs of alleged subversives. Extending a practice begun during the Roosevelt years, the FBI also used wiretaps in violation of the Federal Communications Act of 1934. In 1949 Truman rejected the American Civil Liberties Union's suggestion that a special commission investigate the FBI. "Hoover has done a good job," the president told a press conference. The Attorney General's List of Subversive Organizations, first issued in 1947, demonstrated the Justice Department's insensitivity to guilt by association. Noncommunists who happened to belong to one of these groups sometimes found themselves branded as reds, "pinkos," or "fellow travelers." Libertarians charged that the government too often equated legitimate political dissent with communist subversion.

How real was the domestic threat of communism? Did the White House and the Justice Department exaggerate the dangers? Although no researcher has uncovered hard evidence that procommunists shaped United States policies, the government did obtain reliable intelligence about the activities of communist agents and the passing of military information to the Soviet Union. The FBI captured several authentic spies, and J. Edgar Hoover firmly believed that "the ignorant and the apologists and the appeasers of Communism in our country" consistently minimized the "danger of these subversives in our midst." Still, the amount of subversive activity and the danger to national security remain open questions. Some historians, for example, contend that the Justice Department possessed only flimsy evidence against Ethel and Julius Rosenberg, who were executed in 1953 for passing atomic secrets to the Soviets, and that the couple fell victim to anticommunist hysteria. But until the government allows scholars to examine FBI files, debates over the full extent of the communist threat will continue.

The Communist Issue

Whatever the real danger from communism, the Truman administration had other reasons to mount a vigorous anti-Red crusade. Since the late 1930s, anti–New Deal Democrats and conservative Republicans—particularly members of the House Un-American Activities Committee (HUAC)—had claimed that communists and fellow travelers infested the Roosevelt administration. Charges of communist influence in the federal government often accompanied general attacks upon the "socialistic" New Deal welfare programs. Responding to Republican taunts of being "soft on communism," the Truman administration tried to improve its anticommunist credentials. Truman hoped that a tough policy of his own would prevent Republicans from seizing the anticommunist issue for themselves.

The alleged existence of an active communist conspiracy within the United States also dovetailed with the administration's strong anti-Soviet foreign policy. During the immediate postwar period, public opinion polls revealed that few Americans considered communism a major problem. And some Americans, remembering the wartime alliance with the Soviet Union, believed that Russia presented no great threat to the security of the United States. Truman's advisers feared that such attitudes—along with the strong popular sentiment to avoid expensive overseas commitments—might hamstring the president's foreign policy. A tough stand against a supposedly growing Red menace at home and a constant barrage of anticommunist rhetoric, administration strategists hoped, would counteract domestic resistance to Truman's sweeping foreign policy proposals. Consequently, the Truman administration publicized its plans for dealing with internal subversion; officials continually stressed the need for greater vigilance; and the government orchestrated a vigorous pro-American campaign. In 1947, for example, Attorney General Tom Clark developed the "Freedom Train" program. This historical society on rails carried important documents, including a copy of the Truman Doctrine, to more than two hundred major cities. When the train returned to Washington in the fall of 1947, the government staged a "week of rededication." At a series of patriotic demonstrations, government employees took a "freedom pledge" and everyone sang "God Bless America." In a similar vein, the Office of Education promoted its "Zeal for Democracy" program: Washington encouraged local schools "to vitalize and improve education in the ideals and benefits of democracy and to reveal the character and tactics of totalitarianism."

Government leaders, of course, did not simply manufacture a spirit of 100 percent Americanism. But their efforts did strengthen the inevitable postwar nationalism and gave it an increasingly anticommunist tone. The actions and rhetoric of the Truman administration helped shift attention from the specific problem of Soviet espionage to the highly emotional issue of a general communist "invasion" of American institutions. Many people became less concerned about Russian spies in Washington than about communist sympathizers spreading heretical ideas throughout a too tolerant society.

The more extreme anticommunist spokesmen claimed that government leaders, even President Truman, failed to perceive the nation's grave peril. To these modern Paul Reveres, Soviet spies were only part of the problem. Anticommunists could find sinister forces almost everywhere. Self-appointed vigilantes, for example, moved against

38

"communist" movie stars, left-wing writers, and "subversives" in the radio industry. People whose political ideas seemed suspect found themselves unofficially blacklisted. Some on the blacklist could find no work at all. Others were luckier. Writing under the pseudonym of "Robert Rich," blacklisted screenwriter Dalton Trumbo even won an Academy Award. Protectors of 100 percent Americanism also invoked official sanctions. The Post Office obtained authority to ban communist materials from the mails; many states adopted laws which barred subversives from state government jobs; bar associations and school boards required prospective attorneys and teachers to take loyalty oaths. The House Un-American Activities Committee examined "communist penetration" into the entertainment industry and the federal bureaucracy. Members of HUAC—including young Richard Nixon—claimed that their committee had discovered extensive procommunist activity in the United States. Critics of the committee charged that members had only smeared the reputations of innocent people in order to advance their own political careers.

A series of disturbing events appeared to give credence to the tales about communist machinations. The fall of China in 1949 and Russia's first atomic test frightened Americans who wrongfully believed that the United States had "lost" China to the communists and that the "backward" Russians had stolen vital atomic secrets from the United States. Stories about communists in the State Department and atomic spies offered attractive explanations. The year 1950 brought new shocks: the government uncovered a Soviet spy ring in the United States, and American troops entered the Korean conflict. If these were not troubling enough, there were other disturbing events: a series of scandals within the Truman administration, corruption in the Internal Revenue Service, a televised investigation of organized crime, and even an assassination plot against the president by Puerto Rican nationalists. Although only a few people blamed all these problems on one giant communist conspiracy, the events did generate the kind of anxieties and fears which encouraged a paranoid style in American politics.

McCarthyism

Militant anticommunism reached its apogee—and eventually took its name—from Senator Joseph McCarthy. "McCarthyism" existed before McCarthy ever discovered the anticommunist issue, and other "McCarthyites" made even wilder charges than the Wisconsin senator. But McCarthy captured most of the headlines. His tactics were disarmingly simple: he flung accusations as fast as newspapers could print

39

them but avoided specific proposals for fighting the communist "menace." When an acquaintance asked McCarthy how he would change the Voice of America's allegedly ineffective programs, "the Senator looked blank; obviously he had never thought about it." Neither did McCarthy spend much time documenting his sensational charges. His famous Wheeling, West Virginia, speech—in which he charged that the State Department employed more than two hundred communist sympathizers—rested upon a hodgepodge of questionable evidence from old congressional files. Even though the Senate later gave him broad investigatory powers, McCarthy never bothered to pursue his allegations against the State Department. Instead, he went after new demons who he claimed were hiding in other government bureaus. According to social critic Dwight McDonald, McCarthy dealt in "dead souls." His targets were not "actual, living breathing Communists" but rather people who once were or may have been" communists.

Because of the wide publicity he received, McCarthy soon gained an undeserved reputation as a powerful new political force. The Wisconsin senator, his opponents feared, led a massive right-wing movement which seemed to appeal to the great numbers of lower-middle-class people with little formal education. McCarthy, who looked more like a heavy in a B movie than a tribune of the people, exaggerated his image as a tough guy and a rebel. He railed against "establishment Democrats" such as Alger Hiss, a former New Dealer who was charged with espionage for the Soviet Union, and Dean Acheson, Truman's Yale-bred secretary of state. All these "bright young men who were born with silver spoons in their mouths" and all those "striped pants diplomats," McCarthy charged, were "selling the nation out." As McCarthy escalated his attacks, many liberals and moderates worried about this new threat from the radical right.

In fact, however, McCarthy's power did not come from the support of great numbers of fanatics. Instead, he gained attention because important people, such as members of the United States Senate, either supported his attacks or failed to oppose him. Influential Middle Western Republicans, who formed the traditional base for anti–New Deal conservatism, gave McCarthy vital political assistance. His charges of communist influence in government, which linked Democratic liberalism with socialistic ideas, reechoed the familiar theme of GOP conservatives. Republicans who would not personally stoop to McCarthy's smear tactics—Robert Taft of Ohio, for example—tacitly encouraged the Wisconsin senator. Anything that hurt the Democrats, Taft reasoned, would help the Republican party regain power. In addition to aid from conservative Republicans, McCarthy received help from other important sources. Most newspapers, regardless of their political allegiances, splashed McCarthy's unproven charges over their pages. Sensational scoops about communist influence provided good copy— and greater sales. Many prominent liberal politicians avoided direct confrontation with McCarthy and his supporters for fear of being labeled "soft" on communism.

The passage of the McCarran Internal Security Act of 1950 demonstrated most politicians' fear of opposing anticommunist measures. Rather than openly fighting Senator Pat McCarran's harsh proposals, the White House and Democratic congressmen offered their own internal security bills. In so doing, they accepted the McCarthyites' basic position: communists should not expect the same civil liberties as other Americans. In its final form, the McCarran Act required communist and "communist-front" organizations to register with the attorney general, barred foreign communists from entering the United States, and authorized secret prison camps for detention of domestic subversives during wartime. Only seven senators and a handful of representatives voted against the McCarran Act. In one of his most courageous political acts, Truman vetoed the bill, but Congress quickly overrode the president's action. McCarthyism and McCarthy continued to influence national policy.

Eventually, however, McCarthy ran out of obvious targets and overstepped even his fertile imagination. By 1953 he was charging that Voice of America, the new Republican administration of Dwight Eisenhower, and the United States Army had played into the hands of the communists. In one celebrated incident two of McCarthy's aides traveled around Europe to search for procommunist literature in libraries run by the United States Information Service. His agents and other witnesses charged that these libraries contained many communist books and few pro-American works; one investigator even suggested that librarians manipulated card catalogs so that readers would not find books critical of communism. Finally, McCarthy's charges of communist influence in the army resulted in a special Senate investigation. The Army-McCarthy hearings—a daytime television spectacular as popular as the later Watergate investigation—contributed to McCarthy's demise. Some people resented his brash manner and bullying tactics. Many others simply became bored with the whole communist issue. Emboldened by McCarthy's problems, his critics escalated their attacks. Some of his Republican allies began to temper their support, and a few anticommunists claimed that McCarthy's extremist position discredited the fight against Moscow and unwittingly aided the Kremlin. Finally, the United States Senate, the source of his prestige, turned against him. In 1954 a majority of senators voted to "condemn" McCarthy for conduct unbecoming a member of the Senate. Stripped of his prestige and influence, McCarthy disappeared from the headlines, began drinking heavily, and died in 1957 at the age of forty-eight.

The Cold-war Consensus

McCarthyism represented only the most visible, extreme segment of a general anticommunist consensus. Influential American leaders, people who dismissed Senator Joe as a simplistic vulgarian, espoused a more sophisticated brand of anticommunism. Most prominent American leaders agreed that a vicious totalitarian conspiracy threatened "the American way of life" and that Marxism was a pernicious doctrine without any intellectual respectability. The United States, virtually every writer and commentator argued, was engaged in a kind of holy war against world communism. In the words of liberal journalist Tom Braden, this was a war "fought with ideas instead of bombs." During the 1950s many prominent American intellectuals joined the Congress for Cultural Freedom, an international organization devoted to promoting the doctrines of liberty and opposing "state-sponsored ideologies" such as Soviet communism. In fact, the CCF and its influential journal, *Encounter*, received secret funding from the United States Central Intelligence Agency. Although the CIA certainly did not tell members of the CCF what to say or write, the leaders of the organization rarely sponsored writers who seriously criticized United States policy.

The American press remained free from government censorship, and many papers vigorously criticized official execution of specific programs. But except for ultraconservatives who decried communist influence and Democratic welfare schemes, few journalists questioned basic domestic and foreign policy assumptions. Making the round of fashionable cocktail parties and listening to official off-the-record explanations, influential Washington journalists almost became members of the government themselves. Rather than reporting the news, accounts of real events which they had researched, the Washington press corps sometimes provided outlets for carefully contrived pseudo-events— trial balloons, distortions, and outright lies which government officials and prominent politicians wanted to place before the public. The line between reality and these pseudo-events, such as Joe McCarthy's "communists" in the State Department or a nonexistent "missile gap" between the United States and the Soviet Union, often seemed hazy. Truly independent journalists such as I. F. Stone, who assumed that every government statement was suspect until proven otherwise, were rare in Washington during the 1950s. Serving as reporter, editor, and publisher, he made *I. F. Stone's Weekly* an impressive example of democratic journalism.

The same cold-war consensus pervaded the American academic community. Only a few radical professors ran afoul of witch-hunters and actually lost their positions; no government or academic censors prevented scholars from writing studies which stressed social conflict or expressed an anticapitalist viewpoint. Instead, radical analysis simply became old-fashioned and was dismissed as too simplistic. The undeniable terrors of Stalinist Russia and the Soviet–American cold war caused many former Marxists to renounce communism and to reject the Marxist and class-conflict theories which had been so important during the 1920s and 1930s. After World War II writers invariably emphasized the positive side of American society—the general social harmony, the political democracy, the material abundance, and the economic opportunity. Most political scientists, for example, praised American politicians for their pragmatism and for creating an open system in which all legitimate groups could compromise their differences. At the same time, most historians contended that consensus rather than conflict had always characterized the American experience. Louis Hartz, a professor of government at Harvard, spoke for most academicians and journalists when he concluded that the United States had always been—and would undoubtedly remain—a nation of moderate capitalists.

Although scholars and social commentators still criticized specific shortcomings—the inefficiency of government bureaucrats was a popular theme—they generally praised the kind of pragmatic liberalism represented by Harry Truman's Fair Deal. Rejecting both romantic conservatism and radical social theories, the vast majority of American intellectuals believed that tough-minded problem-solvers could unravel even the most complex social puzzles. Moderate liberal reformers in the tradition of Franklin Roosevelt, they concluded, would advance social and economic justice without any fundamental restructuring of capitalist institutions or change in basic social values. During the late 1940s and 1950s, most influential Americans occupied the broad middle ground between the political right and socialism: Arthur Schlesinger's "vital center." Prominent left-wing dissenters like C. Wright Mills and I. F. Stone were not officially silenced as they would have been in totalitarian regimes; their kind of passionate radicalism simply went out of style.

SOCIETY DURING THE TRUMAN YEARS

Science and Technology

Most Americans praised the tremendous new developments in science and technology. The atomic explosions which ravaged Hiroshima and Nagasaki reflected the United States' growing scientific and technological prowess. "The bomb" raised terrifying images of worldwide destruction, but it also seemed to offer more hopeful possibilities. Correctly developed and properly harnessed, atomic energy could power America's growing cities, run naval vessels, even carry people into outer space. And radioactive material promised exciting new advances in scientific research and in the treatment of diseases such as cancer. But first, the United States needed a way of regulating atomic activities.

In response to a request from President Truman, Congress passed the Atomic Energy Act of 1945. The military implications of nuclear power, of course, made some system of national control imperative, and the act gave the president sole authority to order use of atomic weapons. In addition to regulating military uses, the law of 1946 vested day-to-day control over nuclear energy and materials with the Atomic Energy Commission. Run by civilians, the AEC possessed authority to conduct nuclear research and make policy decisions affecting the use of nuclear energy.

The national government became more involved in a wide range of other scientific activities after World War II. The wartime experience demonstrated the need for continued support of military research, and advocates of federal aid also urged the government to appropriate more money for nonmilitary experimentation. In a report to the president entitled *Science—The Endless Frontier* (1945), Vannevar Bush called for creation of a single national agency to administer grants for scientific research. Scientists, he argued, were about to make important breakthroughs, new discoveries that could protect Americans from foreign enemies and dramatically improve the quality of their daily lives. In 1950 Congress established the National Science Foundation, and NSF grants soon allowed scientists to explore subjects unknown a generation earlier.

Encouraged by government funds (and by grants from tax-exempt private foundations), scientific activity accelerated in postwar America. Ever since the late nineteenth century the number of scientists and technicians had been growing faster than the general population, and this trend continued after 1945. The United States had always been a nation of backyard tinkerers: people like Thomas Edison simply applied their common sense and mechanical aptitude to existing knowledge and came up with new inventions. But the corps of highly trained specialists who dominated science and technology after World War II could not proceed by trial and error or build their own laboratories like Edison's at Menlo Park. The new discoveries—breakthroughs in fields like chemistry, biology, electronics, and nuclear energy—rested upon highly sophisticated equipment and complex scientific theories about the physical universe. Researchers in electronics, for example, did not tinker around until they made a better vacuum tube; they applied recent discoveries in solid-state physics and eliminated vacuum tubes altogether.

New developments in science and technology promised almost unbelievable changes for American society. Instead of merely adapting human institutions to the natural environment, scientists could now go beyond the natural to create an artificial world. Knowledge of scientific theories permitted them to rearrange molecular structures and to produce synthetic fibers, high-strength adhesives, manmade construction materials, and many other new products. In 1944 scientists at Rockefeller Institute isolated a compound, called DNA, which opened the secrets of genetic reproduction. Throughout the 1940s biochemists tried to unravel the molecular structure of DNA, and finally in 1953 an American and a British scientist constructed a model of a DNA molecule. Science, it seemed, was on the threshold of creating life itself. Abstract theoretical knowledge and sophisticated technology were becoming important national resources like iron and coal. In the coming years, people predicted, scientific knowhow and up-to-date technology would be the most vital resources of all.

The computer revolution perhaps best symbolized the possibilities of the new science and technology. World War II had provided the impetus for development of machines capable of storing and retrieving great amounts of data and of systems capable of organizing and analyzing all this information. Not until 1946, however, did scientists and engineers construct the first really usable computer—ENIAC. Later, technicians improved design and efficiency, and Remington Rand marketed the first commercial computer in 1951. But IBM soon came to dominate the industry, providing systems for government, private business, and academic institutions. Computers enabled doctors to check their research more closely, social scientists to analyze human behavior more effectively, and business institutions to control accounts and other records more efficiently. Everyone, it seemed, had a use for computers. During the 1960s one enterprising promoter even used computers to simulate radio versions of imaginary prize fights between all of the heavyweight champions of the twentieth century. Fortunately, the computer decided that the relatively young Rocky Marciano should meet Muhammed Ali in the filmed finale, and the promoter could stage various scenarios, complete with plenty of ketchup, to fit the computer's "authentic" version; a mock battle between septuagenarians like Jack Dempsey and Gene Tunney, even with buckets of artificial gore, would have left too much to the imagination.

Some of the most beneficial scientific discoveries came in medicine. After World War II the United States experienced severe epidemics of poliomyelitis. This disease, which generally crippled those it did not kill, between 1947 and 1951 struck an annual average of 34,000 Americans, mostly children. (Between 1938 and 1942 the annual average had been only 6,400, a figure which rose to 16,800 between 1942 and 1947.) In 1952 doctors reported some success using gamma globulin as a preventative, and three years later Dr. Jonas Salk pioneered the first truly successful vaccine. A nationwide program to inoculate people with this and the later Sabine vaccine resulted in the virtual elimination of polio by the 1960s. After World II doctors also introduced a series of "wonder drugs." Penicillin, first discovered by Dr. Alexander Fleming in the 1920s and refined during the war, came into general use between 1945 and 1952; a powerful set of antibiotics—streptomycin, aureomycin, terramycin, and magnamycin—appeared after World War II; and antihistamines, which proved important in the treatment of allergies, became available in the late 1940s. These drugs and new surgical techniques allowed many Americans to lead fuller and more comfortable lives, and they also encouraged more determined research into cures for cancer and heart disease, two afflictions which became more common as the United States became more urbanized and industrialized.

New developments in medicine, however, did not automatically bring better health care to all Americans. Exotic new drugs, complicated treatment procedures, and lavish hospital facilities increased the costs of medical care. The very poor and many elderly people simply could not afford the new "wonder" cures; many rural areas and small towns, unable to compete with metropolitan areas for younger physicians, found themselves short of competent doctors as well as of up-to-date hospital facilities. Largely as a result of this maldistribution of medical services, the United States actually lost ground, compared to other industrial nations, in its infant mortality rate. Between 1950 and 1970 the United States' worldwide ranking on infant mortality dropped; by 1970 the world's richest nation ranked only fifteenth, slightly behind England and significantly behind Scandinavian countries such as Sweden.

In addition to the unequal distribution of the new developments, advanced medical technology created other problems. Increased specialization produced considerable dissatisfaction about the disappearance

46

of the family doctor—the general practitioner often pictured in Norman Rockwell's paintings—and about the proliferation of specialists trained to diagnose and treat only a limited number of conditions. Indeed, after World War II new medical technology meant that large hospital complexes, with their costly array of machines and their large staffs of specialists, did replace the home and the doctor's office as primary treatment centers. Fewer and fewer doctors made house calls; more and more people went to hospital emergency rooms or outpatient centers. At the same time, people who needed extensive medical care discovered that the new medical discoveries often meant a costly stay in the hospital. In 1946 only 1 of every 10 Americans was admitted to a hospital for inpatient care; twenty years later the figure had risen to 1 of every 6.5 persons. Unfortunately, a hospital visit did not always result in either an instant cure or, in some cases, even the proper treatment. A number of prominent physicians have contended—and several studies have substantiated their claims—that perhaps one-half of many common surgical operations, particularly those performed upon women and children, are unnecessary. Other critics of the medical establishment have gone further: citing information in medical journals, they claim that a sizable percentage of people suffer from iatrogenic illnesses, ailments brought on by the "treatment" for some other malady. Many of these iatrogenic illnesses, these critics argue, result from some doctors' naive faith in new medicines, from improper testing and regulation of supposedly effective drugs, and from the popular belief that doctors possess a miracle cure for every ache and pain. Although such critics point to some undoubted failures of modern medicine, their indictments tend to slight the examples in which new discoveries have aided millions of Americans. Certainly, breakthroughs in the treatment and prevention of diseases such as tuberculosis and polio represent positive gains.

Agriculture

Postwar science and technology affected all segments of American society. Perhaps no one saw more changes than farmers, traditionally the slowest people to alter settled ways. Farming became more mechanized and scientific than ever before. Sophisticated biological knowledge resulted in new types of seeds, such as hybrid corn. Introduced in some areas during the 1930s, hybrid corn spread to all parts of the country by the 1950s. Equally important to grain producers, the chemical industry provided the knowledge to make cheaper fertilizers and pesticides. Farmers quickly turned to these chemicals to boost output; they used three times as much fertilizer in 1950 as they had ten years earlier. Farmers also began to adopt labor-saving machines on a massive scale. Between 1940 and 1960, for example, the number of tractors increased by more than 200 percent, and the number of grain combines rose by nearly as much. Meanwhile, engineers were increasing the size of these machines, boosting their horsepower with higher-compression engines, and offering a variety of attachments. The new machinery and chemicals drastically reduced the number of farm laborers needed to bring in key crops (see chart 1).

As a result of all the new developments, American agriculture changed significantly after World War II. For many years agricultural production had been increasing, but now—with hybrid seeds, better equipment, cheaper fertilizers, and new irrigation facilities—output rose at a much faster rate than before. Farmers could cultivate hitherto unproductive land and areas once set aside as pastures for horses and mules. (In 1920 farmers had used more than 90 million acres of potential croplands to graze draft animals; by 1960 they needed less than 10 million acres for pasturage.) In addition, the new agricultural methods permitted farmers to utilize their old land more effectively, and the yield per acre rose substantially after World War II.

Ironically, postwar changes probably created as many problems as they solved. Irrigation required massive amounts of water, while fertilizers and pesticides raised health hazards for both farm workers and consumers. Most important, steadily increasing production kept farm prices low: after 1947 agricultural prices leveled off until the sudden

Chart 1 Declining demand for farm labor accelerated the rush to urban areas and left pockets of rural poverty.

Mechanization of agriculture: Man-hours per 100 bushels of selected crops

Crop	1945–49	1955–59	1962–66
Corn for grain	53	20	9
Sorghum grain	49	20	9
Wheat	34	17	11
Hay	6.2	3.7	3.0
Potatoes	12	6	5
Sugarbeets	6.3	2.9	2.1
Cotton	146	74	39
Tobacco	39	31	25
Soybeans	41	23	20

Adapted from Nathan Rosenberg, *Technology and American Economic Growth* (New York: Harper & Row, 1972), p. 136.

rises of the early 1970s. While most of the world's people spent almost half their incomes for food, Americans needed only about 20 percent of their paychecks to feed their families. The majority of farmers did not enjoy the rising incomes of most other Americans, and only the largest and most efficient operations could show substantial profits. Although Washington tried to support farm incomes by using the same basic programs devised during Roosevelt's New Deal—direct subsidies and various plans for restriction of acreage—nothing really solved the problem of low farm incomes.

The New Conservatism

Despite all the postwar scientific developments, some Americans felt pessimistic and called for a return to traditional institutions and settled ways. Arch-conservatives like Senator Kenneth Wherry of Nebraska and radio commentator Fulton Lewis, Jr., had long fought a rearguard action against New Deal–Fair Deal liberalism, but the younger conservatives of the late 1940s and early 1950s displayed both a new militancy and a new self-confidence. They condemned the growth of the national government, the "no-win" policy toward communism, the expensive social welfare programs, the increased government restraints on private enterprise and individual liberties, the decline of old moral and religious standards, and the supposed upsurge in lawlessness. (Unlike the situation in the mid-1960s, when crime really did increase, the "crime wave" of the immediate postwar period, as sociologists like Daniel Bell have argued, was primarily a myth.) Observing the strong opposition to any significant extension of the New Deal and the growing challenge to Democratic foreign policy, some liberals began to fear that conservatism might eventually become the new consensus.

Many liberals held a simplistic view of postwar conservatism. They believed that conservatism, with its emphasis on private property and social order, appealed primarily to insecure people who felt overwhelmed by the complexities of the modern world. A classic social science study, *The Authoritarian Personality* (1950), seemed to support the theory that the "radical right" was composed of confused people who desired greater stability in their lives. This analysis probably did explain some of the appeal of postwar conservatism; many right-wing groups seemed to attract people who adopted simple, conspiratorial explanations for their own and the nation's problems. But this social-psychological interpretation tended to deny any validity to the conservative critique. Taking almost all the assumptions of Fair Deal liberalism for granted, many liberals considered any serious dissent,

49

from the right as well as from the left, as mostly silly and probably irrational.

The "new conservatives," as they called themselves, defied easy categorization. Russell Kirk, one of the most pessimistic of the postwar conservatives, condemned democratic reforms like universal suffrage and direct election of senators for disrupting social harmony and urged conservatives to provide voters with a sense of deference to society's "natural leaders." To Kirk, the "creeping socialism" of the Democratic party's welfare state was a giant step toward left-wing totalitarianism. Not all the new conservatives shared Kirk's views. More progressive conservatives, such as historians Peter Viereck and Clinton Rossiter, accepted the idea of political democracy and even praised the New Deal. Viereck, for instance, saw welfare programs like Social Security as stabilizing influences and necessary guarantees of economic security. And while Kirk favored tight censorship of "dangerous" ideas, the libertarian conservatives displayed a much deeper respect for individual liberties and diversity of opinion.

Most of the new conservatives could have agreed on a few central tenets. Dissenting from modern liberalism, they criticized social innovation and glorified custom and tradition; they saw people as basically evil and distrusted popular opinion; they supported organized religion and expressed distress about the declining influence of religious institutions; and they favored order and stability and instinctively feared innovation and change.

Despite their loud criticism of the basic direction of postwar society, however, the new conservatives gained little popular support. If Truman and his liberal advisers could not rally the country behind a new crusade for reform, conservatives discovered even less enthusiasm for rolling back the Democratic welfare state. The essence of the conservative movement remained literary and cultural: even during the 1950s, when a popular Republican president preached the importance of reviving traditional virtues, militant conservatism found itself isolated from the mainstream of American life.

The Taint of Scandal

Although the ultraconservative position remained in the minority, many people did feel a sense of disquietude about certain signs of corruption in postwar society. In 1950 and 1951 a politically ambitious senator from Tennessee, Estes Kefauver, dramatically alerted people to the supposed dangers of organized crime. Exploiting the still new medium of television, Kefauver brought underworld figures—from top mobster Frank Costello down to petty gamblers and prostitutes—into the living rooms of millions of people. The show held all the drama of a Hollywood production. "It was difficult at times to believe that it was real," said the *New York Times*. For eight days, the Kefauver committee kept viewers near their sets; people stopped going shopping or out to eat during the hearings. To sociologists like Daniel Bell, Kefauver had only revealed the obvious: certain "criminal" activities, particularly gambling, had become big business for their operators and a way of life for many Americans. Like earlier bootlegging operations, the gambling industry provided opportunities which poor boys could not find in "legitimate" enterprises. Discovering plenty of customers clamoring for their product, mobsters had become modern Horatio Algers. Kefauver and most viewers took a less detached view, preferring to see the hearings as a morality play, a confrontation between good and evil.

Kefauver's committee also highlighted connections between some gambling figures and urban Democratic political machines. Political sociologists quickly noted that such ties resulted, in large part, from the flow of tax revenues to Washington since the 1930s and that many urban governments needed funds, from whatever source, to carry on necessary programs. Ironically, money from gambling and other illegal activities, when used to aid Democratic politicians, helped support social reform in some urban areas. These observers, of course, were not condoning corruption; they were trying to explain it as a social phenomenon rather than simply as a result of evil people. An exchange between former Mayor William O'Dwyer of New York and Senator Charles Tobey of New Hampshire dramatized the contrast between this pragmatic view and the outraged moralism of other Americans. When O'Dwyer admitted that he knew mobster Frank Costello, the Senator quickly interrupted. "It almost seems to me as though you should say, 'unclean, unclean' . . . and that you should leave him alone. . . ." Admitting that organized gambling existed in New York, O'Dwyer replied that there was a lot of bookmaking in the senator's own state and that he wondered whom the local bookies supported for political office. "There are things that you have to do politically if you want to get cooperation," O'Dwyer concluded.

Other stories of corruption appeared during the early 1950s. In 1950 the United States Military Academy, the citadel of gentlemanly honor and patriotic values, expelled ninety West Pointers, including nine starting members of the football team, for cheating on examinations. That same year, prosecutors in New York uncovered a point-shaving scandal in college basketball. Star players on several top teams—including national champion City College of New York and the University of Kentucky—were taking bribes in exchange for rigging game scores in favor of professional gamblers.

People reacted in different ways to these revelations. Some condemned the commercialism which had invaded college athletics. Some, like Senator J. William Fulbright of Arkansas, blamed the spirit of corruption on a general decline in moral principles. The National Collegiate Athletic Association banned the basketball players from further competition, and the new professional league, the National Basketball Association, blacklisted them forever. But others were not so quick to accept or to assign moral blame. The young West Point cadets eschewed contrition, claiming that they were being punished for a practice followed by most of their classmates. Army's football coach, Colonel Earl Blaik, whose son had been one of those dropped from the Academy, refused to condemn his players and publicly reaffirmed his faith in football as a character-building sport.

In the end, stories of corruption reached into the White House. Along with McCarthyite charges of being soft on communism, accusations about "the mess in Washington" drove Truman's popularity lower and lower. During his last years in office, scandals seemed to pop up everywhere. An old crony, Harry Vaughn, was accused of accepting a deep freeze; Senator Fulbright (an old Truman foe known as Senator Halfbright around the White House) uncovered examples of apparent political favoritism in the Reconstruction Finance Corporation; the wife of a former RFC official received a $9,500 mink coat as part of a questionable transaction; the *New Republic* leveled charges of bribery or political favoritism at no less than six federal agencies; the chairman of the Democratic National Committee appeared guilty of influencing a government decision in exchange for legal fees; and Republicans constantly complained that the Truman administration was full of "five-percenters" who traded their political influence for kickbacks on public contracts. Cantankerous and stubborn as ever, Truman lashed out at his critics. Despite clear evidence to the contrary, he proclaimed that "my house is always clean." By the fall of 1951 liberal Democrats as well as Republicans were demanding that Truman take decisive action. He did appoint an investigator to probe the charges in February 1952, but allowed his attorney general to fire the prober two months later. Although no one ever connected any of the scandals with Truman himself, he left Washington with the reputation of being soft on corruption as well as on communism.

BIBLIOGRAPHY

Eric F. Goldman, *The Crucial Decade—And After* (1960), remains a useful introduction to the postwar period. Rexford G. Tugwell, *Off Course: From Truman to Nixon* (1971); and William E. Leuchtenburg, *A Troubled Feast: American Society since 1945* (1973), are more recent interpretations.

Harry Truman's *Memoirs* (2 vols., 1955–56), contain some useful information, as do Bert Cochran, *Harry Truman and the Crisis Presidency* (1973); Margret Truman Daniels, *Harry S. Truman* (1972); and Merle Miller, ed., *Plain Speaking* (1974). Cabell Phillips, *The Truman Presidency* (1966), is a readable journalistic account. Barton J. Bernstein, ed., *Politics and Policies of the Truman Administration* (1970); and Richard S. Kirkendall, ed., *The Truman Period as a Research Field* (2nd ed., 1974), contain more scholarly analyses of different aspects of Truman's presidency. Alonso Hamby, *Beyond the New Deal: Harry S. Truman and American Liberalism* (1973), offers a broad view of the Fair Deal. Barton J. Bernstein and Allan J. Matusow, eds., *The Truman Administration: A Documentary History* (1966), is a useful compilation of primary materials.

Specific subjects are covered in Susan Hartman, *Truman and the Eightieth Congress* (1971); Richard O. Davies, *Housing Reform during the Truman Administration* (1966); Allen J. Matusow, *Farm Policies and Politics in the Truman Administration* (1967); R. Alton Lee, *Truman and Taft-Hartley* (1966); and Arthur F. McClure, *The Truman Administration and the Problems of Postwar Labor* (1969). On civil rights, see Richard M. Dalfiume, *Desegregation of the U.S. Armed Forces* (1969); William C. Berman, *The Politics of Civil Rights in the Truman Administration,* (1970); and Donald R. McCoy and Richard T. Ruetten, *Quest and Response* (1973).

James T. Patterson, *Mr. Republican* (1972), is the first scholarly biography of Robert A. Taft and an important book on postwar politics. Samuel Lubell, *The Future of American Politics* (rev. ed., 1965), is still a useful reference on voting patterns. See also the relevant chapters in V. O. Key, *The Responsible Electorate* (1966); Angus Campbell et al., *The Voter Decides* (1954); and Walter Dean Burnham, *Critical Elections and the Mainsprings of American Politics* (1970). On Henry Wallace and his drive for the presidency in 1948, see Norman D. Markowitz, *The Rise and Fall of the People's Century* (1973).

There is a substantial literature on McCarthyism and the postwar consensus mentality. The best of the older accounts include Richard H. Rovere, *Senator Joe McCarthy* (1959); and Daniel Bell, ed., *The Radical Right* (1963). For more recent views, see Michael Rogin, *McCarthy and the Intellectuals* (1967); Athan G. Theoharis, *Seeds of Repression: Harry S. Truman and the Origins of McCarthyism* (1970); Robert Griffith, *The Politics of Fear* (1970); Richard M. Freeland, *The Truman Doctrine and the Origins of McCarthyism* (1972); and Robert Griffith and Athan G. Theoharis, eds., *The Specter* (1974). Earl Latham, *The Communist Controversy in Washington* (1966); and Christopher Lasch, *The Agony of the American Left* (1969), also contain relevant material.

The friendly smile of Dwight David Eisenhower dominated American politics during the 1950s. "Ike" read little and was noted for neither brilliance nor wit, but his straightforward honesty made him a beloved father figure to many Americans. A successful general in World War II, Ike surely was shrewder than his simple popular image projected. Army promotions and success as a commander required ambition and a politician's keen sense of timing. But to Americans of the fifties he epitomized moderation and down-home common sense. Even his nickname had a folksy ring, lacking the efficient staccato of "JFK" and "LBJ" or the distant formality of "Richard M. Nixon."

The Elections of 1952 and 1956

In 1952, encouraged by the Truman administration's many problems, Republicans anticipated the victory which had slipped away four years earlier. Still, GOP leaders wanted to take no chances, and the desire to pick a winner worked in favor of Dwight Eisenhower.

Some people doubted that Eisenhower would run for the presidency. In 1948 the popular general had firmly rejected the idea of a presidential race because of the "necessary policy" of subordinating the military to civilian rule. And despite a Republican background, his cur-

3

Affluence and affability: America in the 1950s

rent political affiliation remained a mystery. As late as 1951 Truman had suggested that Eisenhower become the Democrats' standard-bearer. But while president of Columbia University from 1948 to 1951, Eisenhower formed close ties with influential members of the Republican party's Eastern establishment, and he came to share their belief that another GOP defeat would greatly strengthen the more conservative McCarthyite wing of the party. A moderate on almost every issue, Eisenhower did not want the GOP to swing so far to the right. He also believed that the United States must play an active role in Europe, and he feared that Senator Robert A. Taft, a leading contender for the Republican nomination, was not firmly committed to NATO. When Eastern supporters convinced Eisenhower that Taft's reputation as a Midwestern reactionary would prove a serious political liability, the old soldier decided that both the GOP and the nation needed him.

Not all Republicans welcomed their party's new savior. GOP leaders and Republican voters from the Midwest and South resented the power of their party's more liberal Eastern wing; influential senators such as Everett Dirkson of Illinois supported "Mr. Republican" Taft and strongly opposed Eisenhower. Throughout the Republican nominating convention, speakers proclaimed domestic policies closely attuned to Taft's ideas and trumpeted the militant anticommunist rhetoric of Joe McCarthy. After hearing speeches from McCarthy, Herbert Hoover, and General Douglas MacArthur, one reporter concluded that Eisenhower had walked into the wrong convention. A few Republicans even feared that the party might split apart, as it had done in 1912 when Taft's grandfather had battled Teddy Roosevelt for the nomination.

Despite several angry confrontations, the GOP could not pass up a seemingly sure winner: Eisenhower won a first-ballot victory. To soothe ruffled feelings, he selected Richard Nixon, a man with impeccable credentials as a Republican regular and anticommunist crusader, as vice-presidential candidate. The thirty-four-year-old Nixon was also expected to attract younger votes.

During the 1952 presidential campaign, Eisenhower encountered some difficulty in transforming himself from General of the Army to good old Ike. Without his familiar Eisenhower military jacket he looked much like any other sixty-one-year-old politician, and early appearances revealed his inexperience as a stump speaker. In addition, the necessities of campaigning clashed with his personal distaste for the phony familiarity of political life. Gradually though, Ike developed a more natural style and accepted most of the rituals of American politics. To the displeasure of some, he even made symbolic concessions to right-wing Republicans, holding a highly publicized session with Senator Taft and campaigning alongside several outspoken McCar-

Looking forward to victory, 1952.

thyites. In a Wisconsin speech Eisenhower deleted a favorable reference to General George Marshall, his close personal friend but one of McCarthy's favorite targets. And though Ike piously announced, "I shall not and will not engage in character assasination, vilification and personalities," Nixon and other McCarthyites gathered votes by extravagant attacks on communist influence in Washington, corruption in government, and the "no-win" war in Korea. Nixon even reverted to the communist-conspiracy theme when stories about an improper political slush fund threatened his place on the ticket. His televised reply to the charges featured insinuations that the "reds" wanted to deny him the vice-presidency and contained self-pitying comments about his wife's "Republican cloth coat," his worn-out Oldsmobile, and his one political payoff—his daughters' little dog Checkers. The "Checkers Speech" saved Nixon's career and made him an even greater asset to the Republican ticket.

By contrast, Democrats found few bright spots in 1952. Their presidential nominee, Governor Adlai Stevenson of Illinois, won the plaudits of liberal columnists for his cleverly phrased, well reasoned speeches. But critics in both parties complained that the erudite Stevenson aimed his addresses well over the average voter's head. His image as an intellectual egghead, coupled with a recent divorce, became frequently noted handicaps. In addition, Stevenson had to outrun the unpopular shadow of Harry Truman, who insisted upon taking part in the campaign. Political pollsters, who had substantially revised their techniques after the miscalculations of 1948, discovered that many voters simply felt that the Democrats had been in power too long. Election results corroborated their predictions.

Eisenhower appeared to be a person who could restore old-time American virtues to government, and most voters seemed satisfied. Four years later, when the Eisenhower–Stevenson presidential contest was replayed, Eisenhower's popularity as a national hero remained undiminished. Retaining Richard Nixon as a running mate (after several unheeded hints that Nixon might prefer a cabinet post), Eisenhower received almost 10 million more popular votes than Stevenson. Ike's popularity, however, did not carry over to the party as a whole. The Democrats took control of both houses of Congress, showing that the Democratic coalition of the 1930s remained basically intact.

The Eisenhower Presidency

Eisenhower promised a "constitutional presidency." Holding great reverence for the traditions of local government and state autonomy, he felt that Democratic administrations had extended national power too far. Similarly, Eisenhower believed that Harry Truman, whom he held in very low esteem, had provoked Congress, needlessly embittering relations between the White House and Capitol Hill. Ike came to Washington determined to get along with Congress; such cooperation became a necessity after the Democrats gained control of both houses in 1954. Eisenhower instructed cabinet members to avoid antagonizing members of Congress. The art of leadership, he told one associate, did not require "hitting people over the head. Any damn fool can do that. . . . It's persuasion—and conciliation—and education—and patience. That's the only kind of leadership I know—or believe in—or will practice." During his two terms he received much help from congressional Democrats led by two cagey Texans, Sam Rayburn and Lyndon Johnson. Political moderates themselves, Rayburn and Johnson approved many of Eisenhower's policies; one historian described their version of "loyal opposition" as three parts loyal and one part opposition. Although the executive branch and Congress were not on an eight-year "honeymoon," there was little of the bitterness which characterized relations during the late 1960s and early 1970s.

Eisenhower also tried to bring harmony to members of his administration. Believing that Democratic administrations had ignored sound managerial practices, Eisenhower filled his first cabinet with Republican businessmen. "Engine Charley" Wilson, Secretary of Defense, came from General Motors; Treasury Secretary George Humphrey had headed the giant Mark Hanna Company; Postmaster General Arthur Summerfield owned a huge car agency in Michigan. A liberal magazine dismissed Eisenhower's appointees as "eight millionaires and a

United Press International

President Eisenhower's Cabinet. Clockwise around the table: Henry Cabot Lodge, Jr., Chief of the U.S. U.N. Delegation; Secretary of Interior Douglas McKay; Secretary of the Treasury George M. Humphrey; Vice-President Richard Nixon; Attorney General Herbert Brownell; Secretary of Commerce Sinclair Weeks; Secretary of Health, Education and Welfare Oveta Culp Hobby; Presidential Assistant Sherman Adams; Budget Director Joseph M. Dodge; Acting Defense Mobilizer Arthur S. Flemming; Secretary of Labor Martin P. Durkin; Postmaster General Arthur Summerfield; Secretary of State John Foster Dulles; President Eisenhower; Secretary of Defense Charles E. Wilson; Secretary of Agriculture Ezra Taft Benson; and Mutual Security Director Harold Stassen. Standing: Civil Service Chairman Philip Young; Robert Cutler, Assistant to the President for National Security Matters.

plumber." The plumber was Democrat Martin Durkin, president of the United Association of Plumbers and Steamfitters. Eisenhower hoped that a union man might smooth relations between his administration and organized labor, but appointment of a Democrat only enraged conservative Republicans. Within eight months, Durkin was gone. Eisenhower also drew heavily from business and the military to fill White House staff positions.

The president shrewdly managed his new team. He picked Sherman Adams as his chief aide (some people called Adams the assistant president) and granted him broad authority. Adams acted as the president's gatekeeper, allowing entrance to people who had important business but blocking those who might waste time. He also handled many sensitive duties which Eisenhower himself wished to avoid. Adams soon became notorious for his brusque phone calls—he made more than 200 every day—in which he barked orders and then abruptly hung up without waiting for a reply. This style of operation gained Adams many enemies in Washington, but it also allowed Eisenhower to avoid some ticklish situations. In foreign affairs and economic policy Eisenhower adopted a similar strategy, letting Secretary of State John Foster Dulles and George Humphrey take the heat while he remained above the battle.

Eisenhower's skillful use of subordinates as political lightning rods reflected his deep conviction that, after all of Harry Truman's troubles, he must restore the prestige of the presidency. Although he had formed no church ties during his army career, Eisenhower quickly joined Washington's National Presbyterian Church (seven previous presidents had been members), and became a Sunday regular. He opened cabinet meetings with a silent prayer and began the tradition of "prayer breakfasts" at the White House. His inaugural parade contained a hastily constructed entry called "God's Float." Flanked by slogans proclaiming "In God We Trust" and "Freedom of Worship" and topped by a curious structure which was supposed to resemble a nondenominational church, the creation struck one clergyman as "an oversized model of a deformed molar left over from some dental exhibit." But Eisenhower rarely stumbled in his public-relations efforts. Unlike Lyndon Johnson and Richard Nixon, who unsuccessfully used many of the same symbols during their stormy presidencies, Eisenhower apparently convinced most people of his sincerity. Although many journalists questioned the wisdom of Eisenhower's policies, few doubted his integrity or decency. And through his much-publicized addiction to golf and bridge, pastimes which millions of ordinary citizens also enjoyed, he projected the image of the common man. No one would have thought of writing slashing invectives like *McBird* or *An Evening with Richard Nixon* about Dwight Eisenhower.

In recent years, most historians have raised their estimates of Eisenhower's leadership. Once dismissed as a weak president and an incompetent politician, Eisenhower now gains higher marks. Although he lacked interest in many areas of government and party politics, he did demonstrate a sound grasp of other issues. According to his associates, he skillfully presided over cabinet sessions and meetings of the National Security Council. For a long time, people believed that strong figures like Dulles, Humphrey, and Adams dominated Eisenhower and really ran the government. Early in the first term a familiar joke asked, "What if Ike died and we got Nixon as president?" "Yes," went the punch line, "but what if Adams died, and we got stuck with Ike?" But events seemed to demonstrate that Eisenhower retained a firm, though oftentimes unseen, rein in areas he considered critical. During his second term, all three of his key advisers resigned (a kickback scandal forced Adams's resignation, Humphrey returned to business, and Dulles fell victim to cancer), yet Eisenhower carried on without any noticeable disruption.

Still, many questions about Eisenhower's presidency remain unanswered. Did Eisenhower, who left office with an extremely high rating in the opinion polls, defer too much to popular attitudes and exert too little leadership from the White House? Did not the Eisenhower administration ignore crucial domestic problems such as pollution and urban decay? Did Eisenhower's lack of sympathy with the black civil rights movement help inflame racial tensions? (See below, chapter 5.) And was he as shrewd a president as his close associates claimed, or did he have extraordinarily good luck in handling the affairs of state? All these questions and many others await further research and contemplation. But one thing is clear: at a time when many Americans wanted some sign of stability, the former general from Kansas provided a national symbol of old values and traditional virtues.

Economic Policies

Two weeks after taking office Eisenhower announced that "the first order of business is the elimination of the annual deficit" in the federal budget. Guided by Secretary of Treasury George Humphrey and Budget Director Maurice Stans, Eisenhower curtailed federal spending whenever possible. To this Republican administration—the first since Herbert Hoover's—mounting unemployment and possible recession were always less frightening than inflation or the "creeping socialism" of big government.

Eisenhower attempted to reduce government's role in the economy. During his first year in office he turned over certain nationally owned offshore oil deposits to the states of California, Louisiana, and Texas for subsequent lease to private oil companies. He also attempted to undercut the federal government's Tennessee Valley Authority by giving the privately owned Dixon-Yates utility a contract to supply power for the Atomic Energy Commission. (Public furor over the questionable circumstances surrounding this deal, however, forced the government to repudiate the Dixon-Yates agreement.) Ike frequently used his veto power against housing, public works, and antipollution bills; after the end of the Korean War he quickly lifted economic controls (many economists believed too quickly); and his secretary of agriculture attempted to lower farm subsidies. Following his vision of moderate Republicanism, Eisenhower did not dismantle New Deal programs—during his eight years as president Congress raised Social Security payments, minimum wage rates, and unemployment benefits—but the president clearly opposed large government.

One new spending program that Eisenhower did support had a profound effect on the style of American life. The interstate highway program, begun in 1956, committed the federal government to a thirteen-year, $26 billion program to help states construct interstate highways according to a national plan. As the costs mounted to $37 billion in 1961 and $50 billion in 1968, Congress continued to appropriate additional revenues. The program represented a major national commitment to the internal combustion engine; in effect, it subsidized the trucking industry and those Americans who could afford cross-country travel in private automobiles.

Interstate construction brought a host of spin-offs: construction companies boomed; new gas stations sprang up; lines of motels stretched out along the highways. Around big cities the maze of interstate exchanges stood as monuments to human ingenuity, and technology lent its latest techniques to the planning and control of traffic flow. But the positive effects of the interstate program often obscured its drawbacks. Railroads, a less expensive and less polluting method of transportation, could not compete with truckers who used free interstate highways, and rail lines fell into deep financial trouble. In New York City mass transit facilities decayed; in Los Angeles and many other cities they were never constructed, and miles of concrete and asphalt crisscrossed the landscape. Americans became more car-crazy than ever. And the more they drove, the more there was no alternative to driving. Those without cars—the old, the handicapped, the poor—were the losers. The "highway lobby," a loose alliance of auto manufacturers, oil producers, and construction companies, were the winners. The graft sometimes associated with the purchase of right-of-ways and the award of contracts tainted local politics and reminded historians of the railroad corruption of the late nineteenth century.

61

Despite the interstate highway program, Eisenhower kept federal spending down, and the economy grew at a slow rate. Moreover, Ike's failure to use government fiscal policy to regulate the economy contributed to economic uncertainty. In 1954, after the end of the Korean War, the country slid into a small recession, but Eisenhower's advisers refused to pump in additional federal money to promote recovery. Again in 1957, economic indicators showed an alarming downturn. By spring of 1958 unemployment had reached 7.5 percent and the recession seemed serious. Even members of the business community, Eisenhower's strongest supporters, began to worry that the Republican administration would not move rapidly enough to stimulate growth. Still fearing an inflationary spiral, Eisenhower opposed tax cuts or increased federal spending, the usual prescriptions for correcting economic slowdowns.

Liberal economists faulted Eisenhower for his policies of moderate growth and limited spending. America's economic growth rate, they pointed out, lagged behind the Soviet Union's. Worse still, some economists claimed, the low rate of growth did not expand employment rapidly enough to keep up with population growth. The large baby-boom generation, after all, would soon be on the job market. In addition, some charged that the lack of new federal programs stemmed not from a dearth of pressing problems but from a determination to ignore them. Pollution, central-city blight, inadequate mass transit, and inequitable health care had not reached the crisis proportions they assumed in the 1960s and 1970s, but they were nonetheless real problems which, if dealt with, might not have become acute.

In *The Affluent Society* (1958), liberal economist John Kenneth Galbraith denounced the parsimony of public welfare programs. He contrasted the personal affluence of most Americans with the lack of decent public services, writing of the travelers who steer their "mauve and cerise air-conditioned, power-steered and power-braked car" through badly paved and littered streets; who "picnic on exquisitely packaged food from a portable icebox by a polluted stream and go on to spend the night at a park which is a menace to public health and morals." Galbraith scathingly attacked the American tax system which permitted such a disparity between public services and private comfort. He called for higher levels of taxation and greater government spending.

Despite such advice, Eisenhower and his advisers held fast to their economic policies. Defenders pointed out that real wages for an average family had risen 20 percent during Ike's years in office, a gain which meant a great deal to most Americans. In addition, policies of modest growth kept the inflation rate low, and this price stability moderated labor disputes and helped maintain a relatively healthy dollar abroad. If

Ike's administration deferred problems until later, most Americans probably wanted it that way. Eisenhower, after all, had not promised to reform and crusade but to soothe and assure. Many years later, Ike proudly remembered his principal accomplishment as creating "an atmosphere of greater serenity and mutual confidence."

But all was not serene and calm during the 1950s. The population was expanding at a tremendous rate; people were flocking to the suburbs in unprecedented numbers; affluence allowed many people to enjoy the products of a booming popular culture industry; and at the other end of the economic spectrum people, many of them nonwhite, found it difficult to believe that the United States really was a land of affluence.

SOCIAL TRENDS

Baby Boom

During the ten years after World War II the number of children born each year in the United States rose by nearly 50 percent, the biggest increase in births ever recorded anywhere. Throughout the fifties, towns and cities busily constructed the brick-and-glass schools which would hold these youngsters until they were about seventeen, socializing them into the American value system and economic structure. Everywhere children of the baby boom turned, they spilled out of conventional facilities. They needed unprecedented quantities of diapers, toys, books, and teachers. Their very numbers gave them a generational identity and tagged them as somehow extraordinary. During the fifties, the pressure of this generation was contained in homes and schools; later it would find its way into overcrowded subways, unemployment lines, student revolts, and a "counterculture." Understandably, many of the products of this baby boom would later take up the cry for zero population growth.

Demographers seeking explanations for the postwar baby boom have arrived at a few tentative conclusions. From 1940 to the mid-fifties couples began marrying and having children at a much earlier age than their parents. There has always been a close correlation between average age of marriage and number of children—the two factors rise or fall inversely—so the extraordinarily high birth rate comes as no surprise. But why did couples marry early and have large families?

Economic security was one reason. The tremendous economic expansion which came with the war opened new jobs and created a general scarcity of labor. The shortage of younger workers throughout the late forties and fifties meant unusually rapid economic advancement, especially for white males. Not only did pay scales within each job category shoot up, but upward occupational mobility was far greater than in the 1930s or even in the 1920s. Throughout the fifties, business analysts noted a decline in the average age of corporate executives, and older people grumbled at how easily the younger generation could reach positions which had taken them years to attain. Favorable employment and high income levels gave young couples greater security than ever before.

Certain economic innovations also contributed to the affluence of young, particularly white, couples. Government-sponsored benefits for veterans provided extra sources of income; unemployment compensation made savings seem less necessary. The whole array of New Deal programs—FHA home loans, AAA soil bank, REA electrification, FDIC insurance, and Social Security payments—particularly assisted middle-income Americans. In addition to these welfare state measures, wider use of credit allowed families to spend beyond their incomes. Installment buying, finance agencies, charge accounts, and credit cards coaxed Americans to buy whatever they wanted, whenever they wanted it. The financial well-being which encouraged early marriage and large families was based upon certain employment, rising income, the new welfare role of government, and the availability of credit.

The baby boom probably also had psychological foundations. Its beginnings in the war years may have stemmed partially from the fears associated with separation, as men entered the military. After the war, the bright economic picture provided couples with the self-confidence and optimism which are important ingredients in decisions to marry and have children. Then too, Americans had deferred having children throughout the depression, and the meteoric rise of the birth rate during the fifties must always be viewed against the backdrop of its previous decline.

Domesticity

The baby boom was associated with an upsurge in the ideal of domesticity, the notion that a woman's place was in her home and with her children. Although the employment of women increased in the postwar years in response to the generally favorable economic situation (by 1960 one-third of the women of working age were employed), most women occupied low-paying jobs. The greatest gains came in the field of clerical work where wages were low. Although women received college educations in unprecedented numbers, fewer women attained advanced degrees, and employment of women in prestigious professions dropped. For the well-educated wives of white-collar professionals, homes seemed more attractive than the low-status careers earmarked for women. The fifties was a decade of clubwork, not of crusading for equal job opportunities. In 1949, for example, women who had graduated fifteen years earlier from some of the nation's top women's schools (Barnard, Bryn Mawr, Mount Holyoke, Radcliffe, Smith, Vassar, and Wellesley) were polled to determine what they had done with their college educations. Eighty-eight percent considered marriage more important than a career, and only about 12 percent of the married respondents worked full-time. One of every four responded that playing bridge was a major activity in her life.

Widely accepted concepts of "scientific" childrearing reinforced the flight into the home. Dr. Benjamin Spock, who would later lead some of "his children" (as he phrased it) in antiwar protests, guided the baby-boom generation through childhood. His book *Baby and Child Care* rivaled the *Holy Bible* in sales and stood next to it as a guide to appropriate conduct in most middle-class homes. Spock made motherhood a challenging task. Although he cautioned women against becoming too tied to their children and spelled out the consequences of allowing the child to become a tiny tyrant, the overall effect of the book left mothers feeling uneasy about their responsibilities. If a child's budding capabilities depended upon the proper application of "scientific" principles, then the mysteries of child-raising deserved a woman's full attention. Any act, it seemed, could have far-reaching consequences upon the child's behavior and psychological makeup. When a mother heard cries, for example, should she ignore them for fear the baby might become spoiled, or attend to them so that the child would not feel afraid and rejected? Spock tried to provide guides to action, but no book could solve every problem. Often he simply left women in a quandary, feeling vaguely guilty about their uncertainty.

Managing the family's spending also took much of a wife's time. As incomes rose, as credit facilities became more complex, and as advertisers stimulated demand, women tended to become full-time consumers, deciding what foods to buy and what products deserved priority. Advertisers geared their appeals to women, even for expensive durable goods such as automobiles. This strategy both reflected and reinforced the role of the woman as prime consumer. *Better Homes and Gardens*, a women's magazine (edited by men) with a circulation of millions, exemplified the trend. Advertisements took up far more than half the space while the remaining pages contained tips on running a household efficiently and "scientifically"—how to plan quick meals, how to determine what washing machine fit the family needs, how to spruce up a back yard. Women's magazines often emphasized money-saving, but their net effect was to stimulate consumer tastes. The word *housewife* less frequently evoked images of sewing and baking and became virtually synonymous with the word *shopper*.

Suburbia

Rising incomes, the baby boom, and the emphasis on domesticity accelerated the flight to the suburbs. Throughout the country, city dwellers built new residences on the edge of town to accommodate their larger families, to flee the inner city, and to achieve new levels of comfort and status. In major cities and even in smaller towns with populations of twenty-five to fifty thousand, neat rows of homes intruded upon the surrounding countryside. Real estate builders and developers such as Levitt & Company pioneered tract homes, which were cheaply constructed according to a preestablished plan. Building innovations, in addition to the FHA loan program, brought suburban "paradise" within the reach of millions. One-fourth of all the housing which existed in 1960 had been built in the 1950s.

On the surface, suburban living seemed to bring contentment. The predominantly white, middle-class residents aspired to economic success, and although their preoccupation with status often bred rivalries, the shared value system also brought a sense of comfort and community. Conformity was a balm for rootlessness and a cushion against the anxiety of change. But every glimpse of suburban happiness had its darker side of unforseen problems. Burgeoning residential sections often overcrowded existing facilities, creating the congestion that residents had hoped to escape. Payments for mortgages, autos, and consumer goods sometimes brought new financial worries, and the mounting personal indebtedness among Americans alarmed many economists. Distances to work grew longer and longer; those who commuted in comfortable private cars only contributed to clogged freeways and polluted air.

Suburban life easily lent itself to caricature and derision. Folksinger Malvina Reynolds labeled suburban homes "little boxes made of ticky-tacky" and jabbed at the conformity of men who all "drink their martinis dry" and of children who all "go to summer camp and then to the university." In the 1960s Andy Warhol made the slickly packaged consumer culture a subject of pop art, creating still-life portraits of monotonous rows of Campbell's soup cans. Upper-class critics of suburbia snorted at its bad taste—the lack of greenery (except for the spindly tree per lot which FHA mortgages required); the cheap construction; the clutter of too many autos, tricycles, lawnmowers, and children. Poor people and nonwhites, trapped in the inner city, also attacked the suburbs, envying the comparative space and quiet while resenting the drain of tax revenue to outlying areas. And toward the end of the decade a group of West Coast "beats," seeking escape from middle-class monotony, began to form a subculture which rejected the values, aspirations, and behavior of suburbanites.

J. R. Eyerman, TIME-LIFE Picture Agency, © Time Inc.

Moving day in suburbia.

Organization Men and Women

The large business organization dominated the lives of many suburban men during the 1950s. The person whom William H. Whyte called the *Organization Man* (1956) established his roots not in a particular town or region, but within a corporate structure. The business corporation provided the society in which he defined and understood himself: within its structure he gauged his status; within its values he subsumed his individual morality. He did, of course, withdraw from the corporate world to his suburban home and family each day, but this retreat occupied only a few evening hours. Sociological studies revealed that success as a husband and father and occupational advancement often varied inversely. Home and office were separate and competing spheres, and the organization often won out as the primary frame of reference.

The economic growth and occupational mobility of the 1950s reinforced corporate loyalty. With dedication, a young executive was almost sure to rise. But advancement often meant moving around the country at the company's behest. "We never make a man move," one company president explained. "Of course, he kills his career if he doesn't. But we never make him do it." Geographic mobility only strengthened the bond between man and company, for it hindered development of strong ties to a local community and brought the organization right into the family circle as a most important decisionmaker.

The relationship of women to the large business organization was quite different. Especially to young women, corporate life seemed to promise excitement and independence. But during the 1950s most corporations hired women only for positions in the secretarial ghetto, where pay was low and a woman remained a "girl" no matter what her age. The illusion of glamor and independence darkened into the reality of boredom and bare subsistence. Research showed that illicit relationships between boss and secretary, the subject of endless jokes at corporate conventions, were largely male fantasies, seldom duplicated in reality or in the thoughts of the secretaries. For most organization women, love for boss or for business did not transcend dollars and cents, and many rapidly deserted secretarial jobs for domestic life. The rapid turnover of women in corporations bolstered the myth that they were poor risks at any level in the business hierarchy. Organization "girls" were entrapped in a vicious cycle of low pay, rapid turnover, and discrimination.

Wives of most corporate employees were also organization women, deriving income and status from their husbands' jobs. At home, as in the office, the great corporations contributed to female sub-

68

servience. A wife's identity came through her husband—upon meeting a suburban woman many people did not ask, "What do you do?" but "What does your husband do?"—and this relationship could limit her sense of personal esteem. Restricted to the sphere of home and children, the model corporate wife was nonetheless supposed to feel devotion to the business world which she seldom saw. But this obligation of loyalty, together with the husband's unfamiliarity with her domestic routine, drove subtle wedges between married couples. To some women, the organization became a rival for their husbands' attention.

POPULAR CULTURE AND THE ARTS

After World War II, middle-income Americans could enjoy an ever-expanding array of "popular culture," entertainment aimed at a mass audience rather than a small, highly educated elite. The generally rising level of economic prosperity made this pop culture explosion possible. As most American workers gained shorter hours, paid vacations, and higher take-home pay, the entertainment business became more profitable than ever before. Farsighted promoters and entrepreneurs refurbished old products, like popular music, and exploited relatively new ones, such as television and paperback books. By 1950 Americans were spending twice as much money on entertainment as on rent; the total expenditure equaled one-seventh of the gross national product.

Travel and Sports

The travel industry, for example, grew tremendously after World War II. For those who could afford the price, travel agencies marketed package tours to Europe. In only two weeks Americans could absorb the culture of the Old World—from Paris, to Brussels, to Geneva, to Rome, to Vienna, to Hamburg, and finally to London. For those who lacked the money to visit Europe (or who had already toured the Continent), the United States provided its own vacation spots. New motels, their quality certified by motor clubs or franchise owners, began to replace the old independent tourist cabins. When affluent travelers reached destinations such as Southern California, Las Vegas, or Miami Beach, they found luxury resort complexes which offered expensive nightclubs for adults, professional recreation directors for children, and deluxe kennels for family pets. The vacation and travel industries would continue to grow after 1960, but the basic pattern was already established by the fifties.

After the reduced schedules of the war years, sports promotions regained their earlier pace. Promoters welcomed back the young men who had served in the armed forces, abandoning the lesser talents and fading veterans who had performed during World War II. (The supply of quality baseball players became so low that during the war the St. Louis Browns employed a one-armed outfielder). Although all levels of professional baseball revived, the late 1940s and early 1950s proved to be the last hurrah for baseball's minor leagues. Before the full impact of competition from network television, many American cities and smaller towns eagerly supported their own professional teams. And with only sixteen major-league clubs, there was a surplus of good players, particularly blacks, to stock the minor leagues. Until the late 1960s black people complained, with much justification, that only outstanding athletes like Jackie Robinson could play in the majors; white ball players generally received preference for jobs like second-string catcher or reserve infielder. Even talented white players found themselves tied to a monopolistic business system in which major-league teams owned vast numbers of players whom they could freely transfer from team to team, from league to league. In the patriotic spirit of the cold war, baseball served as a symbol of the openness and equality of American society. Sports writers, following in the star-struck tradition of Grantland Rice, lavished praise on the game, celebrating it as an integral part of the American way. One prominent writer-broadcaster, Bill Stern, constantly invented uplifting stories about the national pastime. A dying Abraham Lincoln, Stern solemnly claimed, had told an aide to "keep baseball going: the country needs it."

Professional boxing, plagued by hints of fixed fights and underworld connections, lacked baseball's hallowed reputation but had good-sized audiences. Large promotions, battles for world championships, and small neighborhood clubs made money during the late 1940s and early 1950s. During these years, Joe Louis finally ended his long reign as heavyweight champion, the flamboyant Sugar Ray Robinson captured both the welterweight and middleweight crowns, and a young Italian-American from Massachusetts, Rocky Marciano, battered forty-nine opponents into submission before retiring in 1955 as the undefeated heavyweight champion. Meanwhile, thousands of other boxers suffered in the small clubs, fighting for meager purses and hoping for a shot at the "big money" of a television bout. Professional boxing quickly became one of the staples of network television; at one time during the 1950s, boxing aficionados could watch four nationally televised bouts every week. Such overexposure quickly exhausted both the viewers' attention and the country's supply of good fighters. By 1960 old-timers were already lamenting the declining quality and quantity of professional matches.

70

Professional wrestling, one of boxing's prime competitors for television time, continually demonstrated that lack of quality did not necessarily halt the flow of entertainment dollars. Resting upon spectators' ability to suspend almost all their critical faculties, wrestling enjoyed tremendous popularity during the late 1940s and early 1950s. Obviously contrived and apparently prechoreographed, professional wrestling (as distinguished from the authentic amateur sport) offered a familiar morality play: stereotyped villains, often posing as Germans or "Japs," abused long-suffering heroes until a dramatic reversal sealed the bullies' fate. A flexible catalog of "rules" allowed promoters to vary the scenario slightly and keep fans coming back for the next contest. Only Roller Derby, another pseudosport which enjoyed renewed popularity in the early 1970s, offered a comparable blend of mayhem and mindlessness. To the uninitiated, it seemed like wrestling on wheels, but millions of television viewers eagerly followed the careers of Roller Derby's kings and queens.

The violence and sadism which generally remained muted in professional wrestling and roller derby too often became explicit in paperback and comic books, two other highly profitable forms of popular culture. The exploits of Mike Hammer, Mickey Spillane's brawny crimefighter, titillated paperback readers; by 1950 Americans had bought more than six million copies of Spillane's semiliterate potboilers. The Mike Hammer stories, critics charged, reflected the mindless, superpatriotic, vigilante spirit of the cold war era. With a single-minded devotion to 100 percent Americanism, Hammer loathed communists, sexual perverts, and bleeding-heart libertarians. Spillane's hero expressed only contempt for legal niceties and for civil liberties. He relentlessly pursued the forces of evil, judged them according to his standards, and then exacted his special kind of retribution. Scores of communists and thugs fell before Hammer's righteous hands. "He came right at me with his head down," wrote Spillane-Hammer, "and I took my own damn time about kicking him in the face. . . . He smashed into the door and lay there bubbling. For laughs I gave him a taste of his own sap on the back of his hand and felt the bones go into splinters." Hammer was as deadly with women as with his fists; no female could withstand the Hammer charm. The comic-book industry offered similar doses of gratuitous violence and sex. In one of the most notorious examples, comic-book ghouls played baseball with various parts of a dissected human body.

Comic books and cheap paperback thrillers attracted readers of all ages, but they remained firmly identified with young people. Merchandisers of popular culture aimed more and more of their products at the baby-boom generation, the mass of young people who began to come of age during the 1950s.

Rock Around the Clock: The Popular Culture of Youth

The fifties did not seethe with student activism or talk of generation gaps, but throughout the decade a distinctive youth culture formed
which did provide a point of departure for the more explosive sixties.
The youth culture associated with early rock-and-roll music did not
overtly break with dominant values—popular song lyrics seldom dealt
with social problems or challenged traditional institutions such as marriage, religion, or patriotism. But seeds of rebellion lay just beneath the
surface. When singer Bill Haley advised teenagers to "rock around the
clock," parents looked askance; when kids seemed to find meaning in a
seemingly unintelligible string of "bee-bops" and "shoo-bee-do-whas,"
many older people were uneasy; and when Elvis Presley wriggled his
hips, most parents were horrified. (In deference to such sensibilities,
television producers limited Elvis's first appearance to camera shots
from the waist up.) "Elvis the Pelvis," forging his music from traditional
black blues and Southern hillbilly music, created a sensual sound which
contrasted sharply with most popular songs of previous decades and
which struck many people as somehow indecent. New dances like the
bop, the chicken, or the mashed potatoes seemed to threaten conventional morality. Helping to create a nationwide youth community, Dick
Clark's nationally televised show, "American Bandstand," spread the
latest rock hits and dances.

The loud, heavy beat of rock and roll provided the theme song for
a largely middle-class youth movement which made a cult of the hot
rod, sanctified a few special drive-ins as gathering places, and sprouted
halos of greasy ducktail haircuts. The rock generation was not interested in political protest, but many of its heroes were rebels. James
Dean, the ill-fated young actor, became a special symbol, and many
young whites were drawn to black rock stars such as Chuck Berry and
Little Richard. Many teenagers began to feel that their culture broke
sharply from the past and from the world of their parents.

Like rock and roll, automobiles became a special passion of the
youth culture. Automobiles—especially the increasingly common second car—made young people mobile and provided status symbols, entertainment, and makeshift bedrooms. They provided transportation to
teenage gatherings out of parents' sight and gave the freedom of privacy. In the rapidly growing South, stock-car racing became a preeminent sport. Auto manufacturers vied to contribute innovations which,
by giving dare-devil drivers an edge on the track, would win loyalties
within the vast new youth market. In both North and South, in city and
small town, this was an age of souped-up hot rods, of dual exhaust systems, of raked bodies, of rolled and pleated interiors. For many young
men, transformation of one of Detroit's stereotyped products into a spe-

United Press International

Dick Clark's American Bandstand.

cial personal creation may have represented a subtle, though tangible, revolt against the mass-produced world of their parents. Although only a small proportion of young people actually owned such a creation, the "Kandy-Kolored Tangerine-Flake Streamline Baby," to use writer Tom Wolfe's phrase, was the envy of the teenage "scene."

The youth culture thrived, especially in the suburbs, where the general affluence trickled down from parents to children. The youth market became a multimillion dollar business. Sales of the new 45 rpm records and long-play albums exploded, and a teenager's collection of the latest hits provided an important status symbol. Other items also tempted teenagers to spend money: record players, the latest in penny loafers or saddle shoes, and charm bracelets displaying pictures of rock idols. The youth generation of the 1950s was a peculiar amalgam: in its crass commercialism and unabashed materialism, it mirrored, even caricatured, the rest of society; in its hedonism and stylistic iconoclasm, it set itself decisively apart.

The Critique of Popular Culture

The postwar boom in popular culture disturbed some academi-cians and social critics. Popular culture, they maintained, glorified all that was ugly and irrational in American life; it represented an assault on good taste, traditional notions of decency, and even common sense. The culture of the masses, its detractors charged, indicated the sorry state of American society.

Popular culture, a diverse group of critics agreed, lacked any artis-tic value; it represented instead a banal extension of the United States' sophisticated technology and its mass production–mass consumption economic system. Like automobiles and ready-made clothes, the trivial items of mass culture rolled off assembly lines with no concern for qual-ity or durability. In contrast to "high culture," the popular arts made no attempt to increase understanding of nature or to sharpen perception of fundamental human problems. Instead, popular culture was not meant to be preserved and restudied; like candy and chewing gum, it was to be consumed as rapidly as possible and then quickly discarded. And unlike true folk culture, which ordinary people created from their authentic traditions, popular culture came prefabricated, stamped out by carefully trained manipulators of mass desires. Thus, according to semanticist S. I. Hayakawa, the folk blues of Bessie Smith, though rough by the standard of classical music, sprang from the lives of poor blacks in the rural South; the pop songs which dominated the Hit Pa-rade contained only the trivial fantasies and sentimental clichés manu-factured by the songwriter-technicians on Tin Pan Alley. By its very existence mass culture represented an affront to all that was supposed to be noble and uplifting in human society.

But the effect of pop culture, its most vigorous detractors charged, was even more insidious than this. It acted as a kind of intellectual cancer, eating away at American society and culture. The popularity of mediocre mass culture, some critics contended, inevitably harmed high culture: talented artists succumbed to the monetary rewards of mass culture; popular tastes became too vulgar to recognize good art; and people's senses became too brutalized to recognize the threat of a cor-rupt totalitarianism which employed mass art to manipulate popular opinion. Inevitably, high culture would be destroyed or, at best, be merged with mass culture into some bastard form of "middle-culture."

In addition to causing the erosion of artistic values, popular cul-ture, some writers argued, undermined American society by diverting attention from real problems and reducing people's intellectual level through constant immersion in junk. Citizens became passive receivers, deferring their critical judgment to the manipulators of mass tastes.

Other writers indicted mass culture for fomenting social unrest. The violence of children's comic books, for example, supposedly corrupted young minds and helped produce juvenile delinquents. Some social psychologists hypothesized that the simplicity of any comic-book story, violent or not, hindered young people's intellectual development, teaching them to ignore the complexity of life and conditioning them to expect quick, simple solutions for their problems. Pressure groups urged the government to ban comic books or to force companies to censor antisocial material.

Popular culture, of course, had its defenders. Some writers, though finding little that was uplifting in popular culture, doubted that it could cause all these problems. The history of Western civilization indicated that high art had traditionally been the preserve of a small elite and that the "custodians of culture" had always decried the effect of popular and folk arts. Complex social problems like juvenile delinquency could hardly be traced to comic books or to the novels of Mickey Spillane. Some people observed that no amount of sermonizing could retard the growth of popular culture: new technological developments could only increase its influence. Finally, many observers of mass culture found cause for optimism. Journalist Gilbert Seldes, for example, contended that almost every area of mass culture showed a trend toward more sophistication and artistic craftsmanship. The history of the movie industry and of television after World War II provided some support for the view that the popular arts need not be a cultural wasteland.

The Hollywood Film Industry

Many critics, as well as some filmmakers themselves, expressed contempt for the Hollywood motion picture industry. Director Billy Wilder's 1950 film *Sunset Boulevard* bade a cynical goodby to the old Hollywood. It began with a shot of a corpse floating in a Beverly Hills swimming pool. This dead man, a second-rate screenwriter, narrated the rest of the story. A middle-aged film star, played by Gloria Swanson, lived under the illusion that she would return to the screen in triumph. But a call from a famous director turned out to be only a request for the use of her antique auto, and increasingly she retreated into a fantasy world. The end of the film revealed that the actress had killed the screenwriter and become completely mad. Wilder's message was clear: like the aging actress, Hollywood sustained itself on myths, awaiting an artistic rebirth that would never come. Yet Hollywood survived the 1950s, wounded by anticommunist witch-hunts during the McCarthy years but still able to ignite the fantasies of millions while making some films of real artistic value.

Between 1945 and 1960 most Hollywood filmmakers stuck to traditional forms. The large studios still relied upon the star system, introducing new celebrities like Elizabeth Taylor, Kirk Douglas, Burt Lancaster, Marilyn Monroe, Tony Curtis, and Rock Hudson. Most producers operated on the premise, which often proved correct, that the names of popular stars could sell the most mediocre picture. Recognizing the impact of television, moviemakers increasingly tried huge spectaculars. Cecil B. DeMille remade his silent classic, *The Ten Commandments,* and directed a sprawling circus epic, *The Greatest Show on Earth.* And in other efforts to surpass the technical limitations of television, Hollywood developed new visual techniques: Cinemascope, Cinerama Todd-Ao, and three-dimensional films.

Hollywood also managed to offer some films which broke away from tested formulas. A few offbeat films which featured no great stars and eschewed glamor appeared during the 1950s. Adapted from a successful television production, *Marty* told the simple story of a Bronx butcher, played by Ernest Borgnine, who fell in love with a woman who considered herself plain and unexciting. After the decline of McCarthyism, several films treated controversial social issues. *Paths of Glory* indicted the values of military leaders and portrayed war as anything but a glorious enterprise. Shot in black and white, *Paths of Glory* did poorly at the box office but gained much critical acclaim for its director, Stanley Kubrick. Kubrick would become recognized as one of the United States' most innovative directors during the 1960s. Racial tension provided the backdrop for several films, the most popular being *The Defiant Ones,* a chain-gang story in which brotherhood triumphed over bigotry. Although the film would seem trite and overly cautious to many later viewers, Stanley Kramer's production appeared at a time when racial prejudice was still considered a dangerous subject in Hollywood.

During the 1950s a prominent school of film criticism, popular in both the United States and France, praised those Hollywood directors who could surmount the restraints of the industry and use their films to make personal statements. These critics generally concentrated on so-called lesser films, finding much to admire in the work of directors like Budd Boettcher. A bullfighter turned filmmaker, Boettcher added new dimensions to the most American of all film forms, the Western. Traditionally, the Western had served as action-filled entertainment for children (the B westerns of Ken Maynard and Gene Autry) or as tributes to the glories of the American frontier (the epics of director John Ford). Boettcher's low-budget Westerns lacked both the nonstop action of the B Western and the nostalgic qualities of Ford's films. Boettcher concentrated upon a lone hero, skillfully played by Randolph Scott, who drifted through a hostile, or at best indifferent, world. Like a bullfighter, or like modern man in a mass society, or like a sensitive director in Hollywood, the Boettcher-Scott character found himself constantly tested, constantly forced to demonstrate his individual skill and courage. He rarely initiated a situation but instead reacted to the moves of others. Most of Boettcher's villains, often played by actors who had been or would become leading men, seemed little different from his hero; in Boettcher's amoral world, they certainly did not fit the stereotyped role of the Western bad man. Boettcher carefully selected his locations, his films emphasizing the harsh beauty of the physical world. Boettcher's Westerns not only made money but greatly influenced younger directors, like Sam Peckinpaugh, who would create the much-acclaimed anti-Westerns of the 1960s.

Television

TV sales soared throughout the 1950s. Before World War II, few people had ever seen television; by 1957 there were 40 million sets in the country, and most cities and towns boasted a local station. Within the family, however, the impact of TV was never clear. It did bring popular entertainment into the living room, but it may have become a substitute, not a stimulant, for communication among family members. It may simply have contributed to what Paul Simon called the "sounds of silence . . . people talking without speaking, people hearing without listening." By the 1960s affluent families could afford a set for every member, and each could retreat to his room to watch his favorite programs.

Expansion of television ultimately revolutionized politics, education, and culture. During the 1952 presidential campaign Richard Nixon used a nationwide television address to defend his beleaguered reputation and save his political career; two years later the televised Army-McCarthy hearings helped expose Joe McCarthy as a crude and irresponsible demagogue; and toward the end of the decade, John Kennedy's media image speeded his drive for the 1960 presidential nomination.

The tube had a less immediate impact on education and American culture. Despite hopes that television would dramatically change education, establishment of a separate, nonprofit educational network—and shows such as *Sesame Street*—did not come until the 1960s. Meanwhile, the three commercial networks beamed a steady stream of assembly-line programs which, cynics charged, appealed to the lowest common denominator and widest possible audience. One hit show begat a dozen imitators, and viewers watched endless rounds of standardized variety shows, stereotyped situation comedies, rigged quiz shows, and low-budget Westerns. But in its few good moments television displayed the promise of something better. Many of Sid Caesar's shows featured highly sophisticated comedy sketches; CBS' *Playhouse 90* presented some fine original drama, including Rod Serling's *Requiem for a Heavyweight;* some of Edward R. Murrow's documentaries rivaled the best products of journalism; and all-too-rare specials brought "highbrow" entertainment such as the New York Philharmonic to the small screen.

Some theorists claimed that the media would change people's perceptions. Radio had broadcast the sound of far-off places, but television stimulated visual senses as well. Events seemed more real on TV; viewers became caught up in actual news happenings. Critics complained that television actually manufactured and manipulated news. Some demonstrations, press statements, and human-interest stories might have taken far different shapes had the television camera not been poised to record them. But television's defenders claimed that it offered exciting possibilities: worldwide programming and the instant dissemination of information might ultimately create common values. Just as television homogenized and standardized American culture, it could do the same for the world. Marshall McLuhan prophesied a "global village" in which people of all different cultures experienced a bond of sensory awareness, abandoning themselves to what he called the "cool medium" of television.

Art and Music

Many of the realist painters of the 1930s continued their work after World War II. Abandoning New York for his native Missouri, Thomas Hart Benton established himself as the preeminent regional artist. His murals depicted the American past in scenes filled with vigorous working people; they presented an optimistic view of American society and its potential. While most art critics dismissed Benton's work as old-fashioned and sentimental, Harry Truman called his fellow Missourian "the best damned painter in America." Other regional artists, who continued in the realist style, won similar plaudits from noncritics. Andrew Wyeth's paintings generally presented quiet (and sometimes gloomy) views of the New England countryside and of many real people who lived near his farm in Maine. Peter Hurd failed to gain the popular attention of Wyeth, his brother-in-law, but his stark landscapes of the vast, windswept Southwest easily made him the most famous artist of that region.

If painters like Benton, Hurd, and Wyeth recalled the American past in their realist styles, an influential group known as the New York School experimented with new forms of abstract art. Oftentimes ridiculed in popular publications as a wildman who literally attacked canvases, hurling paint in all directions, Jackson Pollock became the most famous of the abstract expressionists or "action painters." He had studied for two years with Benton before branching into abstract art in the late 1930s; later, like other artists working in New York City, he was influenced by various European "modernists" who fled to the United States during the late 1930s and early 1940s. Gradually, Pollock began to depart from traditional techniques, dropping different kinds of paint onto canvases and later adding other materials, such as broken glass and pieces of string, to his creations. The works excited his admirers and baffled, often repelled, his detractors. "The source of my painting," he subsequently explained, "is the Unconscious. I approach painting the same way I approach drawing, that is directly, with no preliminary studies. . . . When I am painting, I am not much aware of what is taking place; it is only after that I see what I have done." The result was a series of paintings with no apparent geometric order, few rhythmic lines, not even the suggestion of images.

By the 1950s Pollock and other abstract expressionists had gained worldwide attention. Painters such as Willem de Kooning went beyond Pollock to experiment with other styles and techniques. While many people simply shrugged in bewilderment at the melange of lines and blotches of paint, a younger generation of critics praised the imagery and energy of the action painters. Tilting against the new New York art establishment, represented by the Metropolitan Museum of Art, the abstract expressionists and their admirers proclaimed the importance of freedom from restrictive forms and the necessity for total imersion in the process of creation. They produced a major revolution in American art and provided inspiration for the innovators of the 1960s and 1970s.

According to the judgment of most critics, American music also flourished after World War II. A growing population and the general affluence provided new financial support, and philanthropic foundations made generous contributions to help symphony orchestras and to underwrite new musical compositions. Development of 33-1/3 rpm albums—the same discs which boosted the growth of rock-and-roll music—and establishment of FM radio stations greatly enlarged the audience for serious music. As a result, many cities expanded their orchestras or developed new ones. And while established groups, such as the Philadelphia Orchestra under the direction of Eugene Ormandy and the New York Philharmonic, continued to dominate, smaller groups such as the Louisville (Kentucky) Orchestra used money from foundations to create innovative programs.

New directions in jazz indicated the vitality and diversity of post-war American music. Jazz not only became more acceptable to serious music critics but diverged into newer, more complex forms. Although they both played different music than they had during the 1920s and 1930s, Louis Armstrong kept alive the New Orleans tradition, and Duke Ellington continued the style of Big Band swing. Increasingly, Ellington also experimented with other forms and gradually became recognized as a major force in modern American music. At the same time, younger jazz musicians—including Miles Davis, John Lewis, and Dave Brubeck—incorporated various musical techniques, as well as different instruments, into their brand of "cool" jazz, a form suited to the concert stage rather than to the dance hall. In contrast, artists such as Dizzy Gillespie and Charlie Parker developed the harder, less stylistic sound of be-bop or bop. And by the end of the 1950s a new kind of free-form jazz, usually called "the new thing," made saxophonists John Coltrane and Ornette Coleman influential figures, especially to younger black musicians. The black nationalist movement of the early 1960s drew upon the free-flowing, deeply emotional sound of "the new thing."

Even opera became more popular and more innovative during the 1940s and 1950s. With the arrival of a dynamic new manager, Rudolf Bing, in 1950, the New York Metropolitan Opera strengthened its reputation as the leading American company. Its well produced and lavishly mounted productions appealed to a growing number of New Yorkers and continued to reach a nationwide radio audience every Saturday afternoon. While the Metropolitan tended to rely heavily upon traditional works, some other companies and composers adapted American themes. Gian-Carlo Menotti's *The Saint of Bleecker Street* was set in New York's "little Italy," and Virgil Thompson's *Mother of Us All* integrated American themes and even American folk music into the operatic form. Menotti's works, such as *The Medium* and *The Consul,* played to large crowds in New York and in other cities during road-show engagements; his most popular work, *Amahl and the Night Visitors,* debuted on network television in 1951, and NBC produced annual revivals during the 1950s and early 1960s.

In contrast to the general conservatism of most composers during the preceding two decades, many younger artists eagerly embraced new musical ideas during the forties and fifties. The twelve-tone method, which had been pioneered by Arnold Schönberg, became increasingly popular. Discarding keys and scales as the basis of composition and substituting new principles based upon the twelve tones of the octave, this method allowed for freer rhythms and less restrictive use of chords. Going beyond the Schönberg method, other innovators such as Milton Babbitt (who had professional training in mathematics as well as in music) expanded twelve-tone music into an exceedingly complex system of composition. During the mid-fifties Babbitt also began to explore electronic music, composing directly onto magnetic tapes with electrically generated sounds. By the end of the decade he and other experimental composers could employ the new synthesizer, developed by RCA, and even consider the possibilities of using computers to make music.

John Cage soon became the most famous of the experimental musicians. An early convert to twelve-tone music, he continually extended his basic principle that the artist should not dominate his music but should let it happen. During the early 1950s, for example, his experience with sound-free chambers inspired him to create "silent music": a performer would sit at a piano and play nothing; a stopwatch designated the beginning and the end of the "piece"; and, as their own sounds became part of the performance, the audience enjoyed this "total musical experience." Cage also used diagrams and charts, based upon Oriental religious texts, and open-ended compositions to produce works which removed, as much as possible, the creator from his creation. Some of his works contained no master score and allowed musicians to determine the structure and length of each particular performance. In effect, Cage and many of his younger disciples, such as Earle Browne, were attempting to do for music what painters like Jackson Pollock had done for art: to produce works which were filled with energy and spontaneity, to break away from old, confining forms.

Postwar music, however, was not limited to or dominated by such experimentalism. Many so-called traditionalists, such as David Diamond, and people who defied easy categorization, such as Virgil Thompson, continued to compose important works. Enthusiastic about the new musical trends apparent by the late 1940s, Virgil Thompson indicated that the "way to write American music is simple. All you have to do is to be an American and then write any kind of music you wish. There is precedent and model for all kinds of music. . . ."

THE OTHER SIDE OF AFFLUENCE

As city dwellers fled to the suburbs, many people from rural areas flocked in to replace them. These new migrants were usually not white and not middle-class. For them, the fifties did not bring ebullient affluence; their small economic gains came only against a background of oppressive discrimination and entrapment in decaying central cities.

81

Blacks

Black people from depressed rural areas in the South flooded into Northern cities during World War II to take jobs in war-related industries. But even though employment possibilities increased, the overall quality of life remained low. With the nation's resources pouring into national defense, little money remained for housing programs. In Detroit's new black ghetto, for example, one investigator reported that an old converted one-family dwelling might hold over a hundred black people, one family to a room.

Moving into old ethnic neighborhoods occupied by groups such as Italians, Jews, or Poles, black newcomers confronted large-scale racial antagonism. Detroit's situation was explosive. Half a million people, including about 60,000 blacks, arrived in three years, and the strain of overcrowding was unbearable. During the hot June of 1943 an amusement-park fight between white and black teenagers escalated into a race war which was not calmed until a contingent of six thousand soldiers occupied the streets. There were 34 people killed and 700 injured; there was $2 million worth of property damage. Race riots spread to other cities as well.

But overcrowding, discrimination, and harassment by whites did not curb the flow of black people into urban areas. World War II gave a boost to mechanized agriculture, and many Southern blacks who had traditionally hired out as farm laborers found themselves with little hope of employment. Others who had scratched out livings on small farms felt their always marginal existence slip below self-sufficiency. In 1940, 77 percent of the black population lived in the South, mostly in rural areas; by 1960 nearly one-half lived in the North, and three of every four blacks resided in a city.

Although the gap between the living standards of white and black Americans remained large, the war and Northern migration did advance many black people's economic position. Between 1947 and 1952 median nonwhite family income rose from $1,614 to $2,338, and the gap between black and white narrowed slightly. In 1940, 80 percent of all black workers were employed in unskilled jobs; by 1950 the figure had dropped to 63 percent. Similarly, blacks' life expectancy advanced from 53.1 years in 1940 to 61.7 in 1953 (compared with 64.2 to 69.6 for whites). Throughout the fifties the expanding economy and favorable job market helped maintain the economic gains which many black people had made during the war. For those who stayed in the rural South or found no jobs in the cities, of course, life remained a constant struggle against hunger and disease.

82

Puerto Ricans

Thousands of Puerto Ricans moved to New York City in the decade after World War II, transforming that city's ethnic makeup. New York's Puerto Rican community grew over half a million in twenty years, from 70,000 in 1940 to 613,000 in 1960. A variety of circumstances contributed to this massive migration. Throughout the 1940s, Puerto Ricans had experienced increased contact with the United States mainland through mass media, advertisements, and military life (65,000 Puerto Ricans served in the armed forces during World War II). Especially to young and better-educated Puerto Ricans, life in the United States seemed alluring. New York's unemployment rate was less than half that in Puerto Rico; its schools and hospitals were superior. And comparatively inexpensive air service between San Juan and New York, begun in 1945, facilitated movement to the mainland. The reform-minded administration of Luis Muñoz Marín in Puerto Rico also encouraged the trend, primarily to reduce the island's population pressure and thereby assist economic growth. Once a sizable Puerto Rican community existed in New York, it generated its own growth through a high birth rate and the additional migration of friends and relatives.

The Puerto Rican community crowded into East Harlem and then into other ethnic ghettos throughout the five boroughs of New York. Studies showed that the newcomers generally had a higher level of education and skill than the average Puerto Rican, but their Spanish language, skin color, and close ties with the island left them outside the mainstream of city life. During the 1950s most Puerto Ricans could obtain only the lowest-paying jobs, and few entered New York City politics. Puerto Ricans suffered the fate of many groups which lack economic power and political muscle: they faced discrimination, deteriorating schools, overcrowded housing, and indifference to their problems. Every year around 30,000 people returned to the island, but Spanish Harlem continued its rapid growth.

Mexican-Americans

The attraction of urban jobs and new immigration from Mexico swelled Southwestern cities with another Spanish-speaking population: Mexican-Americans (Chicanos). Before World War II Chicanos, like blacks, lived largely in rural areas; by 1960, 80 percent resided in cities. According to the 1960 census, over half a million Mexican-Americans lived in the Los Angeles–Long Beach area; large Spanish-speaking *barrios* existed in El Paso, Phoenix, and other Southwestern cities; and

Northern industrial centers such as Chicago, Detroit, Kansas City, and Denver attracted growing numbers of Chicano workers.

City life and the favorable job market of the 1950s raised the overall living standards of Mexican-Americans, but racial prejudice kept a lid on opportunity and advancement. Discrimination, coupled with the ethnic awareness which grew in city barrios, produced racial tensions between Chicanos and white "Anglos."

During World War II, for example, street gangs of Chicano boys in Los Angeles defied conventional styles of dress by donning "zoot-suits" (or "drapes") consisting of pleated, high-waisted pants with tight-fitting cuffs and long, wide-shouldered, loose coats. The duck-tail haircut (which would become standard for fans of Elvis Presley in the 1950s) topped off the costume. Many whites, feeling threatened by the display of ethnic separateness, tended to see zoot-suiters as hoodlums. In 1943, after a zoot-suited gang reportedly beat up eleven sailors who were strolling through a Chicano neighborhood, large-scale violence erupted. About two hundred sailors, joined by scores of soldiers and marines, cruised through the city beating anyone who wore a zoot-suit. The Los Angeles police followed, arresting only the injured Chicanos. The one-sided rioting went on for several days, and similar disturbances quickly spread to other cities throughout the country.

Despite widespread racial prejudice against Chicanos, the United States government welcomed additional Mexican migrants under the *bracero* (farm worker) program. The executive agreement between the United States and Mexico which started the bracero program in 1942 was part of an effort to increase manpower during World War II, but under pressure from large agricultural enterprises, Congress continued to authorize migration of farm laborers. Throughout the 1950s the number of entering workers climbed each year, reaching a peak of almost a million in 1959 alone. Mexican migrants provided cheap, unorganized labor to harvest seasonal crops from Texas to Montana, and growers profited enormously. By the early sixties, however, the growing unemployment rate among Americans, combined with anti-Mexican predjudice, convinced Congress to discontinue the bracero program. Over the protests of large growers, but to the satisfaction of labor unions which feared competition from cheap labor, the bracero program ended in 1965.

American Indians

American Indians, like other minority groups, also flocked to urban areas during and after World War II. Army life and lucrative industrial jobs initially attracted Indian people away from reservations, and the federal government's policies during the 1950s substantially increased their flight to the cities. The Indian policy of the Eisenhower administration, as passed by Congress in 1953, called for the government to end Indians' "status as wards of the United States, and grant them all of the rights and privileges pertaining to American citizenship." The plan sought to "terminate" Indians' dependence upon the national government, to liquidate the reservation system, and to permit states to assume legal jurisdiction over Indians. Six bills of termination, applying to tribes who supposedly no longer needed a special relationship with the federal government, passed Congress in 1954.

While pursuing termination, the government also set up a Voluntary Relocation Program (later called Employment Assistance Program) to coax more Indians into urban areas. Begun in 1952, this program helped Indians move to one of ten cities with Field Relocation Offices and paid living expenses until first wages were received. Within about a decade, more than sixty thousand (approximately one of every eight) Indians had migrated from reservations to urban centers.

Termination and relocation greatly disrupted Indian life. Some terminated tribes, now subject to state tax requirements, fell upon hard times. Others sold tribal lands to private developers, gaining short-range economic viability. Indians who moved to the cities found themselves ill-equipped for the transition from semicommunal rural existence to fiercely competitive urban life. Federal officials had hoped that termination and relocation would assimilate Indians into the American mainstream and end federal outlays to support them, but assimilation proved more complicated than a geographical move. Many relocated Indians exhibited the passivity and withdrawal associated with cultural shock; they became the most invisible of all urban ethnic groups. The Bureau of Indian Affairs estimated that 35 percent of all relocated Indians eventually returned to the reservations, but other studies suggest that about 75 percent would probably have returned had the reservations offered more job opportunities.

Few Indians favored the federal policy, and protests mounted against the breakup of reservations and the destruction of Indian culture. Although the Eisenhower administration never abandoned the goal of termination, officials finally promised not to force it upon unwilling tribes. By the 1960 presidential campaign, termination was so discredited that both Democratic and Republican parties repudiated it. During the 1960s the government reversed the policy and attempted to provide opportunity on the reservation rather than to force Indians off.

The "Invisible" Poor

The large-scale migration of nonwhites into the cities, coupled with white flight to the suburbs, transformed urban life. Tax revenues, the life-blood of a healthy metropolis, drained away, and signs of urban decay appeared everywhere. Sanitation facilities deteriorated, landlords moved out of the neighborhood, and housing grew unsightly. Hostility developed between all-white police forces and nonwhite citizens. City schools especially suffered. Many could barely provide a decent education for English-speaking children, much less deal with the large influx of pupils whose native tongue was not English.

Still, despite urban deterioration, those people who congregated in central-city ghettos were often better off than their counterparts who remained on the farm. During the 1950s great agribusiness combinations mechanized operations and engrossed more land. By 1954, 12 percent of the farm operators made nearly 60 percent of total agricultural sales, and the imbalance grew. Unemployment accompanied this agricultural revolution; severe rural poverty became a major, if often unnoticed, problem. Young people often escaped. Throughout the rural Midwest in the fifties, the young left for cities rather than try to make their family farms compete with large agricultural enterprises. A million and a half people left unproductive patches of land in Appalachia. But the many old people who remained on the land were the least able to cope with mechanization and changing markets. Whether a person was a black tenant farmer in Georgia, an Indian on an isolated reservation, a white farmer in the hills of Appalachia, or a Mexican-American migrant worker, poverty was an oppressive reality and there seemed little hope of escape.

America remained polarized into two cultures: one of increasing affluence and one of persisting poverty. While the medium of television made middle-class comforts highly visible to the poor, poverty and degradation grew more invisible to the affluent. Suburbanites in fast-moving automobiles skirted the slums and never penetrated the pockets of rural poverty. A gap grew between the aspiration of the lower sectors and the social consciousness of the affluent. Bitterness mounted in the central city as complacency spread through the suburbs.

Urban Problems

Although the term *urban crisis* did not become a cliché until the sixties, people who studied urban life recognized severe tensions and strains during the fifties. Signs of tremendous growth and some examples of positive change, however, helped mask many uncomfortable facts about American cities. Construction of new office buildings and highways, reduction of the number of substandard housing units, and greater attention to old problems such as education provided evidence for the view that conditions in urban areas were improving. In addition, the diversity of urban life in the United States allowed people to cite vastly different information about "the American city." Obviously, problems such as pollution, racial conflict, and crime varied according to local conditions. But local discomforts increasingly appeared to be variations on general trends such as the continued migration away from small towns and rural areas and the growth of large institutions. By 1960 almost every city confronted serious problems, difficulties that seemed beyond the capacity of established urban institutions.

Clearly most cities were paying the price for more than a century of largely uncontrolled development. Even after the advent of planning and zoning commissions during the early twentieth century, the private decisions of businessmen exerted the greatest influence on the direction and pace of urban change. The needs of business enterprises largely determined what land would be used, how it would be changed, and what groups would pay the highest social costs. All cities confronted another problem with a long history. Unlike Europeans with their long tradition of city living, many Americans continued to hold the old Jeffersonian bias and to view urban life as less natural or virtuous than rural and small-town living. Persistence of this anti-urban attitude created a curious situation: people moved toward cities to find the economic opportunities located there, while feeling that urban life was not really what they wanted for themselves or for their children. (This feeling was not limited to affluent whites; many black and Spanish-speaking parents also feared, with more reason than whites, that urban life might harm their children.)

Whatever their apprehensions about the quality of city life, people still flocked to urban areas after World War II in search of greater economic rewards. As a result, the urban population grew tremendously during the late forties and throughout the fifties. Sprawling across the landscape, urban areas became more fragmented and segmented than ever before. After studying cities along the Eastern seaboard during the fifties, a French geographer called this new social organization the "megalopolis." "We must abandon the idea of the city as a tightly settled and organized unit in which people, activities, and riches are crowded into a very small area clearly separate from its nonurban surroundings," wrote Jean Gottman. A city would spread out "far and wide around its original nucleus" until it melted into the suburban neighborhoods of other cities.

Many people blamed this geographical expansion for many of the failures of the modern American city. Larger urban areas made efficient centralized administration difficult, and any decentralized arrangement left less affluent areas saddled with poor schools, inadequate social services, and too little money to solve their problems. Many sociologists also argued that urban sprawl exacerbated people's sense of isolation and contributed to their feeling of being transients rather than part of a community. As long as urbanites could hope to escape to suburbia, they would hesitate to commit themselves or their tax dollars to projects which aimed at long-range solutions to the new urban problems.

Ironically, many attempts to meet urban needs seemed only to accelerate decentralization and fragmentation. Significant federal aid for construction of low-cost housing rarely reached central cities during the 1950s. Even the modest goal of 810,000 public housing units by 1955, the target of the Housing Act of 1949, was not achieved until the end of the 1960s. In fact, the Housing Act provided authority for another program—urban renewal—which actually reduced the number of dwellings available to poor people. In theory, urban renewal allowed local governments to obtain federal funds to clear out old and dilapidated buildings and to replace them with new public housing units or with other projects, including almost anything from new cultural complexes to concrete parking garages. In practice, however, the Eisenhower administration began to permit urban planners and private developers to evade the responsibility of replacing or increasing the supply of living units. Increasingly, urban renewal concentrated upon construction of nonresident facilities. Many people profited from this: building contractors and construction workers enjoyed steadily rising incomes; the more affluent people could find a greater variety of cultural and recreational facilities; and city officials gained new sources of tax revenue. But too many poor people, the intended beneficiaries of federal largesse, ended up the big losers. In many cities, poorer citizens watched their homes bulldozed into rubble and their neighborhoods transformed into business complexes or even into apartment buildings for middle- and upper-income people.

At the same time, creation of a vast network of multi-lane expressways also brought paradoxical changes to urban life. The new freeways allowed people to travel to work in the privacy of their automobiles rather than on public transportation and enabled those with enough money to live even further from decaying urban centers. In addition to accelerating uncontrolled urban sprawl, the freeways created other problems. The commitment to the new concrete conveyers contributed to the decay of existing mass transit facilities and worked against creation of any new ones. The stream of cars creeping to and from the central cities every day also increased air pollution without noticeably speeding the pace of urban transportation. Finally, the new expressways destroyed even more old buildings and further contributed to the fragmentation of urban life.

88

Despite its ambivalent record, the national government's greater resources required federal officials to take more and more responsibility for the problems of the city. During the presidential campaign of 1960 both Richard Nixon and John Kennedy pledged their support for creation of a new cabinet-level office to coordinate federal assistance to urban areas.

BIBLIOGRAPHY

The demographic trends of the 1950s are analyzed most effectively in Richard A. Easterlin, *The Baby Boom in Historical Perspective* (1962). Blake McKelvey, *The Emergence of Metropolitan America, 1915–1966* (1968), provides a good beginning for understanding the changes occurring in American cities. See also Scott Donaldson, *The Suburban Myth* (1969); and Herbert J. Gans, *The Levittowners* (1967). Four influential writers who addressed themselves to the quality of life in America during the 1950s were John Kenneth Galbraith, *The Affluent Society* (1952); David Riesman et al., *The Lonely Crowd* (1950); C. Wright Mills, *White Collar* (1951); and William H. Whyte, *The Organization Man* (1956). Michael Harrington's *The Other America* (1962) was a pathbreaking analysis of the "new poverty" which persisted in the midst of general affluence. See also Herman P. Miller, *Rich Man, Poor Man* (1972).

The war had important effects on most ethnic groups which were felt throughout the 1950s. See Richard Polenberg, *War and Society: The United States, 1941–1945* (1972); Nathan Glazer and Daniel P. Moynihan, *Beyond the Melting Pot* (1963); and John R. Howard, ed., *The Awakening Minorities: American Indians, Mexican-Americans, Black Americans and Puerto Ricans* (1970), for information on a variety of minority groups. More specialized studies are August Meier and Elliott Rudwick, *From Plantation to Ghetto* (1970); and Donald R. McCoy and Richard T. Ruetten, *Quest and Response* (1973), on black people; Carey McWilliams, *North from Mexico* (1949); Manuel P. Servin, ed., *The Mexican-Americans: An Awakening Minority* (1970); and Matt S. Meier and Feliciano Rivera, *The Chicanos* (1972), on Mexican-Americans; and Stuart Levine and Nancy O. Lurie, eds., *The American Indian Today* (1968), on Indians. Two important and highly readable books on minorities are Oscar Handlin, *The Newcomers: Negroes and Puerto Ricans in a Changing Metropolis* (1959); and Oscar Lewis, *La Vida: A Puerto Rican Family in the Culture of Poverty—San Juan and New York* (1967). William Ryan, *Blaming the Victim* (1971), criticizes the idea of a "culture of poverty."

Various aspects of postwar American culture are discussed in Bernard Rosenberg and David Manning White, eds., *Mass Culture* (1957);

Rosenberg and White, eds., *Mass Culture Revisited* (1971); Charles Higham, *The Art of the American Film* (1973); Gilbert Chase, *America's Music* (2nd ed., 1966); Barbara Rose, *American Art Since 1900* (1967); and Tom Wolfe, *The Kandy-Kolored Tangerine-Flake Streamline Baby* (1965). On postwar conservatism see the relevant chapters of Ronald Lora, *Conservative Minds in America* (1971).

There are now two good introductions to the Eisenhower presidency: Herbert S. Parmet, *Eisenhower and the American Crusades* (1972); and Charles C. Alexander, *Holding the Line: The Eisenhower Era, 1952–1961* (1975). Alexander's book contains a complete up-to-date bibliography of various specialized works.

Eisenhower and Dulles

The new president, Dwight Eisenhower, and his secretary of state, John Foster Dulles, contrasted with their flamboyant, controversial predecessors. For years Eisenhower had reconciled diverse opinions into consensus, first as commander of the world's greatest amphibious invasion, the D-Day attack against occupied France, then as president of Columbia University, and from 1948 to 1952 as leader of NATO's vast military apparatus in Europe. Congress and the American public placed great confidence in this general who vowed to "wage peace." Their future depended upon Eisenhower's grasp of unfamiliar diplomatic issues and upon Dulles's ability to create policies attuned to a complex world situation.

Eisenhower harbored no ambitions to be an aggressive president in either domestic or foreign affairs, and he championed conservative economic principles. Aware of the potential for waste, he scrutinized defense expenditures more carefully than other recent presidents—Truman, Kennedy, Johnson, or Nixon. Ready to delimit the reach of American government where practical, however, Eisenhower was no isolationist. The United States had to protect Western Europe and perhaps to smooth ruffled relations with the Soviet Union. Only international agreement, he believed, could solve the nuclear dilemmas which threatened everyone. Despite domestic retrenchment, Washington would continue its global role.

4

Protector of the free world

John Foster Dulles, the austere corporation lawyer who dominated American foreign policy during the 1950s, had the mien of his Presbyterian ancestors. A sense of orderliness, rooted in the certainty of faith, pervaded his ambitions and his fixations. He even looked the part: a long face, punctuated by a thin nose and round wire-rimmed eyeglasses, almost personified the Calvinist ethos. Containment of communism, a reactive, static policy which grated against the nation's penchant for "getting the job done," affronted Dulles. He stridently called for a psychological and political offensive, presumably on behalf of "the captive nations of Eastern Europe," extending the position of the 1952 Republican platform which condemned Truman's tactics as "negative, futile, and immoral." Though extravagant rhetoric could not substitute for positive policy, it did stymie right-wing Republican senators like William Knowland, who dreamed of "unleashing" Chiang Kai-shek against Asian communism. Dulles never supported preventive wars,

United Press International

Seriousness on their faces, President Eisenhower and Secretary of State John Foster Dulles confer during a stroll through the gardens of the president's villa near Geneva.

but he did sharpen Soviet-American rivalry. He saw himself, one biographer writes, "as the chess master of the free world, daily engaged in a mortal contest against a monolithic adversary."

Dulles argued that Russia's postwar advances had resulted from Stalin's opportunistic probes and from the lack of American opposition. To remedy such weaknesses, the secretary planned to announce the perimeters of the free world, which the United States would defend against "alien subversion," and so prevent miscalculations like the Korean War. A constant counterpressure would not only block communist expansion but also keep America's rival off balance, perhaps even causing its collapse. Soon famous for his willingness, at least during press conferences, to risk war in the pursuit of national objectives, Dulles converted diplomacy into apocalyptic posturing. Though Eisenhower discounted the rhetoric of brinksmanship and probably never considered nuclear war a feasible option, his secretary of state broadened containment into an uncompromising, worldwide crusade to determine the pace, even the nature, of change.

The New Look

Republicans had to adjust their larger philosophies to the realities of a balanced budget and a volatile world. A cost-conscious president, a messianic secretary of state, and Pentagon generals soon recast America's strategic doctrines, relying upon the deterrent of massive retaliation. Modern technology could increase American military power while reducing its cost: Secretary of Defense Charles Wilson quipped that nuclear weaponry provided "more bang for the buck." Doomsday bombs, together with sophisticated delivery systems, could protect the United States from attack, since no nation would risk "second-strike" reprisal.

But Dulles was not satisfied with a nuclear standoff between Russia and America, and new weapons still bloated the federal budget. Determined to stake out the boundaries of the "free world" as broadly as possible, the secretary dramatically expanded the nation's collective security arrangements. He spent months traveling around the world, signing up allies. A succession of bilateral defense pacts with Formosa, Korea, and Japan extended America's nuclear umbrella to the shores of China. Even more grandiose schemes shored up Britain's weakness "east of Suez." The Southeast Asia Treaty Organization (SEATO) in 1954 linked Australia, the Philippines, Thailand, and Pakistan with the United States, Britain, and France. The next year Washington sponsored England's Central Treaty Organization (CENTO) with Turkey, Iraq, Iran, and Pakistan. Turkey tied CENTO with NATO; Pakistan connected SEATO with CENTO. Each of these multilateral covenants pledged that an attack against one member, either by overt aggression or, as Dulles put it, "by internal subversion," would bring all into consultation to decide common action. Eisenhower, already skeptical about the military value of large American army reserves, thought that local native forces, financed from Washington and linked to a network of alliances controlled by the United States, could contain regional threats without escalating into nuclear cataclysm.

The New Look perversely increased America's obligations while decreasing its security—the opposite of Republican aims. Adopting penny-wise–pound-foolish economy, Dulles and Eisenhower had hampered themselves as much as their opponents. Deterrence institutionalized an arms race. Technological innovation could upset the exquisite balance of terror which massive retaliation required. A scientific breakthrough might tempt one side, for example, to strike before its opponent deployed a new device. Everyone understood the predicaments of nuclear weaponry, so the only solution was a carefully balanced arms build-up. Then, too, eagerly sought allies proved unmanageable. France, for example, reacted angrily against America's refusal to share its nuclear power. Regional pacts often involved the United States in local disputes outside the range of its national interests. Most restricting of all, the Republicans had postulated a communist world of monolithic unchangeability, of necessary hostility. Events quickly undermined such assumptions.

Korea

Korea ruined American calculations. Armistice negotiations with the North Koreans and Chinese had broken down in October 1952, largely because of a complicated impasse over prisoners of war (POWs). The United States insisted upon voluntary repatriation. Since most enemy soldiers wanted to stay in South Korea, this formula meant that the South would gain, and the North would lose, an army of about 40,000 trained men. The communists therefore demanded a forced return of all POWs to their original home. Stalemate also continued on the battlefield. True to his campaign promise, Eisenhower toured the front in November and then, with Dulles, orchestrated an exercise in New Look diplomacy, punctuated with threats and more fighting. The two sides resumed armistice talks in April 1953, after Eisenhower pointedly mentioned retaliation, perhaps with Chiang Kai-shek's aid. But negotiation broke down almost immediately, again over the POW issue. Then the president wired General Mark Clark, the United Nations commander, that the United States might "carry on the war in new ways never yet tried" if the communists remained intransigent. Dulles was more specific: America might drop atomic bombs.

The appeal to apocalypse worked. Within two weeks both sides had initialed armistice terms: Korea would stay divided, as before the war, into a communist North and a pro-West South. Neutral powers were to tackle the POW repatriation issue, presumably by maintaining the regional balance of power. Certain that only a complete victory could counter leftist discontent with his increasingly dictatorial regime, the South Korean president, Syngman Rhee, aborted the compromise. He released over 27,000 communist POWs, who immediately disappeared into the Southern population. China attacked along much of the front, apparently to demonstrate that it could maintain a balance of power on the peninsula, regardless of South Korean action. Yet neither side wanted the war to continue, and Rhee's action alienated many in Washington. Dulles bluntly ordered him to sign the armistice "or else." So on July 27, 1953, a truce—not a peace treaty—ended a war which had killed over two million people, mostly civilians.

THE CERTAINTIES DISSOLVE: EUROPEAN ICING AND RUSSIAN THAW

American bluster may have worked in Asia, but the Republicans soon discovered that it failed in Europe. The tangled peace in Korea had foreshadowed the limitations of a struggle against ideology, and difficulties with NATO countries and dramatic changes within the Soviet Union finally forced Republicans to rethink most of their strategic plans.

The Troubled Alliance

Of all its criss-crossed security pacts, America's alliance with Western Europe was the only one not simply an anticommunist marriage of convenience. A common heritage and economic ties bound these nations together into an Atlantic community. In military matters, however, the Europeans had neglected their rearmament, relying more and more upon America's immense power. Washington had strongly urged an integrated NATO force, armed with conventional weapons. A joint effort would force Europe to finance a larger portion of its defense, increase pressure against the Soviet Union, and rope German power into a regional enterprise. Diplomats set up a European Defense Community (EDC) by 1953, but many, particularly the French, opposed its transnational approach and lack of nuclear weapons. So Dulles ruminated at a press conference about "an agonizing reappraisal" of America's rela-

95

tions with Europe if EDC foundered. President Eisenhower reiterated that the United States would maintain its troops in Europe "for the long term," easing European fears of a precipitous withdrawal.

Yet stick-and-carrot tactics only angered politicians in France and England who asserted national defense to be the province of their own parliaments, not of foreign statesmen. Specialization—an American nuclear force paired with conventional European armies—would continue Europe's second-class status in the NATO alliance. Would the United States risk nuclear war, and thus its own destruction, to save Western Europe? Conversely, might not Washington and Moscow compromise a "war" after mushroom clouds rose over Paris and, say, Warsaw? When the French National Assembly finally refused to ratify the EDC treaty on August 30, 1954, most Europeans happily acquiesced. Britain and France accelerated their plans for nuclear rearmament. New Look maneuvering had again secured the opposite of its goal, this time in wasteful duplication and the continued presence of large numbers of American troops in Europe.

The Bogey Fades: Russia

If assumptions about allied pliability went awry, so too did New Look calculations about the Soviet Union. Dulles predicated his view of a conspiracy against American values upon Russia's firm control over its Eurasian empire and Stalin's rigid police state. The fifties ruined both estimates. On March 5, 1953, the Soviet dictator died, and his tyranny partially withered. Stalin's theories had proved wrong: world war had revived liberal capitalism, not doomed it. The troika which replaced Stalin—Foreign Minister Vyacheslav Molotov, Defense Minister Nikolai Bulganin, and Nikita Khrushchev, First Secretary of the Communist Party—went along with Premier Georgi Malenkov's plan to ease relations with the United States. But internal rivalries soon complicated Soviet diplomacy. Traditionalists like Bulganin wanted to continue Stalin's defensive priorities and his domestic emphasis upon heavy industry. In contrast, Khrushchev argued for a more flexible approach. Detente with the United States would slow the arms race and permit a higher standard of living within Russia. At the same time, Khrushchev advocated vigorous policies to expand Soviet influence in the third world and perhaps break down Dulles's ring of alliances. The clash between expansionism and detente did not much bother the first secretary, who relied on the deterrent of nuclear war to insure American patience. Within three years, Khrushchev had triumphed over the others, largely because the Soviet people, tired of fear and poverty, enthusiastically responded to his promises of "peaceful coexistence" and more consumer goods. After Khrushchev denounced Stalin's "Gestapo tactics" in 1956, Russians dreamed of less regimentation, less sacrifice. This new direction in Soviet policy not only substituted competition for confrontation but also outflanked massive retaliation and containment. The Soviet Union reduced its armed forces from four million to less than three million men by the mid-1950s. Though primarily an effort to shift economic priorities toward consumer industries, the unilateral gesture did belie the Dulles prognosis. It also calmed European fears of a Red tide and further complicated American relations with its NATO allies. A change of tactics in the third world brought the Soviets stunning gains in India, Afghanistan, Burma, and the Middle East— precisely the area of declining British influence. Russians usually linked up with anticolonial movements, pointing out that the Russian Revolution was more relevant to the twentieth-century problems of industrialization and mass culture than a system based upon individual liberty, a luxury which many developing nations felt they could not afford. The Soviets promised to concentrate national energies more efficiently, without the paternalism of empire.

Eisenhower's Summitry

Ignoring prospects for detente, Dulles indulged his preconceptions about the communist menace. But Eisenhower hoped that new men and different techniques might at least prevent war. Working outside the State Department, the president and White House advisers like C. D. Jackson and Nelson Rockefeller aimed to refashion America's relationship with the Soviet Union, perhaps by easing the nuclear arms race. During the halcyon months of Russian thaw, the English had urged a conference of heads of state to settle European problems, particularly German reunification. The idea of a summit meeting intrigued Eisenhower, despite Dulles's pessimistic admonitions. Summitry offered not only an alternative to grim crusades but also a new forum for long-stalled disarmament negotiations.

During July 1955 the president traveled to Geneva, where he met with his counterparts among the Big Four: Premier Bulganin and First Secretary Khrushchev, Prime Minister Anthony Eden of Britain, and Premier Edgar Faure of France. The drama of face-to-face sessions obscured otherwise desultory talks about Germany's future and East–West cultural exchanges. Then Eisenhower submitted a unique plan for disarmament. The United States and the Soviet Union should exchange blueprints of all military installations and permit reconnaissance flights over each other's territory. Surprise attacks would become impossible, and each power could assess the other's true intent. The brief summit conference itself could neither resolve the enormous complexities involved nor convince military leaders in both countries who vigorously opposed the idea. But the "open skies" proposal did counteract recent Soviet propaganda gains and, more important, inaugurated "the spirit of Geneva." Many people sensed that something better than mutual terror and animosity might be possible.

Yet the president's dramatic overture achieved nothing permanent. Later that fall, at a meeting among the Big Four foreign ministers, the Russians gently sidetracked open skies. No one wanted to reunite Germany. Such a change would only upset the European balance of power so painfully achieved during the Stalin-Truman years. Germans themselves, particularly in the Rhineland and Bavaria, did not want to bear the cost of rebuilding the Eastern zones, heavily looted by the Soviets. But even if Eisenhower's effort solved no problems, Russians and Americans began to see each other as something more than the mirror of their own suspicions. Leaders in the two blocs moderated their intractable rhetoric, and after 1955 cultural exchanges eased popular misconceptions. The gains, though small, seemed worthwhile: nuclear war no longer appeared inevitable.

Superpower Challenges: Egypt and Hungary

Even if Russia and America could compose their differences, discontent fractured the unity of both power blocs. The New Look, based upon America's strategic superiority, communist hostility, and a more efficient globalism, became irrelevant. Russia's thaw spread throughout its East European empire, creating unrest—even outright rebellion. After September 1957 the Soviet Union and the United States still sought diplomatic advantage, but without the certainty of European subservience. Nations on both sides of the Iron Curtain rejected crucial parts of their overlords' prescriptions for the future.

Nowhere were hopes for mastery wrecked more consistently than in the Middle East. Nationalism and charismatic leaders, not economic theories or political systems, defined the contours of change. In Egypt, for example, a military coup destroyed King Farouk's corrupt monarchy in 1952, intending to modernize the country and escape Britain's economic domination. Two years later, a "colonels' revolt" gave Gamal Abdel Nasser near-dictatorial power. The new president dreamed of making Egypt the chief military power in the Middle East so that he could lead Arab nationalism. Popular resentment at Israeli statehood and English control over much of the Middle East's political life encouraged rearmament programs; "positive neutralism" garnered money and technological aid from both East and West. Nasser's successes soon enraptured Arabs but alienated Britain and frightened Israel. Then, during June 1956, Nasser announced that he would use Egyptian cotton to buy advanced weapons from the Soviet Union. Angry with this threat to the Western-dominated status quo, London banks and John Foster Dulles blocked loans for the Aswan Dam, a huge project which would improve harvests and provide hydroelectric power for Egypt's developing industries. Nasser then seized the Suez Canal on July 25, assuming that its duties could finance the dam's construction.

Britain, France, and Israel resolved to act. Israelis saw the Suez crisis as a pretext for preventive war; Europeans hoped to destroy Arab nationalism in the Middle East. French Premier Guy Mollet also reckoned that a militant response would shore up his foundering coalition in the French Assembly. Then too, a blow at Nasser would discourage Arab rebels in Algeria, where France was attempting to suppress an anticolonial guerrilla movement. Meanwhile, the British had created their own domino theory: Nasser was a Hitlerian figure who, if unopposed, would unite the Arab world and confiscate Britain's most valuable investments. Communications between London and Washington became more and more self-deluding. When Eisenhower cleverly ducked the Suez crisis during his 1956 presidential campaign, the British Foreign Office chose to interpret his obscure statements as a negative endorsement of intervention in the Middle East. The United States, they thought, could not abandon its closest ally once military operations began.

On October 29, Israel attacked Egypt, and several days later Anglo-French forces retook the Suez Canal. The war ended quickly, partly because Egypt's armies proved surprisingly inept, but largely because of superpower reactions. The United States angrily reasserted its leadership of the Atlantic community. Opposed to "any aggression by any nation," Eisenhower threatened to destroy the English pound by refusing to renew British loans from the International Military Fund unless London called off the attack. Unencumbered by alliances with former colonial powers, the Russians condemned Britain and France more forcefully and even hinted at a nuclear strike. Eden and Mollet could only acquiesce in a Canadian-American plan for United Nations troops to police the Sinai Peninsula.

The affair severely damaged America's prestige in most parts of the world. Egyptians did not forget that the "American peace" had stationed foreign soldiers in their country, but not in Israel, the aggressor. The Suez crisis ensconced Russia in Egyptian affairs, especially after the Soviets took over financing the Aswan Dam, and insured Nasser's leadership of the Arab world. Neither prospect pleased Dulles.

99

Washington's criticism had also alienated the Europeans. Franco-American relations never quite recovered. Suez convinced most Frenchmen that Washington had sacrificed their national interest; Europe must now chart a new course. The British were stunned. Unwilling to give up their "special relationship" with the United States, English leaders did not know what to do. England's long walk away from world commitment toward European integration began in 1956.

Strains within the Western alliance during the Suez crisis coincided with a similar emergency within the Soviet bloc. After the war, Stalin had backed pro-Soviet regimes throughout Eastern Europe. These "satellites" embarked upon industrial programs designed to complement Soviet reconstruction. Never content with Stalinist tactics and the distortion of national economic needs, some Eastern Europeans challenged these local regimes once the Russian thaw began. Yet how much liberalization would Moscow's new rulers allow? In June 1956 over 15,000 factory workers rioted at Poznan in Poland. Their three-day rebellion set off a popular upsurge in favor of Wladyslaw Gomulka, a former minister removed by Stalin when he publicly opposed collectivization and advocated national development regardless of Russian orders. After complicated maneuvers with Poland's old guard and Moscow's politburo, revisionists forced Moscow to accept the unorthodox Gomulka. Events had caught Soviet leaders off-guard, but their recognition of Gomulka seemed to indicate that economic reform which did not threaten the integrity of the Soviet bloc would be feasible.

Misunderstanding this subtlety, Hungarians reached for true political independence a few months later. Emboldened by Poland's success and suffering from the same Stalinist exploitation, a huge mob demonstrated on October 23. Students and workers, intellectuals and housewives paraded for hours, demanding the return of Imre Nagy, like Gomulka a former minister disgraced for his liberal views. Nagy formed a new government, but strikes and unrest continued. Protests against subservience to the Soviet Union turned into armed rebellion in the countryside and within days paralyzed the capital as well. Misled by overly optimistic broadcasts from America's Radio Free Europe, the revolutionaries dreamed of United States assistance in gaining freedom. Nagy pledged free elections and a multi-party system: "No nation," he declared, "can intervene in our internal affairs." Although Moscow tried to negotiate, the lure of independence betrayed the Hungarians into tragic illusions. As violence continued, the Russians sent a huge army into Hungary. Brutal repression drew the line of de-Stalinization at economic reform. Moscow would not tolerate more, not even political neutrality. At the same time, the Kremlin could no longer assume that the communist bloc would passively follow its dictates.

America's Relations with Europe: An Odd Irresolution

The new mood of self-assertiveness in Europe aggravated tensions within the Atlantic community, especially over the old issue of nuclear control. Because the United States insisted upon taking independent action, European foreign ministers still feared that Washington might start a war or compromise one at their expense. Unable to dissuade France from building a national atomic force, the United States finally suggested that NATO become "a fourth nuclear power." Joint control would maintain America's power over the alliance and reassure the Europeans about its intentions. A nuclear NATO could also curb West Germany, the country that by 1960 provided nearly two-thirds of NATO's conventional troops. No one really liked the idea, however, and it faded away. The problem remained.

More than debates about nuclear warfare fueled Europe's restiveness. By the late 1950s, returning prosperity had repaired Hitler's destruction. Many Europeans, and even Americans, believed that economic integration would accelerate this revival and discourage Soviet adventures. France, Germany, Italy, Belgium, the Netherlands, and Luxembourg pooled steel and coal production in 1952. The Common Market treaties, signed five years later at Rome, pledged to end barriers to the movement of commerce, capital, and workers among the "Inner Six." Uniform external tariffs gave the Common Market enormous bargaining advantages with other nations. This trend toward economic unity excited the people of Germany and Italy so much that their leaders depended upon its progress to remain in office. The situation in France differed dramatically. Nearly self-sufficient economically, the country's popular president, Charles de Gaulle, could ignore integration. Under French leadership, he believed, Europe should escape the confines of a bipolar world. De Gaulle saw the Common Market as the vehicle for French glory. Clearly, the Atlantic nations faced difficult adjustments in the sixties, not only between Europe and America but also within Europe itself.

Soviet–American Relations: Machiavellian Goodwill

The late 1950s became a strange interlude, halfway between cold war and unsteady peace. Both Eisenhower and Khrushchev fashioned innovative proposals for ending the nuclear arms race and embarked upon personal diplomacy.

The threat of a nuclear holocaust frightened many into a search for security. In mid-1958, the Russians unilaterally stopped nuclear testing, presumably to probe American intentions while converting more of their economy to consumer production. Britain and the United States followed later that year. During the fall of 1958, Khrushchev visited the United States for twelve days. He addressed the United Nations, talked to Iowa farmers, and watched Hollywood stars make a movie. Then premier and president conferred privately at Camp David, a mountain retreat in Maryland. Though achieving nothing concrete, both leaders reached for accommodation, for something better than an inevitable atomic war. This "spirit of Camp David" moderated the rhetoric of rancor in both countries. At the same time, their leaders embarked upon much-publicized goodwill trips. Eisenhower went to Europe, the Middle East, Latin America, and the Far East, though anti-American riots protesting a bilateral defense treaty forced him to cancel a trip to Japan. Khrushchev appeared in Western Europe, Afghanistan, and India.

But goodwill tours could not erase old problems. Early in November 1958 Khrushchev once again revived unresolved German issues. Four-power occupation of Berlin, he announced, must end. Although the enclave could not threaten the Soviet bloc, the showpiece city embarrassed the Russians. Its black market in Western currencies upset financial planning in Eastern Europe. Then, too, Khrushchev wanted to test Eisenhower. Easy concessions could check domestic critics unhappy with the premier's conciliatory approach toward the United States. So the Soviet leader demanded a "satisfactory settlement" within six months or he would sign a separate peace with East Germany. The West had no legal claims to the city; its right of access depended upon communist consent, not treaties. Tensions soared, but the Western allies abandoned neither their nerve nor the West Berliners. Khrushchev's bluff failed. The deadline expired quietly only weeks before the premier's visit to the United States.

An even more bizarre incident occurred during Eisenhower's last year as president. In early 1959, Khrushchev called for another summit meeting, perhaps to exchange Berlin for an understanding in the Middle East. The dilemma of German reunification still haunted diplomats, and the paradoxes of nuclear armament apparently required personal solution. Recent troubles and the "spirit of Camp David" propelled leaders toward a summit, this time scheduled for Paris. Preliminary talks made little progress, however, and on May 1, 1960, the Soviets shot down an American U-2 spy plane over their territory. Both powers used the U-2 affair to box the opponent into a diplomatic corner. Khrushchev could have muffled the incident, but instead he trumpeted Russia's injured innocence, demanding an apology and an end of such flights. Determined to score as many propaganda points as possible, the premier travelled to Paris, but his diatribes soon angered Eisenhower.

After all, the U-2 flights demonstrated that American technology could police any nuclear agreement. Was Khrushchev now trying to back out of serious disarmament talks? Or had he simply lured everyone to Paris, not to negotiate but to embarrass the West? Skeptical of Russian good faith, Eisenhower ignored Anglo-French efforts to rescue the summit. It was a curious epitaph to the oscillating course of Soviet–American relations. Both powers pursued national advantage, at times almost recklessly, but the terrors of nuclear war restrained any ultimate threat. Their rivalry brought neither peace nor war.

FRUSTRATIONS IN THE THIRD WORLD

The pretense of a bipolar world fell apart during the 1950s as superpowers lost more and more control over the course of events. The focus of international affairs shifted toward Asia, Africa, and Latin America, where charismatic leaders often pursued economic self-determination and control over natural resources—no less than political freedom. Most nationalist modernizers in the nonwhite world thought disputes over ideology useless; results alone mattered. The third world took from both Russian and Yankee. So long as a nation, like India, remained genuinely independent and balanced communist against capitalist, neutralism was feasible, even logical. If a country came to rely almost exclusively upon one or the other, two alternatives loomed: the giant power might become dangerously involved in purely local issues or, less likely, disputes in the third world among surrogates could lead to nuclear war between their sponsors. It was a delicate game. For nearly two decades diplomats and warriors alike worked to refine America's military strategy into a new flexibility.

Vietnam

America's most perplexing involvement in third-world politics came in Southeast Asia. Financed largely from Washington, French armies had struggled with the nationalist leader Ho Chi Minh for control of Vietnam since 1945. Frenchmen had systematically destroyed much of Vietnamese culture in their eighty-year occupation. Ripped from their villages to work on vast plantations or to serve in colonial bureaucracies, many natives had lost both the will and the means to resist. But Japan's initial victory in 1940 discredited France and galvanized a coterie of nationalist intellectuals into a movement for postwar independence. Ho Chi Minh, an able Marxist scholar dedicated to spreading the class struggle to his country of peasants, assumed leadership of the Viet Minh, a popular front of all revolutionary parties. And as Japanese power collapsed at the end of World War II, Ho declared Vietnam's independence (on September 2, 1945). Although his provisional government wanted to negotiate, France almost immediately launched a war of reconquest. Ho and an exceptionally skillful general, Vo Nyugen Giap, countered with guerrilla tactics seeking to avoid defeat in the field while winning the people over to their nationalist-communist cause.

After nearly nine years of a frustrating succession of French generals, the rebels apparently abandoned their war of stealth and psychology. In early 1954 Giap sent his main force into Laos, resorting to conventional tactics to conquer territory and lure the French away from their coastal supply depots. General Henri Navarre quickly followed. Anxious to trap the communists into a major assault, he concentrated 25,000 men at a frontier outpost, Dien Bien Phu. Giap surrounded the fort, and the battle became one of attrition. A constant artillery barrage cut off Navarre's reinforcements. Using a complicated system of tunnels and munitions backpacked into the mountains by thousands of peasants, the communists began a slow advance. As the French public watched the sure strangulation of its army, the government under Pierre Mendes-France pledged to end the war, even if that meant leaving Vietnam to national communists under Ho Chi Minh. The French prepared for a peace conference in Geneva.

Shocked that yet another area might "go communist," Dulles and some Pentagon figures—notably Admiral Arthur W. Radford, chairman of the Joint Chiefs of Staff—proposed an air strike against Giap's army. Some even speculated that American troops could revitalize the French war effort. Eisenhower did not want to "lose" Indochina so soon after the Chinese debacle, but he was aware of America's limited power in so remote a place and worried about the federal budget. Typically, the president turned to Congress. Its leaders refused to authorize intervention unless the United States first secured foreign support, and Britain quickly refused. After the army outlined cost and manpower estimates, Eisenhower concluded that intervention was impossible. Chief of Staff Matthew Ridgeway predicted that a million men, huge draft quotas, and enormous construction might win this political-guerrilla war, but he thought that even then most Vietnamese would more likely support the Viet Minh.

Meanwhile, peace negotiations at the Geneva Conference had reached an odd démarche. France wished only to get out of the war. The Russians, afraid of aggravating Washington, and the Chinese, searching for international legitimacy, urged Ho Chi Minh's Hanoi-based communists to accept a compromise. Paris granted Vietnam,

Laos, and Cambodia full independence, though none of the new states could join foreign alliances or permit foreign soldiers on its soil. French troops were to regroup in Vietnam south of the Seventeenth Parallel, communist forces north of it. A nationwide election during 1956 would provide a single government for the reunified country. This solution—a graceful exit for the defeated French and a neutralized Indochina in exchange for a probably communist cabinet for Vietnam—gratified most everyone concerned.

Everyone, that is, except John Foster Dulles and his followers. He saw a way to "save" at least some of Indochina, though it required unilateral action. The secretary refused to sign the Geneva accords and announced instead that the United States considered North and South Vietnam two separate entities. The State Department hurriedly completed plans for SEATO and gratuitously extended its coverage to South Vietnam, Cambodia, and Laos. After Bao Dai, the legitimate Vietnamese emperor who had served the French, stepped down in 1955, the Eisenhower administration pledged vast amounts of economic aid to his pro-Western successor, Ngo Dinh Diem. Diem, with American backing, called off the scheduled national elections in which a communist victory appeared certain. And the Republican administration updated an old doctrine, long applied to Europe, to justify these expedient maneuvers: the domino theory. If South Vietnam "fell," Thailand would be next; then the rest of Indochina, and perhaps even India or Australia. If the West stood firm now, as Britain and France should have stood up to Hitler in 1936, communist subversion would fail. A model for democracy in Southeast Asia could serve conveniently as an example for the third world. So American experts and much of the American public, anxious to forestall another "defeat" yet stymied by the all-or-nothing finality of nuclear war, pinned much on Diem's frail regime. But the connection was so one-sided that Vietnam became more colony than sovereign state. Dependency reinforced the arguments for continued United States intervention.

For six years after the Geneva conference ended the first Indochina war, Republicans richly supplied South Vietnam's pro-West Premier Ngo Dinh Diem with economic aid, military know-how, and diplomatic protection. The results at first vindicated their gamble that a limited commitment might yield jackpot gains, not only in staving off another communist victory but also in building a capitalist model for the third world. Between 1954 and 1957 South Vietnam ended wartime economic controls, started toward reconstruction, and began industrial development. Diem redistributed land confiscated from French landlords to peasants in the Mekong River delta. His steadily improving army ended gangsterism in Saigon and forced allegiance from the semifeudal reli-

105

gious sects in the countryside. But Diem could never really centralize the nation, and his Catholicism alienated the predominately Buddhist population. To ensure at least the appearance of popular support, Diem replaced local officials with his stooges. A grandiloquent "population relocation" program degenerated into political witch-hunts. Land reform ultimately benefited a new kind of absentee owner, the Saigonese bureaucrat. The regime's dependence upon the United States frightened nationalists. Corruption oozed through the dike of American aid, diluting help to villagers trapped in the war-ravaged countryside and to refugees hounded into inflation-ridden cities. Smiling strangely, clad only in white, Diem retreated more and more into a contracting circle of family and army generals.

To protest such abuses, an odd amalgam of anti-Diem intellectuals, nationalists, harassed politicians, and Viet Minh communists organized the National Liberation Front (NLF) in 1957. Its platform promised a return to village rule, immediate land ownership for the peasants, and a coalition cabinet in Saigon. Discontent in the countryside propelled many recruits into the NLF's makeshift army, the Viet Cong. Communist cadres soon dominated both groups, partly because of their experience during the earlier guerrilla struggle against France. Then too, they represented the communal traditions of the village rather than the alien dictatorship in Saigon which relied on American "round-eyes."

A communist-led war for national liberation set in motion a dangerous spiral of escalation. The renewal of serious fighting panicked Washington into supplying Diem with billions of dollars and a growing corps of American advisers—900 by 1960. In response, Hanoi aided the insurgents, training recruits in the North. Then, after a five-year plan had made their country the most heavily industrialized state in Southeast Asia by 1959, the North Vietnamese shipped large amounts of war materiel south along the Ho Chi Minh Trail. Although this primitive line of communications depended as much on human backs as on gasoline engines, it permitted the Viet Cong to make great progress despite America's reinforcements. After all, a little guerrilla action went a long way against conventional armies. Raiders could strike anywhere, shielded behind popular resentments. Their opponents could only garrison the entire country. Thus the cycle of Saigon corruption and communist rebellion led to American reinforcement and then, to more aid from Hanoi.

Washington tried to break this chain reaction by asking Diem to reform his regime. Instead, the mandarin hinted at turning the land over to the Viet Cong. Partly because of larger problems elsewhere, the Republicans avoided any final answers, a natural result of the uneasy tension in Eisenhower-Dulles diplomacy. The secretary blurted out during a press conference that "the free world would intervene in Indochina rather than let the situation deteriorate." Once involved, Dulles thought, America's prestige required victory. The president demurred. A charter member of the Never-Again Club—a group of generals who resolutely opposed another land war in Asia after their experiences in Korea—Eisenhower flatly contradicted his chief adviser on foreign affairs. "I can conceive of no greater tragedy," he said, "than for the United States to become engaged in all-out war in Indochina."

Intervention: Lebanon, Guatemala, Cuba

Vietnam was only the most prominent riddle in America's relations with the third world. Because its experience in nonwhite regions was so limited, the administration tried to formulate a general approach, the Eisenhower Doctrine. After weeks of dickering during the spring of 1957, Congress finally authorized the president to defend countries in the Middle East "against overt armed aggression from any nation controlled by international communism." The new doctrine reordered politics in the area: a three-cornered contest among the capitalist West, communist East, and Arab nationalists replaced older imperial tensions.

During the summer of 1958, when rioting broke out in the small Middle Eastern country of Lebanon, the doctrine had its first test. Lebanon's government blamed the riots on saboteurs from the newly organized United Arab Republic (Egypt and Syria), but animosity between Christian and Moslem, city and countryside, Nasserites and moderates had long ago turned the tiny land into a tinderbox. Then nationalists in Iraq murdered King Faisal and his premier, Nuri el-Said. The new leaders took Iraq out of the CENTO alliance, thus nullifying it, and made overtures to the UAR. As violence in the Middle East accelerated, the established elements in Lebanon and Jordan asked the United States and Britain to "stabilize" the situation. Both powers quickly complied, anxious to check Nasserism and protect their dangerously exposed oil pipelines. Over 14,000 Marines eventually waded ashore on Lebanese beaches in an intervention notable for its bloodlessness, military polish, and short-range success. American troops set up a new coalition government in Beirut, more representative than before, though still strongly anti-Nasser. Meanwhile in Jordan, the British restored King Hussein's control over his army. Despite its superficial innocence, the Anglo-American intrusion provoked new fears of Western imperialism. The Eisenhower Doctrine may ultimately have pushed many

Arab nationalists toward Moscow. Some Arabs began to turn away from the United States, not because they were pro-communist but because they suspected American motives.

Efforts to mold reality into preconceived theories about containment of communism also beset Latin American policy. Republicans reacted to communist advances by isolating the symptoms rather than treating the causes. In some parts of that region landed aristocrats, allied with the military, perpetuated an almost feudal system of economic and social regimentation. Because the landlords invested their profits in safer havens overseas, most of the smaller nations lacked capital, and their farmers suffered the wild fluctuations of world prices for raw materials. Eisenhower's policymakers argued that such countries must avoid unsettling social experiments in order to attract private enterprise.

The Guatemalan crisis convinced Republicans that only strong governments, not necessarily democratic ones, could forestall radicals. Discontent in that Central American land against an autocratic ruler and the Yankee-owned United Fruit Company helped bring leftist Jacobo Arbenz into power in 1954. Afraid of the new regime's connections with the communists, the United States CIA covertly intervened, destroying the fledgling government and establishing a dictator more to its liking. But repression only aggravated social hatreds in Guatemala and elsewhere. During Richard Nixon's goodwill tour of Latin America in 1958, for example, thousands of Venezuelans mobbed the vice-president's car in Caracas, upsetting not only Cadillac limousines but also American illusions. Once again, Eisenhower reacted belatedly. He organized a government-financed Development Bank to stabilize commodity prices. The State Department stopped awarding medals to dictator allies and shifted its praises instead to such liberal reformers as Venezuela's Romulo Betancourt. But only the image changed. Price supports helped the landowners, not the peasants, and judicious American military aid prevented coups except by approved anticommunists.

American policy did not "contain" revolution everywhere in Latin America. In 1959 a guerrilla leader in Cuba, Fidel Castro, converted his mountaintop rebellion into a social revolution which not only deposed the country's dictator, Fulgencio Batista, but also ended the island's dependence upon the United States. The Cuban revolution surprised many Americans who were unaware of conditions in Cuba. The rich sugar crop had benefited foreigners and the upper class, while the working population suffered long hours and miserable living conditions. The prospect of honest government, social equality, and land redistribution provided support for the bearded, thirty-two-year-old Castro, like Nasser a charismatic leader. Initially welcomed by Americans as an alternative to the repressive Batista, Castro soon encountered hostility as he tried to reduce his country's economic dependence on the United States. Castro nationalized some American companies; Eisenhower retaliated by curtailing the amount of Cuban sugar the United States would import; Castro stepped up nationalization and turned toward the Soviet Union for aid. When the spiral of deteriorating relations had ended, Castro had nationalized over a billion dollars worth of Yankee assets, taken reprisals against thousands as "enemies of the people," and frightened most of the Cuban upper-middle class into exile in Florida. During a visit to the United States, Castro appealed to America's racial minorities to follow his example. Later he joined hands with Krushchev at the United Nations.

Although many Americans wondered whether Castro was a true communist or just an opportunist playing Moscow against Washington, the Republicans moved methodically to drive him from power. Eisenhower wholly cut off Cuba's sugar quotas, which had maintained the island's prices above world market levels. Under great pressure from Washington, the Organization of American States expelled Cuba, thus cutting off all aid. These heavy-handed measures only reaffirmed the Cuban people's belief in Castro and forced him to rely upon the Soviets. Anxious to take advantage of American blunders and, no doubt, to check domestic critics, Khrushchev bought up Cuba's sugar crop in 1960 at an inflated price. CIA operatives also began training a Cuban invasion force in Guatemala and plotting other bizarre moves against Castro's regime, but threat of American intervention only justified further swings to the left by Castro. Shortsighted containment in the Caribbean, no less than in the Middle East, produced nationalist reactions often hostile to American goals.

REEVALUATION OF THE NEW LOOK

Sputnik

On October 4, 1957, the Soviet Union orbited the first space satellite, Sputnik I; a month later Sputnik II, which weighed over 1,300 pounds and carried a live dog, spent several days in space before landing. The accuracy and large payload of the Russian rockets tilted the symmetry of nuclear statemate. Some alarmists warned that if the Soviet Union could neutralize America's second-strike deterrent, Moscow might risk a preemptive atomic attack knowing that the United States could not retaliate. Alternately, Soviet sophistication might release Russian forces for conventional operations, since Washington now could not escalate to nuclear levels. Sputnik ended America's easy confidence in its technological ascendancy and created new fears of Soviet strength.

A false sense of vulnerability pervaded American life. Defense planners wondered whether the country should continue to focus on solid-fuel missiles like the Minuteman and Polaris or switch priorities toward liquid-fuel rockets, like those the Russians used. Though more economical and reliable, America's rockets required very complicated engineering and more time for deployment. Even if the United States accelerated its liquid-fuel programs, some experts feared a lag-time of four, perhaps even seven, years before a balance could be restored. They predicted a "missile gap," especially after Defense Secretary Neil McElroy announced that "the United States does not intend to match the Soviet Union weapon for weapon." The beeping satellites did frighten the Pentagon into deploying intermediate-range rockets in Britain, Turkey, and Italy. The Defense Department also channeled more and more money into research and development (R and D) programs. But most high officials recognized that America's manned bombers far outclassed Soviet defense systems. Though spectacular, Sputnik in no concrete way threatened the safety of the United States.

The Eisenhower administration's measured response to Sputnik did more to alarm than to reassure large segments of the American public. Long restive about New Look economies, some military people publicly worried about the emphasis on bombers and carrier-based fighters. General Maxwell Taylor, Army Chief of Staff, argued for "armament in depth," so that the United States could fight "low-level, conventional battles," if nuclear stalemate produced "brush-fire wars on the periphery of the free world." Sensing political advantage, many liberal Democrats saw more military spending as a means to stimulate the lagging economy. Defense intellectuals, gathered into research institutes by governments and universities, explained that atomic armaments required constant technological innovation to keep pace with scientific discoveries. This Alice-in-Wonderland world asked citizens to run faster and faster just to stay in the same place. Only exotic new weapons, like submarine-based missiles, could provide real security against surprise attack. The Korean War had spawned an industry dependent upon arms contracts. Research and development money produced ever more complicated weapons. Powerful interests in such politically important areas as Long Island, Texas, and Southern California pressed to begin lucrative mass production. This combination of American generals, Democratic politicians, and enterprising businessmen coalesced into a powerful group which lobbied for more and more armaments. Eisen-

110

hower's immense prestige, his skepticism about Pentagon claims, and his resolute search for peace temporarily quieted the clamor. But opponents of the New Look wondered whether Eisenhower's economies had not misled the country.

The Cold War as Future

Eisenhower left the presidency a discouraged man. He confided to John F. Kennedy that "foreign affairs are in a mess" and warned the American people of "a burgeoning military-industrial complex." The Republican record was mixed, even confused, because of its disorientation and the growing complexities of world affairs.

Aware of the limits of American power, a cost-conscious Eisenhower pursued peace. Dulles, on the other hand, launched an open-ended ideological crusade to refashion the world into a mold compatible with United States interests. Expansive rhetoric and restrained action produced an attitude among Americans that ignored risks. Neither nationalistic rebellions nor opportunistic neutrals dissuaded American policymakers from their determination to control events. The New Look aggravated this singlemindedness. Massive retaliation did not guarantee security but instead required more and more doomsday weapons. Even then, deterrence could affect only the Soviet Union; elsewhere nuclear omnipotence was useless. Yet Dulles helped convince many Americans that those third-world movements which were not carbon copies of liberal capitalism were necessarily "communist" and threatened American security.

Limitless objectives matched America's apparent inability to deal with change. A chain of anticommunist military alliances and the proliferation of bases abroad entangled the United States in local complexities more often than they contained radicalism in the third world. Misunderstanding of Castro, for example, presaged tragic miscalculations about Southeast Asia. Prosperity and a mellowing Russia diverted Western Europeans from the cold war and slowly ended their dependence upon Washington. From one perspective, these trends were expected. That Europe wanted to escape American tutelage was natural, not the fault of obtuse diplomats. And could an advanced technological power understand the seemingly strange demands of underdeveloped countries?

Despite complexities in Europe and the third world, the central concern of American foreign policy during the 1950s always remained its relationship with the Soviet Union. Here too the prod of events dictated a new departure. Survival demanded a steady arms race but, curiously, it also spawned a growing desire to escape the all-or-nothing options of atomic power. Eisenhower institutionalized this paradox, less by noteworthy innovation than by avoiding nuclear confrontation for eight years. Krushchev mirrored the pattern, and the superpowers tacitly agreed not to drop their bombs. It was a modest achievement, one to be balanced against the animosities of brinksmanship and distortions the Republicans had introduced into American policy toward both allies and neutrals, but it was the decade's most comforting accomplishment in foreign affairs.

BIBLIOGRAPHY

The relevant volumes of Council on Foreign Relations, *The United States in World Affairs* (1945–1961), contain excellent year-end summaries of Eisenhower's diplomacy. Important documentary collections include Robert L. Branyan and Lawrence H. Larsen, *The Eisenhower Administration, 1953–1961: A Documentary History* (2 vols., 1971); the appropriate parts of Arthur M. Schlesinger, Jr., ed., *The Dynamics of World Power: A Documentary History of United States Foreign Policy 1945–1972* (5 vols., 1972); and *Documents on American Foreign Relations* (1953–61). The president's sometimes less-than-candid memoir is Dwight D. Eisenhower, *The White House Years: Mandate for Change,* and *The White House Years: Waging Peace, 1956–1961* (1963). See also Mark W. Clark, *From the Danube to the Yalu* (1954), and Matthew B. Ridgway, *The Korean War* (1967), especially for the difficult armistice negotiations.

The best survey of American foreign policy during the 1950s is David Bernard Capitanchik, *The Eisenhower Presidency and American Foreign Policy* (1969), a careful effort at balanced analysis. Cecil V. Crabb, *Bipartisan Foreign Policy: Myth or Reality?* (1957), warns against increasing "politicization," while Doris A. Graber, *Crisis Diplomacy: A History of U.S. Intervention Policies and Practices* (1959), justifies Washington's actions in terms of national security. Richard J. Barnet, *Intervention and Revolution* (rev. ed., 1972), is more critical. Many scholars have tangled with Dulles and his diplomacy. Louis Gerson, *John Foster Dulles* (1967), though more summary than analysis, sketches the secretary's busy, sometimes secretive life. Robert R. Randle, *Geneva 1954: The Settlement of the Indochinese War* (1969), admires Dulles's "accurate appraisals" of containment diplomacy. The best, most trenchant study is Townsend Hoopes, *The Devil and John Foster Dulles* (1973), an account strongly critical of Dulles's moralistic, shortsighted crusade against the devil of communism. Michael Guhin, *John Foster Dulles: A Statesman and His Times* (1972), is more sympathetic.

112

For specific episodes or topics, consult David A. Baldwin, *Economic Development and American Foreign Policy, 1943–1962* (1966); Keith Eubank, *The Summit Conferences, 1919–1960* (1966), especially good on the two Paris summits; Foster Rhea Dulles, *American Policy toward Communist China, 1949–1969* (1972); Nadav Safran, *The United States and Israel* (1963); Herman Finer, *Dulles over Suez: The Theory and Practice of His Diplomacy* (1964); Philip E. Mosely, *The Kremlin and World Politics: Studies in Soviet Policy and Action* (1960); John G. Stoessinger and Robert G. McKelvey, *The United Nations and the Superpowers: United States–Soviet Interaction at the United Nations* (2nd ed., 1970); David Wise and Thomas B. Ross, *The U-2 Affair* (1962); Lionel M. Gelber, *America in Britain's Place: The Leadership of the West and Anglo-American Unity* (1961); and Herbert Nicholas, *Britain and the U.S.A.* (1963).

The Making of a President

A 1973 bestseller by one of John Kennedy's closest aides expressed a general sentiment: *Johnny We Hardly Knew Ye*. The title was revealing. The Kennedy administration was always shrouded in legend, and books by his associates helped the myths grow larger. But historians now know to peek through the clouds of adulation which surrounded the thirty-fifth president.

Few fathers groom their sons to be president, but wealthy Joseph P. Kennedy, an Irish Catholic outcast in properly Protestant Boston, wanted one of his sons to gain the nation's highest office. When his oldest boy died during World War II, his other war-hero son picked up the family colors. Young John Kennedy attended an elite prep school and then graduated from Harvard, all the while refining his social graces and developing a tough-minded view of public affairs. He learned to listen well, to absorb the ideas of others, and to make decisions independently. He also displayed an intolerance for those who did not match his quick, facile mind. People who could not say what they had to say quickly, who moralized or digressed, irritated a busy man like John Kennedy. Sentimental liberals—Adlai Stevenson, for example—seemed suspect: how could a man do great things who took so long to make up his mind? John Kennedy always surrounded himself with bright, ambitious young men who possessed his mental quickness and his distaste for sentimentality. The "public" Kennedy—idealistic, inspirational, and sometimes emotional—was very different from the calculating and restrained politician from Boston.

5

The liberal promise: JFK and LBJ

Kennedy's narrow victory over Richard Nixon in 1960 capped a rather unimpressive political career. In 1946 he won election to the House of Representatives and six years later ousted a distinguished scion of the Boston aristocracy, Henry Cabot Lodge, Jr., from the United States Senate. Like many other bright young men, Kennedy considered that slow-moving, tradition-bound institution undemanding and often boring. Kennedy generally supported liberal expenditures for social welfare programs and championed a strong anticommunist policy, but he sponsored no important legislative measures. During these years Kennedy did marry an attractive wife, who proved to be an important political asset, and he wrote a prize-winning book—*Profiles in Courage*. Between 1956 and 1960 Kennedy took full advantage of the new age of jet travel, personally visiting people in the party hierarchy and accumulating political debts which he could cash during the 1960 presidential campaign. He and his close associates (the Irish Mafia, some called them) put together a smooth-running organization which included pollster Louis Harris, strategist Lawrence O'Brien, speechwriter Theodore Sorenson, his two younger brothers, and a coterie of Harvard intellectuals.

The Election of 1960

The energetic Kennedy dominated the presidential campaign of 1960. As a politician Kennedy did few new things; he simply did the old ones better than most other candidates. His speeches covered the traditional themes—the cold war with the Soviet Union, prosperity at home, and sacrifice for country—but they were cleverly phrased and, after some speaking lessons, effectively delivered. While he brought his wife and baby daughter into the political spotlight, he used them less frequently and with more taste than most other politicians. Kennedy's operatives employed blatant arm-twisting to gain political favors, but they generally knew just how much leverage to use and exactly where to apply it. Unlike Adlai Stevenson, who had let the convention choose his running mate in 1956, JFK made a highly political choice: Senate majority leader Lyndon Johnson of Texas. Even Kennedy's much-discussed "charisma" was not a new phenomenon; throughout the 1950s political observers had analyzed the charisma of President Eisenhower. But Kennedy's most distinctive qualities—his youth, good looks, and charm—did have a special impact upon young people and women. A *Newsweek* correspondent pointed out "the jumpers"—the women of all ages who bounded up and down when Kennedy's motorcade came into view.

115

The Republican candidate, Eisenhower's Vice-President Richard Nixon, tried to contrast his supposed maturity and experience with Kennedy's political record. The tactic backfired in the widely heralded television debates: TV made the sharp-featured Nixon appear old and tired, while it accentuated Kennedy's best qualities. The harsh lights highlighted Nixon's famous five o'clock shadow, suggesting the image of "the man you wouldn't buy a used car from" or of "tricky Dick." Finally, Kennedy's confident manner during the first debate undercut Nixon's claim about his opponent's immaturity. And though Nixon scrupulously avoided any hint of anti-Catholicism during the campaign, some of his supporters, particularly the Reverend Norman Vincent Peale, did not. Catholic voters tended to be Democrats anyway, and JFK piled up large Catholic majorities in several key states. The election of 1960 was very close: Kennedy won by only 120,000 popular votes, and small shifts in several large states would have made Nixon president. The unexpectedly narrow victory probably increased Kennedy's political caution.

Camelot: The New Frontier

Although he could hardly claim a popular mandate, Kennedy quickly built an imposing image for his administration—the "New Frontier," the energetic successor to the New Deal and the Fair Deal. First, JFK assembled his version of Roosevelt's Brain Trust. He appointed his brother and campaign manager, Robert Kennedy, as attorney general; Robert McNamara, president of Ford Motor Company, became secretary of defense; Harvard's brilliant government professor, McGeorge Bundy, assumed the important role of national security adviser to the president; and Dean Rusk, head of the Ford Foundation, got the coveted position of secretary of state. Even the secondary jobs claimed top people. (A promising young intellectual named Henry Kissinger found himself outgunned in such fierce competition and took over Bundy's courses at Harvard, awaiting an administration that would better appreciate his talents.) Few of these advisers had much political experience, but they had all been eminently successful in other areas. Vice-President Lyndon Johnson left the first cabinet meeting dazzled by the intellect which Kennedy had assembled. "You should have seen all those men," he told his old political mentor, House Speaker Sam Rayburn. "Well, Lyndon, you may be right and they may be every bit as intelligent as you say," replied Mr. Sam, "but I'd feel a whole lot better about them if just one of them had run for sheriff once."

116

United Press International

President Kennedy and his Cabinet. From left: Postmaster General J. Edward Day; Ambassador to the U.N. Adlai Stevenson; Vice-President Lyndon Johnson; Secretary of Defense Robert McNamara; Secretary of Agriculture Orville Freeman; Secretary of Labor Arthur Goldberg; Secretary of Health, Education and Welfare Abraham Ribicoff; Secretary of Commerce Luther Hodge; Attorney General Robert Kennedy; Secretary of State Dean Rusk; President Kennedy; Secretary of the Treasury C. Douglas Dillon; and Secretary of Interior Stewart Udall.

The Kennedy White House became a center of art and culture. A telegram which invited people from the arts to attend the inauguration announced that

DURING OUR FORTHCOMING ADMINISTRATION WE HOPE TO EF-FECT A PRODUCTIVE RELATIONSHIP WITH OUR WRITERS ARTISTS COMPOSERS PHILOSOPHERS SCIENTISTS AND HEADS OF CULTURAL INSTITUTIONS STOP . . .

Jacqueline Kennedy, a well-educated woman who spoke several foreign languages, became the special guardian of culture: she invited people such as cellist Pablo Casals to perform at the White House, redecorated the old mansion, and even conducted a tour of it for millions of television viewers. Kennedy parties were lavish productions in the grand style; I. F. Stone, the radical journalist, complained that the atmosphere resembled that of "a reigning monarch's court." Such a comparison probably did not disturb Kennedyphiles. Many of the president's followers reveled in the reputation of "Camelot." (Unlike most older Washington politicians, who preferred large quantities of hard liquor, the Kennedy people drank moderate amounts of fine European wines.)

In addition to intellect and style, the New Frontier emphasized toughness. As John Kennedy noted in his inaugural address, he and his advisers were all tough young men—"born in this country, tempered by war, disciplined by a hard and bitter peace. . . ." Facing the challenges of a dangerous world, they could not afford to be soft. In defending his space program, for example, JFK bragged that Americans would accept the challenges of space "not because they are easy but because they are hard." The Kennedy team displayed its toughness during impromptu touch football games; here the president's brother Robert gained the reputation as the most hard-nosed New Frontiersman. After Floyd Patterson lost his heavyweight boxing title, the attorney general removed the ex-champ's picture from his office. All the Kennedy people prided themselves on their ability to handle any foreign or domestic crisis. Kennedy insiders leaked a story to the *Saturday Evening Post* about Adlai Stevenson's alleged "softness"—his distaste for nuclear confrontation—during the Cuban missile crisis of 1962.

The Kennedy team seemed almost to welcome a good crisis. In 1962, Kennedy massed the full power of the national government to combat a price increase by United States Steel and several other large firms. JFK denounced the companies as unpatriotic, contrasting their actions with the sacrifices of servicemen who were already dying in Vietnam and reservists who had been called up to meet a feared confrontation with the Soviet Union in Berlin. The president coupled his verbal assaults with a massive legal offensive; the Justice Department began to seek evidence of price fixing; FBI agents started to investigate possible illegal activities by steel corporations; the Federal Trade Commission threatened to look into the same questions; and administration sources even hinted at possible antitrust actions to break up the steel giants. At the same time, the Defense Department refused to buy from companies which raised prices, and Kennedy aides pressured corporate friends to resist the lead of U.S. Steel. Confronted by this counterattack, Big Steel retreated and rolled back prices. Throughout the short skirmish, the president viewed the controversy as an extension of foreign affairs, claiming that price increases threatened national security. It was the type of problem, he believed, that required crisis management.

The president's critics viewed the situation differently. Many businessmen predictably denounced Kennedy for using "police state" tactics, but even some foes of large corporations expressed concern. A radical young law professor, Charles Reich (who would later gain fame as author of *The Greening of America*), concluded that it was "dangerously wrong for an angry president to loose his terrible arsenal of power for the purposes of intimidation and coercing private companies and citizens. . . ." Other observers contended that Kennedy's actions reflected a dangerous crisis mentality and indicated the administration's lack of any consistent domestic policies. Within a year the steel firms raised prices twice, and the Kennedy administration did nothing.

Although JFK was more interested in foreign policy than in domestic affairs, he did have some broad goals for his New Frontier at home. In large part, the new Democratic administration revived many of Harry Truman's old Fair Deal proposals: federal aid to education, a national health program, and expansion of other welfare state programs. Kennedy never saw his education program or Medicare pass Congress, but he could take some credit for several less spectacular measures. Congress extended Social Security coverage to more American workers, covered more people by federal wage standards, raised the minimum wage to $1.25 an hour, appropriated nearly $5 billion for public housing, established the manpower training program, and passed an area redevelopment act for West Virginia and other impoverished areas in Appalachia. These were not radical innovations in social policy; rather they reflected JFK's preference for moderate, gradual reforms, and his political caution. Like his intellectual-in-residence, Arthur Schlesinger, Jr., John Kennedy remained committed to "the vital center."

In addition to updating the Fair Deal's social welfare programs, the Kennedy administration tried to refine the techniques of Truman's liberal economists. In his first state of the union address, JFK admitted that "the American economy was in trouble," and he promised both "a prompt recovery" and "long-range growth." Kennedy, of course, blamed the country's economic problems on the Eisenhower administration: the GNP had risen slowly during the late 1950s while the unemployment rate had climbed to around 6 percent. Although Kennedy shared with Eisenhower a limited background in economics—JFK had received a "C" in his introductory economics course at Harvard—he gathered a distinguished group of economic advisers, including John Kenneth Galbraith of Harvard and Walter Heller of the University of Minnesota. According to these advocates of the "new economics," the

119

national government could use its power over federal expenditures and its controls over monetary policy to "fine-tune" the economy.

The Kennedy administration adopted a number of strategies for stimulating production and creating new jobs. Increased government spending pumped vital funds into the economy and brightened the general economic picture. In 1962 the White House persuaded Congress to give businesses a 7 percent tax credit for investments in new machinery and plants. At the same time, the administration granted one of businessmen's top requests and readjusted depreciation schedules for corporate taxes. This action encouraged purchases of new equipment by allowing businesses to write off assets more quickly. Taken together, the investment tax credit and revised depreciation schedule reduced business taxes and theoretically increased corporate spending by about $2.5 billion; the total tax cut amounted to almost 12 percent.

Although the economy picked up considerably, many liberal economists called for further steps to boost production and employment. John Kenneth Galbraith, who had become ambassador to India, suggested massive government expenditures for social welfare programs. Kennedy rejected this as politically impossible but did consider further tax cuts. A cut in tax revenues would increase the federal deficit; it would also, however, expand purchasing power for both consumers and businesses. Walter Heller, chairman of the Council of Economic Advisers, and Paul Samuelson, an influential economist at MIT, were among those who urged an immediate tax reduction to ward off a possible recession. But advocates of a balanced federal budget, particularly Treasury Secretary C. Douglas Dillon and Federal Reserve Chairman William McChesney Martin, rejected this example of the new economics, and Kennedy finally shelved the proposal for 1962. The following year, however, the administration unveiled a comprehensive revenue bill which did include a $10 billion tax cut and tax reforms.

Kennedy's carefully calculated approach to social and economic problems reflected his basic assumptions about the new role of liberal government in America. The "old sweeping issues have largely disappeared," he told Yale's graduating class in 1962. Basic domestic problems were now "more subtle and less simple": how to manage a complex economy; how to ensure increasing productivity and rising prosperity for all citizens. The "sophisticated and technical questions involved in keeping a great economic machinery moving ahead" required "technical answers—not political answers. . . ." The keys to effective government were the rational bureaucrats, the cool technicians who could manage complex institutions. Although his tenure in office tempered some of his early optimism, John Kennedy died confident that his view of government remained correct and that the bright young men around him measured up to its demands.

Assassination

On November 22, 1963, the presidential motorcade was winding its way past unexpectedly friendly crowds in Dallas when a volley of shots—some claimed three, others four or five—raked Kennedy's open-topped limousine. Texas Governor John Connally was seriously wounded, and one shot ripped away the top of Kennedy's head. Within an hour, doctors at Parkland Hospital pronounced the president dead; the thousand days of Camelot were over. Aboard Air Force One, Vice-President Lyndon Baines Johnson took the oath of ofice.

News of the president's death stunned the nation. Most people dropped everything and dashed for the closest television set or radio; Walter Cronkite hurried on camera, covering the story in his shirt-sleeves. The wire services quickly sent out the stark, grim details. For two days the nation watched an elaborate memorial, and most people's respect for their fallen leader grew. Pictures of Kennedy's coffin, his rid-erless horse, and his grieving family clashed with scenes from Kennedy's past. Images of a vibrant JFK—sailing off Cape Cod, laughing with his children, or facing down the Russians in Cuba—made his death seem all the more tragic. The Kennedy mystique expanded.

The television spectacle also began to raise doubts about the cause of JFK's death. Within hours after the assassination, Dallas police officials announced capture of the killer—a young man named Lee Harvey Oswald. A former marine who had lived in the Soviet Union for a short time, Oswald refused to confess and steadfastly proclaimed his innocence. On Sunday, November 24, while Dallas police were transferring Oswald to a different jail, millions of television viewers witnessed the assassination of the alleged assassin. A local night club operator, Jack Ruby, fatally shot Oswald at close range, in the Dallas police station.

Oswald's bizarre death raised further doubts about his guilt. Was he part of a larger conspiracy? Was Kennedy's death somehow tied to pro- or anti-Castro forces? Was Ruby a hit man sent to silence Oswald? Were the Dallas police, or the CIA, or the FBI part of the "plot"? Wanting to squelch such rumors quickly, President Johnson persuaded Chief Justice Earl Warren to head an official inquiry. After a ten-month investigation, the Warren Commission named Oswald a lone assassin and reported no credible evidence of any broader plot. Conspiracy buffs, however, were already offering an amazing variety of scenarios, and the Warren Report merely gave them twenty-six volumes of evidence to piece through. More sober critics of the commission pointed out serious flaws in the hastily researched and sloppily documented report. (None of the government's marksmen could simulate Oswald's feat under more favorable conditions, and critics hotly contested the commission's theory that a single bullet struck both Kennedy and Connally.) Despite an intensive "sell" campaign through the mass media, many Americans refused to accept the Warren Commission's version of what had happened in Dallas. Still, more than ten years later, no one has yet framed a satisfactory alternative to the Oswald–lone assassin theory.

THE GREAT SOCIETY

LBJ

When Teddy Roosevelt succeeded another slain president, William McKinley, a conservative Republican expressed fears about "that damn cowboy"; sixty-two years later, many liberal Democrats felt much the same way about Lyndon Baines Johnson. Except for being a rich Democrat, LBJ had little in common with the cool, urbane Kennedy. Unlike JFK, Johnson loved the Senate, and during the 1950s he had dominated that body as its majority leader. John Kennedy always remembered how, as a senator, he had to beg Lyndon Johnson for favors. But despite years in Washington, Johnson never lost the earthy exuberance of "a good old boy from the ranch." (In his early White House days, Johnson showed a homemade film of deer mating and contributed his own coarse sound track.) In contrast to Kennedy, who had inherited his wealth, the self-made Johnson often was haunted by the hint of scandal. Critics snickered about "landslide Lyndon's" suspicious eighty-six-vote triumph in the 1948 senatorial primary, about his close association with convicted influence peddler Bobby Baker, and about his mysterious financial dealings throughout the Southwest. Lyndon Johnson came to Washington as an ambitious young politician attracted to Roosevelt's New Deal; he left as a former president and a multimillionaire. To some people LBJ looked too much like Jay Gould in a Stetson hat.

Johnson constantly worried about his public image. People would not give him "a fair shake as president," he often complained, "because I am a Southerner." But even Johnson realized that his problems lay deeper. "Why don't people like me?" he asked visitors to the White House. One elderly caller, who felt that his advanced years protected

Wide World Photos

LBJ, the tall Texan, 1964.

him, replied honestly: "Because, Mr. President, you are not a very lik-able man." Defensive about his provincial education in southwest Texas and his social awkwardness, Johnson seemed to require constant reassurance and unswerving loyalty from his subordinates. Around Johnson, no one wanted to be the bearer of bad news. He often flew into sudden rages, publicly berating staff members or arbitrarily summoning them at all hours of the night. He appeared to need the LBJ brand on everything. (His wife inherited the name Lady Bird, but LBJ christened his daughters Lynda Bird and Lucy Baines.) White House employees whom he suspected of antiwar sentiments dropped from favor, and only a few loyalists, such as Walt Rostow and Dean Rusk, stayed until the end. A critical reporter might receive the "Johnson treatment"—a private audience during which Johnson conducted a nonstop monolog on the glories of his presidency. A big man, the president liked to get close to his listeners, overwhelming them with his bulk.

Johnson smoothly handled the transition from the Kennedy administration and initially seemed a worthy successor to JFK. But after 1964 he watched his popularity steadily decline. Johnson often blamed the media for what became known as his "credibility gap." Overly optimistic predictions of an American victory in Vietnam and a few outright lies helped create popular mistrust of the government, but in some ways the president was correct. Stories about Johnson's pettiness, his vanity, and his duplicity entered the media and colored people's perception of the president. Most reporters had genuinely liked Kennedy and had sometimes pigeonholed unfavorable stories about his policies. Increasingly, though, newsmen became more sensitive to charges of government manipulations. Even before Kennedy's death, some journalists reexamined their role and argued that the press must abandon its deference to high political leaders. Johnson, like Richard Nixon after him, became the target of more vigorous investigative reporting, not just from I. F. Stone but from large segments of the Washington press corps. In addition, the media compared Johnson with the still untarnished image of JFK as well as with the vigorous reality of the Kennedy family. John Kennedy's youngest brother, Edward, represented Massachusetts in the Senate, and in 1964 Robert Kennedy overcame charges of being a carpet-bagger, winning election to the Senate from New York. The Kennedys only thinly veiled their distaste for Johnson, and many reporters expressed more sympathy for "Camelot-in-exile"—the intellectuals and politicians who swarmed around Bobby's home at Hickory Hill or the family compound on Cape Cod—than for Lyndon Johnson's entourage.

Toward the end of his presidency, as controversy over Vietnam obsessed both the president and the press, too many people forgot Lyndon Johnson's accomplishments and admirable qualities. He could take much credit for the Great Society legislation passed between 1964 and 1968, and even most critics conceded his sincere commitment to social reform, racial justice, and economic progress. For all his faults, Johnson was an intelligent, complex, sensitive man. The American people, particularly the opinion-making elites, probably misunderstood Lyndon Johnson as much as he misunderstood them. Eric Goldman, an Ivy League historian and LBJ's onetime intellectual-in-residence, believed that Lyndon Johnson was a tragic figure; he was "the wrong man, from the wrong place, at the wrong time."

The Johnson Program

Lyndon Johnson moved to fulfill the Democratic promise of economic expansion. Aided by a reduction in taxes (the Tax Act of 1964, of course, was originally a Kennedy proposal) and by increased federal spending (particularly for the expanding war in Southeast Asia), the economy built upon gains begun under Kennedy. Between 1960 and 1964 the Gross National Product increased by 24 percent while corporate profits went up by 57 percent; during the next year, the GNP climbed by almost 7 percent and corporate profits by 20 percent; and by 1965 the nation achieved what most economists considered "full" employment, an unemployment rate less than 4 percent. The boom lasted throughout Johnson's second term: unemployment never exceeded 4 percent, and the GNP expanded at a rate of almost 5 percent a year.

Not everyone was impressed by the Kennedy-Johnson boom. Some economists correctly warned that the expansion was too rapid and that the Johnson administration was ignoring the threat of inflation. Others argued that LBJ's economic wizardry was largely a fraud. Liberal economist Leon Keyserling contended that the Tax Act of 1964, which came out of Congress without most of its original reforms, primarily assisted the wealthy. According to Keyserling's calculations, the average taxpayer in the $10,000 income bracket received only a 3.5 percent increase in disposable income; in contrast, the $100,000 taxpayer enjoyed a boost of 16.5 percent, while the very wealthy, those in the $200,000 category, got a 31.1 percent windfall. Keyserling charged that the nation's basic economic problem remained an inequitable distribution of income; radical economists such as Marxist Paul Sweezy concurred. They complained that the pace of economic growth was too slow, unemployment too high, and the gap between rich and poor too wide. Citing the tremendous rise in corporate profits during the Kennedy-Johnson years, many radicals argued that large corporations were the main beneficiaries of the high-growth policies of the "new economics."

Lyndon Johnson, the man who sincerely wanted to be "president of all the people," saw the situation differently. Of course, large businesses would benefit from economic expansion, but so would

125

middle-income workers and small businessmen. And galloping prosperity enabled the country to go beyond the limited goals of Truman and Kennedy and extend greater assistance to the very poor in the best LBJ style—with great breast-beating and with promises of much government money. Buoyed by his early successes and the economic boom, he claimed that there was a consensus—what he later called "a broad, deep, and genuine consensus among most groups within our diverse society"—on behalf of social reform. If only everyone would "sit down and reason together," Americans could realize the Great Society. Speaking in the spring of 1964 before an outdoor crowd of almost 100,000 people, LBJ heralded the coming of America's golden age, a society "where the meaning of our lives matches the marvelous products of our labor . . . a place where men are more concerned with the quality of their goals than the quantity of their goods." Even John Kennedy might have blushed at this rhetoric, but then, JFK never approached the impressive string of legislative measures which LBJ watched roll through Congress in 1964 and 1965.

In the wake of Kennedy's death and his own landslide triumph over Republican Barry Goldwater in 1964, Johnson broke what he called "the legislative log jam," the do-nothing congressional stalemate. Never in recent memory had Congress done so much so quickly. When Johnson left Washington in 1969, his cabinet gave him a plaque commemorating the more than two hundred "landmark laws" passed during his administration. In the first full year alone, Congress approved the Tax Act of 1964, a new Civil Rights Act, federally sponsored recreation programs, funds for urban mass transit, and the Economic Opportunity Act (the measure which signaled the beginning of Johnson's "war on poverty"). And this was merely the prelude to the Great Society, a program which Johnson took to the nation in the 1964 presidential race.

The Johnson Landslide

The Republicans graciously handed Johnson the election. Militant conservatives, most of whom lived in the "rim states" from Southern California to Florida or in isolated enclaves in the Middle West, temporarily gained control of the GOP. Bragging that they would offer the nation "a choice, not an echo," they successfully nominated Senator Barry Goldwater of Arizona. The last major party candidate without a college degree, Goldwater had already gained a reputation as an injudicious right-wing extremist. During a series of bitter primary campaigns, his right-wing supporters reinforced this image by vehemently attacking more liberal Republicans, particularly New York's Nelson

Rockefeller. When Rockefeller rose to address the GOP convention, Goldwaterites in the galleries shouted him down. For several minutes Rocky baited the crowd; they yelled back, and he taunted them some more. The conservative faithful loved it, but millions of television viewers saw the Goldwaterites' performance as fanaticism from "the radical right." (Goldwater's official delegates were actually quite restrained, and the candidate's staff consisted of highly-disciplined professionals who borrowed many sophisticated campaign techniques from the Kennedy organization.) Goldwater's acceptance speech increased the apprehension of many moderates. Extremism in the defense of liberty, he challenged his Republican critics, "is no vice. . . . Moderation in the pursuit of justice is no virtue."

Goldwater ran squarely against Johnson's brand of liberalism. Ever since the New Deal, Republican candidates had campaigned against the central government in Washington, but Goldwater really seemed to mean it. His strategists hoped that a militantly conservative effort would bring millions of alienated people to the polls and attract a backlash vote from whites who were frightened by the civil rights movement. A Goldwater administration, he appeared to say, would sweep away all the baneful welfare programs established since the New Deal: agricultural subsidies, pro–labor union legislation, civil rights laws, and all the other "socialistic" laws. "I will give you back your freedom," he promised his followers. On several occasions he even suggested making Social Security voluntary, a position which Democrats falsely translated into the charge that Goldwater planned abolition of the entire system. Along with some missile-rattling statements about the need for a quick victory in Vietnam, his domestic program enabled Democrats to paint Goldwater as a trigger-happy Neanderthal.

With the moderate center of the American electorate deserting the Republican party, Johnson and his running mate, Minnesota Senator Hubert Humphrey, recorded a landslide victory. The Democratic presidential ticket gathered 61.3 percent of the popular ballots and the electoral votes of all but six states. At the same time, Democrats sent thirty-nine additional congressmen to the House of Representatives and gained more than 500 new seats in state legislatures across the country. Johnson celebrated his "politics of consensus," and some nervous Republicans wondered if the "Goldwater caper" would destroy the GOP.

The Great Society

After his smashing victory, LBJ watched more Great Society measures pass through the new eighty-ninth Congress. Medicare and Medicaid programs fulfilled Harry Truman's goal of some government-sponsored health care for people over sixty-five and for the very poor. Two other long-delayed measures, the Elementary and Secondary Education Act and the Higher Education Act, extended federal funds to schools at all levels of the educational hierarchy. The Civil Rights Act of 1965 eliminated barriers against black voters in the South: it suspended literacy tests and authorized use of federal inspectors in areas where the attorney general suspected chicanery. To deal with the problems of urban decay, Congress passed the Housing Act of 1965, which created the new Department of Housing and Urban Development (HUD), and the Demonstration Cities and Metropolitan Development Act of 1966, which provided federal money for local "model cities" projects. Prodded by advocates of automobile safety—many of whom had read Ralph Nader's indictment of Chevrolet's Corvair, *Unsafe at Any Speed*—congressmen passed several bills dealing with highway and traffic safety. One measure, the Motor Vehicle Safety Act (1966), inaugurated federal safety standards for the auto industry and established a uniform grading system for tire manufacturers. As in the case of urban problems, Congress also created a new cabinet post—the secretary of transportation—and gave it the tasks of coordination and enforcement. Finally, Congress passed a number of "minor" pieces of legislation such as a new Immigration Act, which admitted newcomers primarily on the basis of their economic skills rather than their national origins, and a Truth in Packaging Act, which provided some protection against deceptive advertising practices.

Most Americans readily accepted these programs, measures once considered "socialistic," as integral parts of the American welfare state. Controversies still erupted over details—how much should Medicare patients pay from their own pockets or how quickly should auto makers comply with safety standards—but few people suggested repeal of these Great Society laws. The loudest complaints came from social critics who charged that the programs required only minimal sacrifices from special-interest groups and provided too little assistance for citizens. Consumer advocate Ralph Nader, for example, claimed that auto manufacturers blocked truly effective laws while they used the cost of minimal improvements as an excuse to raise their prices. And despite all Lyndon Johnson's promises, basic needs such as better mass transportation systems and effective urban housing programs remained only dreams.

The War on Poverty

In addition to completing the Fair Deal, Johnson launched a crusade of his own—elimination and prevention of poverty in America. Because of their material abundance, middle-class Americans had largely forgotten that one-fourth to one-fifth of the population, mostly white people, still lived in substandard housing and subsisted on inadequate diets. Michael Harrington's *The Other America* helped spark concern for the poor, and Johnson declared his war on poverty. At first glance, the array of programs seemed impressive: federal funds to finance public works projects, particularly new highways in Appalachia; a Job Corps to train young people who lacked marketable skills; a Work-Study program to supplement the incomes of college students; Volunteers in Service to America (VISTA) to send young volunteers into impoverished areas; and the Headstart program to provide compensatory education for preschoolers from "disadvantaged" families. Although these measures went beyond any previous national efforts, even the program's supporters conceded their traditional approach to social problems. In providing federal money and another federal agency (the Office of Economic Opportunity or OEO), the Great Society borrowed the techniques of the New and Fair Deals.

One part of the war on poverty, the Community Action Program (CAP), did represent a significant change in federal policy. Under Title II of the Economic Opportunity Act, Congress authorized funds for local groups—either private nonprofit or public organizations—which developed innovative programs to cure the symptoms of poverty. Sounding a theme that Richard Nixon would later adopt, President Johnson argued that CAP rested upon "the fact that local citizens best understand their own problems and know best how to deal with these problems." At first, many people praised CAP as an attempt to check the extension of federal power into local affairs. Many poor people looked forward to being able to plan their improvements.

Like the conflict in Vietnam, the war on poverty brought Lyndon Johnson few historic victories. Many Republicans and blue-collar Democrats denounced the poverty program for giving money to people allegedly too lazy to help themselves. ("Yeah, I helped the war on poverty," went one sick joke of the mid-1960s. "I threw a hand-grenade at a bum.") Actually much of the available money went to middle-class bureaucrats or into expensive equipment. After their stints in public service, some antipoverty workers established consulting agencies which received government contracts for "expert" advice on the problems of poverty. Early in the fight, some social critics declared that the "poverty-industrial" complex was a far bigger winner than the poor. And congressmen, who were being asked to vote more money for Vietnam, balked at the cost of antipoverty projects. Whether or not Johnson liked it, the nation simply could not afford both guns and butter; it could not wage two "wars" at once. Only a few of the problems, such as Work-Study for students, received generous funding.

The attempt to decentralize reform through the CAP quickly

floundered as established welfare agencies and local political leaders opposed grants of funds to new community groups. Since some of the CAP organizations espoused militant demands such as income redistribution, OEO's bureaucrats often sided with the vested interests and against poor people themselves. Even radicals, after all, could hardly expect the "establishment" to finance its own overthrow. In time, OEO placed more emphasis on "prepackaged programs" from Washington, such as Headstart, community beautification projects, and legal-aid, and employed local CAP groups as administrators rather than innovators.

The fate of CAP perhaps illustrates the basic flaw in the war on poverty; reformers singled out poor people as special targets for uplift by a compassionate bureaucracy. Architects of the program assumed that, with a helping hand from the national government, most poor people could work themselves out of poverty. They gave primary attention, therefore, to people who could be employed—young people and male heads of poor families. The war on poverty offered little, for example, to poor mothers or to old people. They were left to limp along on existing programs such as Aid for Dependent Children or Social Security. Bureaucratic programs, VISTA volunteers, and education could, of course, help the poor, but as sociologist Lewis Coser bluntly concluded, what poor people needed most was money. Despite rhetoric about curing poverty, liberals opposed any serious talk of income redistribution. As a result, figures from the Census Bureau revealed that the gap between rich and poor narrowed very little during the 1960s. Nothing could more coldly illustrate the ultimate failure of the war on poverty.

Had the poverty program been fully funded and carried out, it undoubtedly would have relieved much suffering and improved many people's lives. Johnson, however, promised more than most Americans were prepared to deliver—especially while they fought a costly foreign war. Obviously, poor people derived some benefits. But Johnson's program neither ended poverty nor altered the basic socioeconomic structure of American society. In large part, it merely raised expectations among the poor, created resentment within the middle class, and expanded the central bureaucracy in Washington.

The Warren Court and Liberal Reform

The Supreme Court, too, discovered the difficulties of reform from above. Chief Justice Earl Warren, appointed by Dwight Eisenhower in 1953, and his activist majority believed that they could forecast the path

130

of social progress and could hasten the coming of justice and equality. The result was a flood of landmark decisions during the years of the Warren Court.

Even before Lyndon Johnson became president, controversy surrounded the Supreme Court and Chief Justice Warren. The famous desegregation decision, *Brown* v. *Board of Education* (1954), in which all nine justices held that racially segregated schools were "inherently unequal," angered segregationists throughout the country. In a series of decisions handed down in 1956–57, a divided court also affirmed the rights of alleged communists, and anticommunist crusaders denounced the court. The ultrareactionary John Birch Society erected billboards which demanded "IMPEACH EARL WARREN." And when the court appeared to reverse itself on the communist issue in the late 1950s, civil libertarians criticized the justices, particularly Felix Frankfurter, for caving in to popular pressures. Because it was almost equally divided, the Warren Court established no clear pattern during the Chief Justice's first years on the bench.

During the 1960s, however, the liberal "activists" gained ascendancy. They believed that the court could play an important role in protecting individual liberties and advancing social and racial justice. Led by Chief Justice Warren and two veteran justices, William O. Douglas and Hugo Black, the court began to require state and local governments to conform to the specific guarantees of the Bill of Rights. The activists recognized that effective legal protection remained largely a matter of one's income and social standing. Rich people could afford good lawyers and thereby gain valuable legal protection. Poor people rarely employed attorneys, and they faced powerful government institutions with inadequate knowledge of their rights. In *Gideon* v. *Wainwright* (1963) the court held that states must furnish indigents with lawyers in felony cases. Such decisions expressed the activists' commitment to a single standard of due process and to the principle of equality before the law.

In addition, the Warren Court attempted to invigorate the democratic process. Beginning with *Baker* v. *Carr* (1962), a majority of justices held that malapportioned electoral districts deprived some voters of equal protection. *Baker* v. *Carr*'s "one man, one vote" rule aimed at correcting situations in which rural districts with comparatively few people had the same legislative representation as populous urban districts. Hoping to encourage more vigorous scrutiny of public officials, the court made it more difficult for politicians to sue their critics for libel (*New York Times* v. *Sullivan*, 1964). In a series of highly controversial decisions, the majority declared that Bible reading and prayer in public schools violated the First Amendment's prohibition against establishment of religion. Earl Warren was declaring God himself unconstitutional, grumbled conservatives. Their mood remained sour when the same court struck down laws against pornography. Despite all the criticism, however, the court seemed to have consolidated its new position by the mid-1960s. The Kennedy-Johnson appointees—particularly Arthur Goldberg, Abe Fortas, and the court's first black justice, Thurgood Marshall—offset the increasing conservatism of Justice Black and appeared to ensure an activist majority for years to come.

Then, after 1966, the liberal majority collapsed. One of the court's decisions did much of the damage. In *Miranda* v. *Arizona* the court held that once a police investigation focused upon a particular suspect, the authorities had to inform the defendant that he could remain silent, have a lawyer present during questioning, and request a free attorney provided by the state. More than any other decision, *Miranda* angered the court's critics and united them around one emotional issue. The decision coincided with rising fear of "crime in the streets," and advocates of law and order blamed the Warren Court for handcuffing the police. Although criminologists easily demonstrated that such charges were without foundation, popular criticism and pressure from within the legal establishment increased. Congress considered legislation to overturn the Miranda decision, and politicians such as George Wallace and Richard Nixon promised to appoint new justices who would "interpret the Constitution strictly." (This meant, of course, that they wanted *less* strict protection for individual liberties.)

Amid all this controversy, the Chief Justice announced his impending retirement. President Johnson wanted to replace Warren with his old friend Fortas and then to appoint another crony, Homer Thornberry, to the court. Anticipating a Nixon victory in the 1968 election, Republicans and many conservative Southern Democrats tried to block Johnson's reshuffling. Their job became easy when *Life* magazine uncovered what appeared to be evidence of official misconduct by Justice Fortas. Johnson had to withdraw his nomination, and Fortas eventually resigned in disgrace. Newly elected President Nixon thus gained two vacancies on the court—the Chief Justice's post and Fortas's old seat.

Even before the demise of the activist majority, however, legal scholars were beginning to question the impact of the Warren Court's decisions. Obviously they had eliminated some gross inequities in the American legal system and had established high standards for law enforcement officials. But the court lacked the means—as it always had and always will—to enforce its rulings to the letter. Police departments could effectively evade the *Miranda* decision; publicly-appointed lawyers often acted more as agents of the prosecutor's office than as representatives of their clients; and local pressures made restrictions against formal pornography laws superfluous. In an even more fundamental sense, decisions from five well-meaning activists were not always effective tools for social engineering. Broad interpretations of the law of libel, for example, could not make every journalist into a vigorous crusader for the public interest. Reapportionment of state legislatures did not necessarily produce effective legislative bodies. On the most explosive public issue of the late 1960s, the court took no position at all; it avoided ruling directly on cases which challenged the legality of the undeclared war in Vietnam. And though the Warren Court played a vital role in the early movement for legal and political equality for black people, the justices had no power to effect the sweeping social and economic changes which black militants came to demand. When the black revolution turned away from legal issues in the late 1960s, the judiciary could play only a limited role.

CIVIL RIGHTS TO BLACK POWER

Civil Rights During the Eisenhower Years

In 1954 almost every area of Southern society had segregated facilities for blacks and whites. "Jim Crow" extended to public transportation, restrooms, drinking fountains, even parking lots and cemetaries. Often required by law and always demanded by custom, these separate, but rarely equal, facilities reminded black people of the inferior status assigned them by white society. The National Association for the Advancement of Colored People (NAACP) financed a series of legal challenges; their success in *Brown* v. *Board of Education* (1954) marked an important victory. All nine justices agreed that legally sanctioned segregation of public schools violated the equal protection clause of the Fourteenth Amendment. In a simple, straightforward opinion, Chief Justice Earl Warren argued that separate schools were "inherently unequal" and deprived black children of equal educational opportunities. But one court decision, by itself, could not produce a revolution in race relations. Bowing to political pressures and recognizing the practical problems of education, the Supreme Court later ruled that school integration need not be immediate; it should proceed "with all deliberate speed." Ten years after the *Brown* decision only about 1 percent of black children in the South attended desegregated schools.

Resistance to desegregation hardened after the *Brown* case. Most white Southerners protested this "invasion of states' rights"; some denounced the ruling as part of a communist plot to destroy "the white race"; many pledged massive resistance to school integration. The Ku Klux Klan revived, and a new organization, the White Citizens Council, became a powerful force in many areas of the deep South. Not all members of the KKK and Citizens Council endorsed violent resistance, but some did use force against blacks who "didn't know their place." In 1954 a crowd of whites lynched a young black man, Emmet Till, for allegedly whistling at a white woman.

Southerners also used legal and political stratagems to delay integration. In 1957, 101 congressmen and senators signed the "Southern Manifesto," a protest against "federal usurpation" of states' rights, and Southern senators employed the filibuster to block civil rights legislation. A segregationist image was essential to political survival in many Southern states; after a moderate young lawyer, George C. Wallace, lost badly to a segregationist, he announced that he would never be "outnigraed again." The most spectacular example of official resistance came in 1957 when Arkansas Governor Orval Faubus defied a federal court order to desegregate Little Rock High School and used helmeted national guardsmen to keep black children out of the building. With national authority openly challenged, the Eisenhower administration could not avoid the issue. Although never a supporter of integration, Eisenhower placed the Arkansas national guard under federal control, augmented it with regular army troops, and enforced the court order. The following year, Arkansas officials tried to block desegregation through the courts. Meeting in emergency session, the Supreme Court rejected Arkansas's claim that the state need not obey national court orders and buried once again the states' rights argument. After the Little Rock incident, the Supreme Court declared unconstitutional evasive tactics of closing down public schools and of gerrymandering school districts, and pressed for realistic desegregation plans.

Desegregation of public facilities in the South gained the support of influential people. Fighting a war against Nazi racism and crusading against "atheistic communism" had made American liberals more sensitive to injustices at home. The success of American institutions, they argued, required a greater commitment to racial justice. Foreign policymakers, competing with the Soviets for the goodwill of the so-called third world nations, found it difficult to explain away discrimination against nonwhites in the United States. When diplomats from the new African states experienced segregation firsthand, the whole system of Jim Crow became highly embarrassing to influential whites. Many religious leaders and scientists also lent their prestige to the civil rights cause. Most biologists, for example, rejected old theories about black inferiority, making segregation appear to rest on the superstitions of ig-

134

norant "red-necks" or the subjective research of racist professors. Finally, white leaders found it impossible to ignore black demands, for within the black community new leaders and new organizations were taking the lead in the fight for equality.

New Organizations and New Tactics

A young Alabama minister, Dr. Martin Luther King, Jr., eventually gained recognition as the most influential black leader. Certainly not a radical, King nevertheless went beyond the courtroom tactics of the NAACP and the calm lobbying of the Urban League. While still in his twenties, he led a successful boycott against segregated public transportation facilities in Montgomery, Alabama. For several months in 1955–56, blacks refused to use municipal buses, rode to work in their own car pools, and refused to obey local laws against the boycott. Eventually litigation ended the long impasse—the Supreme Court struck down statutes which required blacks to sit at the back of the bus—but King's tactics of nonviolent civil disobedience and economic pressure became the civil rights movement's newest weapons. Citing the success of Mahatma Gandhi's passive resistance in India, King preached the importance of laying one's body on the line and of loving one's enemy. "If we are arrested every day . . . if we are trampled over every day, don't ever let anyone pull you so low as to hate them. We must use the weapon of love." In 1957 King and other black ministers formed the Southern Christian Leadership Conference (SCLC), which quickly became the most active civil rights organization in the South.

King and the SCLC worked primarily through churches and drew their heaviest support from middle-class black people. The son of a prominent Atlanta minister, King had enjoyed a sheltered childhood and a good education at Morehouse College before going north to get a doctorate at Boston College. He spoke in the measured cadence of the black preacher, the man who traditionally led the black community, but he also had the oratorical power to move white audiences and touch their consciences with his message of Christian love. Whether he sought the role or not, King became the spokesman for the nation's entire black population. Such a position gained him the enmity of angry whites and of more militant black spokesmen.

Several other groups tried to work with the SCLC in the early 1960s. The Congress of Racial Equality (CORE) had employed nonviolent civil disobedience during the 1940s; led by James Farmer and later by Floyd McKissick, it became more active during the early 1960s. Another group, the Student Nonviolent Coordinating Committee

(SNCC), evolved from demonstrations in North Carolina during the winter of 1960. Black college students, polite and neatly dressed, unsuccessfully tried to eat at a dimestore lunch counter. Braving hostile whites—who tossed lighted cigarettes, dumped ketchup, and threw punches—the young blacks remained seated, patiently waiting for service. The sit-in movement quickly spread to other kinds of public facilities, as thousands of young activists, both white and black, joined the protests. In April 1960 a group of these students formed SNCC and accepted King's approach—nonviolent protest. Some of the early "freedom songs" expressed their optimism:

Freedom's Comin' and It Won't Be Long

We took a trip on a Greyhound bus,
Freedom's comin' and it won't be long
To fight segregation, this we must
Freedom's comin' and it won't be long.

Violence in 'bama didn't stop our cause
Freedom's comin' and it won't be long
Federal marshals come enforce the laws
Freedom's comin' and it won't be long.

On to Mississippi with speed we go
Freedom's comin' and it won't be long
Blue-shirted policemen meet us at the door
Freedom's comin' and it won't be long.

Judge say local custom shall prevail
Freedom's comin' and it won't be long
We say 'no' and we land in jail
Freedom's comin' and it won't be long.

Civil Rights: The Kennedy Years

The election of John Kennedy in 1960 seemed to offer hope of greater support from Washington. During his campaign, JFK criticized the Eisenhower administration's reluctant support of integration and promised a new frontier for blacks. Once in office, he appointed a number of prominent black people to federal positions, filed more desegregation suits than his predecessor, and supported a new civil rights act. (The previous civil rights laws of 1957 and 1960 had dealt primarily with voting rights; Kennedy supported a measure which would ban discrimination in public accommodations and give the attorney general authority to file desegregation suits.)

136

Kennedy's political caution, however, tempered his campaign rhetoric. During the campaign he had denounced Eisenhower's refusal to issue an executive order ending discrimination in housing—Ike could do it with "a stroke of the pen," claimed Kennedy—but delayed his own order for two years. Desiring good relations with Southern congressmen, Kennedy often deferred to them on patronage questions, appointing several outright racists to the federal bench. (One Mississippi judge referred to black civil rights workers as "monkeys" and consistently demeaned black defendants.) Kennedy also refused to cross J. Edgar Hoover, permitting the FBI leader to set his own rules in civil rights cases. In effect, this meant that Hoover, no friend of civil rights groups, would do as little as possible to help blacks and to jeopardize his close relationship with law officers in the South. Without thorough background investigations by the FBI, the Justice Department oftentimes lacked evidence to prosecute cases of alleged discrimination.

But a series of dramatic events in the deep South took the initiative away from the Kennedy administration; civil rights activists, not the government in Washington, began to determine the pace of change. In 1961 young activists from CORE and SNCC defied Jim Crow laws on interstate buses and in Southern terminals. Angered by these "freedom riders," segregationists used iron bars, clubs, and finally explosives against the nonviolent invaders. Increasing violence finally forced the government to respond: Attorney General Robert Kennedy dispatched a team of Justice Department troubleshooters and a corps of federal marshals to protect the demonstrators. He also asked the Interstate Commerce Commission to issue an order banning segregation in interstate facilities, a request which the ICC honored in the fall of 1961. The use of federal personnel to protect the freedom riders established a pattern, and the following year President Kennedy reinforced the marshals with United States army troops to quell violence which followed enrollment of one black student, James Meredith, at the University of Mississippi. Kennedy's actions probably prevented bloodshed on other campuses—two people died during disorders at "ole Miss"—and a confrontation at the University of Alabama in 1963 ended differently. After symbolically "standing in the schoolhouse door," George Wallace—the man who had once proclaimed "segregation now and forever"—stepped aside and watched Justice Department officials integrate the university without serious incident.

In the spring of 1963 the focus of integration struggles shifted from Southern campuses to the streets of Birmingham, Alabama. The drive to desegregate public facilities in this Alabama industrial center marked an important turning point in the struggle for racial equality. Police violence escalated into savagery, and people expressed outrage at the tac-

Charles Moore for Black Star

In April 1963 Eugene Theophilus Connor, Birmingham's commissioner of public safety, shocked the world by using police dogs against black demonstrators.

tics of Birmingham authorities. Police Commissioner Eugene "Bull" Connor turned fire hoses and dogs upon black demonstrators, including small children. Club-swinging policemen rounded up thousands of protesters and threw them into makeshift lockups. White vigilantes unleashed a terror campaign which culminated in the bombing of a black church; four Sunday school children died in the blast. "Bull" Connor fit the stereotype of the bigoted Southern sheriff; his exuberant use of force redounded to the benefit of the civil rights movement. Events in Birmingham probably turned the tide of Northern opinion in favor of civil rights legislation and integration of Southern schools.

On the other hand, Birmingham provoked a new militancy within the black community. People who lived in crowded urban slums had never really accepted nonviolence, and many young blacks began to express disillusionment with Dr. King's philosophy. In retrospect, Birmingham began the long years of urban violence which helped change both the black movement and the white response. When blacks began to march in the streets of Chicago, supporters of civil rights were reminded that racial prejudice was a national rather than a regional phenomenon. After facing hostile crowds in Chicago, Dr. King concluded that racism seemed more violent there than in the South.

But in 1963, much of this remained hidden in a glow of optimism and a temporary spirit of cooperation which climaxed in the August March on Washington. Following closely after the disorders in Birmingham, the March produced much favorable publicity for the civil rights movement. Most Northern newspapers and magazines praised the neat appearance, politeness, and commitment of the estimated 200,000 marchers. The unity within the movement also seemed exemplary as young activists from SNCC shared the platform with the NAACP and the Urban League as well as with white church and labor leaders. The speakers effectively captured the attention of participants and television viewers. Just when the August sun threatened to wilt the marchers, Martin Luther King revived their spirits with his "I Have a Dream" speech. A carefully structured series of images, but devoid of any substantive proposals for change, the address confirmed King's reputation

United Press International

The apogee of the civil rights movement: the 1963 March on Washington.

as the movement's greatest spellbinder. With the formalities completed, civil rights leaders adjourned to the White House for a coffee hour with the Kennedys.

The Civil Rights Act of 1964: End of an Era

Even though black leaders recognized JFK's limitations, his death seemed a great blow to their movement; it brought a Southerner with an even more ambivalent record into the White House. But Lyndon Johnson quickly dispelled many doubts about his commitment to civil rights when he helped push a stronger version of Kennedy's bill through Congress in 1964. The new president cultivated the support of Everett Dirkson, Republican minority leader in the Senate, and deputized Hubert Humphrey to pressure wavering Democrats. With this help from the White House, the bill's sponsors gained enough votes to break a seventy-five-day filibuster against the measure.

The Civil Rights Act of 1964 outlawed racial, religious, and sexual discrimination in private businesses which served the general public—such as restaurants and filling stations—and in public facilities such as swimming pools. It also authorized the executive branch to withhold federal grants or contracts from institutions which discriminated against nonwhites, and empowered the attorney general to file school desegregation suits at his initiative. To safeguard voting rights, the law contained a section which established a sixth-grade education as the basic requirement for literacy. This provision, it was hoped, would prevent the use of unfair "literacy" tests against black people seeking to register. (A white voting inspector in Alabama once flunked a black applicant because his test contained "an error in spilling.") When properly enforced, the Civil Rights Act of 1964 produced sweeping changes in the pattern of race relations. The law demanded no less than destruction of a settled way of life, a system of racial discrimination which had evolved since the formal end of slavery. According to the act, blacks could now sleep in any motel, eat in any restaurant, or sit anywhere on any bus.

Although it applied to the entire nation, the law cost many whites very little. Lower- and lower-middle-class whites, particularly in the South and in large Northern cities, had to make most of the adjustments on behalf of the larger white society. Racists would lose the psychological security blanket of Jim Crows, and might have to sit by, eat near, or work with a black person. But such things, important as they seemed, required no basic alteration in America's socioeconomic structure or in the distribution of political power.

By 1964, however, many black people were demanding more than equal access to public accommodations and government facilities; the victories of the early 1960s had raised the stakes. Black militants complained that the government allowed no compensation for the years of discrimination, provided little immediate economic assistance, and gave no significant political power to black people. Such things, white politicians argued, were clearly impossible; it had taken much bloodshed and a great deal of political skill even to obtain the act of 1964. But young black radicals rejected arguments based upon what older black spokesmen and white politicians considered possible. Some blacks charged that their own leaders were selling out to the "white power structure." After the troubles in Birmingham, white philanthropists, perhaps frightened by the spectre of violence moving northward or perhaps sincerely moved by the rightness of the cause, pledged almost a million dollars to the leading civil rights organizations. Militants viewed this as a payoff, denouncing Kennedy's civil rights program as a sellout of the movement. During the march on Washington, leaders had forced John Lewis, the youthful head of SNCC, to rewrite his fiery address. Lewis intended to criticize the Kennedy civil rights bill—"What is there in this bill to ensure the equality of a maid who earns $5 a week in the home of a family whose income is $100,000 a year?"—and to condemn "the cheap political leaders who build their careers on immoral compromises and ally themselves with open forms of political, economic, and social exploitation. . . ." To preserve the harmony of the day, Lewis softened his speech, but other blacks did not attend the march or temper their words. One man who had not been invited asked, "Who ever heard of angry revolutionists all harmonizing 'We Shall Overcome Some Day' while tripping and swaying along arm-in-arm with the very people they were supposed to be revolting against?" The angry young man was Malcom X, an eloquent spokesman for militancy and black pride.

A series of disturbing events in 1964 made nonviolence and peaceful political appeals less attractive to some blacks. In Mississippi three civil rights workers—Andrew Goodman, James Cheney, and Michael Schwerner—were brutally murdered; the only black among the three, Cheney was apparently beaten to death with chains. That same year a group of activists risked their lives to organize the Mississippi Freedom Democratic Party (FDP), only to watch white liberals join with Southern leaders to deny the FDP formal recognition at the Democratic National Convention. And during the "Freedom Summer" of 1964—a SNCC-sponsored campaign to register voters and establish "freedom schools"—racial tensions within the movement itself increased. Blacks frequently expressed their resentment of "paternalistic" whites, "fly-by-night freedom fighters who were bossing everybody around." As SNCC tried to limp along and to test the viability of nonviolence in the South, some Northern blacks expressed their grievances in a very different way.

The Ghettos Explode

In August 1965 a clash between a white highway patrolman and a black motorist touched off four days of rioting, burning, and looting in the Los Angeles ghetto of Watts. Before the disorders ended, authorities had sent in the national guard, thirty-four people had been killed, and property damage totaled more than $20 million. The trouble in Watts inaugurated several years of mass urban violence. The year 1967 was the worst, with disorders in 128 cities and major clashes in Newark, New Jersey, and Detroit. The Detroit "riots," during which regular army units were called to assist police and national guardsmen, caused at least forty-three deaths and produced widespread destruction in the black ghetto. In all the confrontations, blacks emerged the major losers: most of the people killed were black, and property damage generally remained confined to ghetto areas. Investigations later revealed indiscriminate shooting by the authorities and several incidents of outright murder by white policemen. These disorders left behind burned-out buildings, racial hatred, and feelings of uneasiness among most white integrationists. The violence, after all, came during a time of undeniable progress in race relations. What could explain such destruction?

"Official" explanations tried to steer between theories of a grand communist conspiracy and black claims of incipient revolution against capitalist exploitation. Investigating the Watts disorder, the McCone Commission (headed by former CIA director John McCone) propounded what became the common view: the "rotten apple" or "riff-raff" interpretation. A small group of troublemakers, the McCone Report concluded, had precipitated the trouble and fueled the violence. The "riots" were not legitimate protests against substantive grievances but "formless, quite senseless, all but hopeless" outbursts of looting and burning—"engaged in by a few but bringing great distress to all." The commission theorized that most of these "rotten apples" had recently migrated from the rural South and had not yet adjusted to the pressures and demands of urban life. Though it refused to call Watts a ghetto (because it contained mostly single-family dwellings and fairly wide streets) or to concede a serious problem of police brutality, the commission did see some problems in Watts. The black area had inadequate mass transit to jobs, poor educational facilities, and a small number of poorly trained policemen. Suggesting that the situation required no fundamental social or economic changes, the report called for greater job opportunities near Watts, more money for education, and "better understanding" between police and citizens. Throughout the report, McCone and the other commissioners viewed the need to maintain respect for the law enforcement system as the major issue at stake.

Other investigators quickly challenged the basic assumptions and conclusions of the McCone Commission. These observers sympathized with the people of Watts and considered the disorders to be political protests rather than formless riots. The violence in Watts, they claimed, involved a sizable portion of the black community, not a few misfits. The protesters, in fact, represented a cross section of the community: they had lived in Watts for some time, usually held low-paying jobs, and possessed the best education the ghetto could provide. Disputing the idea that the violence had been senseless, some researchers argued that protesters had tried to avoid black-owned businesses and had concentrated upon white firms which were considered dishonest. Critics of the McCone Commission also challenged the idea that Watts was not a ghetto: much of the housing was dilapidated, many businesses exploited black customers and employees, and police brutality was an everyday occurrence. Many of these writers concluded that the violence stemmed from a rational grasp of deep-seated, legitimate grievances.

Thus, the dispute between "riot" and "protest" involved more than a semantical difference. The former view upheld the quick suppression of such disorders and pointed to the need for changes within the existing system; the latter position at least implied the legitimacy of the protest and supported the need for more sweeping changes in American society. Equally as important, the riot view tended to see the problem as one between "good" people and "bad" people, between "haves" and "have-lesses." The protest theory pointed to a deep-seated racial crisis, a conflict which could not be solved through more government-controlled "wars on poverty."

As disorders continued, the official explanation changed very little. The most extensive government investigation, President Johnson's National Advisory Commission on Civil Disorders (commonly called the Kerner Commission), rejected evidence which suggested fundamental problems with the American system. In the end, the commissioners did cite "white racism" as part of the trouble, but not before they had fired 120 staff members who wanted stronger language and had suppressed the staff's radical report, "The Harvest of American Racism." The commissioners' own document recommended a moderate two-pronged approach: increased government expenditures to help black people and more effective use of force to suppress disturbances.

143

Inevitably, the last solution seemed more acceptable to most white politicians, and Congress voted additional funds to beef up local law enforcement agencies and to train the national guard in efficient riot control. Saddled with burgeoning expenditures for Vietnam, the president filed away the commission's other recommendations. Johnson, like most other national leaders, preferred to ignore the implications of "white racism."

Black Power

Lyndon Johnson might have resisted confronting the problem of white racism, but militant black spokesmen were already citing it as a justification for rejecting integration—the traditional goal of the civil rights movement. An established separatist group, the Black Muslims, suddenly gained prominence in the early 1960s. The Muslims preached the superiority of black people and black institutions, predicted eventual collapse for the decadent white society (including the corrupt Christian religion), planned the creation of separate black areas in the United States, and stressed the necessity for hard work and self-discipline. The sect gained a number of converts during the 1950s, including Malcolm Little, a former dope pusher and ex-convict but a self-educated man with a keen intellect. Rejecting his "Christian slave name," Malcolm X became Muslim leader Elijah Muhammed's top aide and the most eloquent spokesman for anti-integrationist ideas. Malcolm's fiery oratory first attracted national attention to the Muslims, and the conversion of the popular heavyweight boxing champion Cassius Clay (who became Muhammed Ali) gained them headlines in the sports section.

In advocating black pride and separation from whites, Malcolm X and the Muslims revived a powerful strain in the Afro-American heritage. Malcolm ridiculed Martin Luther King's philosophy of nonviolence: "If someone puts a hand on you," he preached, "send him to the cemetery." He advised black people to join together "to lift the level of our community, and to make our society beautiful so that we will be satisfied in our own social circles and won't be running around here trying to knock our way into a social circle where we're not wanted." A series of disputes with Elijah Muhammed led Malcolm to form his own movement—The Organization of Afro-American Unity—in 1963. After leaving the Muslims, he slowly began to temper his separatist rhetoric and to suggest a working alliance with a variety of black groups. Such ideas seemed heresy to the more isolationist followers of Elijah Muhammed. Malcolm was assassinated, allegedly by his Muslim enemies, in 1965. After his death, growing numbers of people read his

144

Autobiography, and Malcolm became an even greater hero to young radicals. "Black history began with Malcolm X," proclaimed Eldridge Cleaver of the Black Panthers.

By the mid-1960s the doctrines of black pride and black nationalism seemed to be gaining greater support. Southern resistance to the Civil Rights Act of 1964 and the Voting Rights Act of 1965 produced further bloodshed and death; to some blacks, the urban disorders in the North suggested the possibility that violence might bring more concessions or at least greater psychological satisfaction than nonviolent civil disobedience. In May 1966, SNCC, officially committed to integration, urged blacks "to begin building independent political, economic, and cultural institutions that they will control and use as instruments of social change in this country." Later that summer SNCC joined other civil rights groups, including SCLC and CORE, in a protest march through Mississippi, an effort which widened divisions within the civil rights movement. Stokely Carmichael, SNCC's new chairman, took the spotlight away from Martin Luther King, who was often absent. Carmichael vowed that he would never go to jail peacefully again, and declared that "every court house in Mississippi ought to be burned down to get rid of the dirt." In the most publicized event of the march, he coined the movement's new slogan: "black power!" The media played up the role of the militants, and older black leaders complained that television reporters pushed a microphone in front of anybody who yelled "black power" or "burn, baby, burn."

Behind the sloganeering, young blacks were seriously attempting to frame a workable philosophy. The people in SNCC and CORE had tried nonviolence and cooperation with whites, and they believed that these tactics had failed. Integration, wrote Stokely Carmichael, "reinforces among both black and white, the idea that 'white' is automatically better and 'black' is by definition inferior." And to blacks like Carmichael, political and legal equality, the basis of the old civil rights movement, now seemed less important than immediate economic power. Black people, they argued, had to gain control of their communities and expel the "white power structure"—the "dishonest" businessmen, the "rent-gouging" landlords, and the "crooked" politicians. "Get rid of Whitey," became their rallying cry. Along with independence, young nationalists promoted black pride. Since whites would always see blacks as inferior, they contended, black people must reject the values of white society and seek their own cultural identity based upon their Afro-American heritage. As a means of stimulating black pride and cultural nationalism, militants demanded community control of ghetto schools and, where this was not immediately possible, special black studies courses, taught and administered by blacks.

145

There were many variations on the themes of black power and black nationalism. Identifying with dark-skinned peoples in the third world, some viewed black Americans as colonized people subject to the domination of alien, white masters. Others adopted a Marxist framework, seeing blacks as the most exploited group in an exploitative capitalist society. Violent revolution, a few extremists suggested, offered the best means of redressing grievances. But most others warned against open confrontations with the overwhelming fire-power of white America, and most radicals suggested the need to build a base of support before attempting a revolutionary movement.

The history of the Black Panthers, an organization which spread across the country in the late 1960s, revealed the tensions generated by debates over black power and black nationalism. Beginning as a glorified street gang in Oakland, California, the Panthers gained attention primarily through a shootout with Oakland police and through the literary success of Eldridge Cleaver's *Soul on Ice.* The Oakland group borrowed their name from the short-lived Black Panther party of Lowndes County, Alabama, an organization sponsored by SNCC. Outfitted in paramilitary garb, the Panthers frightened most whites, and law enforcement officials denounced the group as the newest threat to American society. Panther leaders Huey Newton (who was convicted of killing a policeman during the Oakland shootout) and Bobby Seale urged blacks to organize "self-defense groups that are dedicated to defending our black community against racist oppression and brutality." The Panthers also demanded a guaranteed income for all citizens, exemption of blacks from military service, government funds for cooperative housing facilities, reparation payments "as retribution for slave labor and mass murder of black people," release of all black prisoners "because they have not received a fair and impartial trial," and use of all black juries to try black defendants. Such demands borrowed from black nationalist ideas, but they also owed as much to a simplistic Marxism and to the rhetoric of American constitutional law (Huey Newton always carried a stack of law books in his car). In seeking to advance their goals, Panthers found it difficult to fix a strategy: should they ally with white radicals and build for revolutionary action, or should they avoid ties with nonblacks and stress black pride? The Panthers finally did seek ties with both white and black radicals, a course which did not please all of the party's members.

By 1968 neither black power nor black nationalism had carried the day. Most black people—if opinion polls are to be believed—still supported the traditional aims of integration and equal rights, and they considered Martin Luther King the foremost black leader. But the spirit of militancy had prompted black people to reexamine their goals and aspirations. Most saw no real contradiction between greater racial pride and some type of integration with white society, no real conflict between greater political power for blacks and acceptance of the basic American system. Black politicians, gaining crucial white votes to add to their power base, began to obtain elective office in many large cities. Throughout the 1960s the income of black families rose steadily, though it still lagged behind that of whites. New styles of dress—Afro haircuts and dashikis—appeared more than changing fashions; black studies seemed more than a passing fad. When he was killed in 1968, Martin Luther King was trying to use his Poor People's Crusade as a means of bringing together a coalition of "have-nots." He never used cries of black power, but he had begun to recognize the limits of the old SCLC approach and to stress black pride.

The Civil Rights Act of 1968, the last major civil rights measure, indicated the ambivalent attitude of the "white power structure" toward the black revolution. Title VIII of the law prohibited discrimination in the advertising, financing, sale, or rental of most homes and charged the executive branch with acting "affirmatively" to achieve integrated housing. Together with a Supreme Court decision (decided under the obscure authority of a nineteenth-century statute) and state open housing laws, the Civil Rights Act seemed an important step toward integration of the largely white suburbs. If coupled with generous funding for inner-city projects, it promised better urban housing for minority families. But the majority of white congressmen also indicated their fear of the radical implications of black power. At the instigation of Strom Thurmond of South Carolina, Congress added a section which made it a crime to use the facilities of interstate commerce "to organize, promote, encourage, participate in, or carry on a riot; or to commit any act of violence in furtherance of a riot. . . ." In approving this seemingly vague provision, most members of Congress knew exactly what they wanted: a federal law which would stop the activities of black power advocates such as H. Rap Brown of SNCC. The "Rap Brown section" gave national authorities a catch-all statute to halt the travels and organizing efforts of black radicals.

The movement for political and economic power and the renaissance of black pride, then, affected white as well as black people. The sight of young persons shouting "black power" and of black men with sunglasses and Afro haircuts frightened many white people; the new black militancy represented another threat to settled ways. But other whites, particularly the young and better-educated, recognized the need for greater black pride and self-assertiveness. Potentially at least, the message that "black is beautiful" could also liberate white Americans. By suddenly discovering the story of black Americans, many people began to gain a greater awareness of white America's own past, its single-minded commitment to the ideals of a fair-skinned Horatio Alger. Never a people to doubt seriously the superiority of white Protestant values, white Americans perhaps gained a greater appreciation of the need for cultural diversity.

BIBLIOGRAPHY

Books on JFK and various parts of the Kennedy administration already fill many shelves. James M. Burns's campaign biography *John Kennedy: A Political Profile* (1960) remains extremely useful. Theodore H. White, *The Making of the President 1960* (1961), is the best of the semi-official series on the race for the White House. Two sympathetic but highly useful accounts of the Kennedy presidency are Arthur Schlesinger, Jr., *A Thousand Days* (1965); and Theodore Sorenson, *Kennedy* (1965). Much more critical is Henry Fairlie, *The Kennedy Promise* (1972). Two good works on more specific topics are Grant McConnell, *Steel and the Presidency—1962* (1963); and Jim F. Heath, *John F. Kennedy and the Business Community* (1969). A classic analysis of the conflict between the White House and Congress is James M. Burns, *The Deadlock of Democracy* (rev. ed., 1968). A new synthesis of the Kennedy-Johnson administrations is Jim F. Heath, *Decade of Disillusionment* (1975).

Lyndon Johnson, *The Vantage Point* (1972) offers Johnson's view of his stewardship but contains few real insights. More critical accounts include Eric F. Goldman, *The Tragedy of Lyndon Johnson* (1969); Roland Evans and Robert Novak, *Lyndon B. Johnson: The Exercise of Power* (1966); and Lewis Heren, *No Hail, No Farewell* (1970). Theodore H. White, *The Making of the President 1964* (1965), is the standard account. A series of essays, critical of the Great Society from the political left, are collected in Marvin E. Gettleman and David Mermelstein, eds., *The Great Society Reader* (1966). The role of the Warren Court is analyzed in Archibald Cox, *The Warren Court* (1968); Anthony Lewis, *Gideon's Trumpet* (1964); and the concluding chapters of Paul Murphy, *The Constitution in Crisis Times, 1918–1969* (1972).

Louis E. Lomax, *The Negro Revolt* (1962); and Anthony Lewis, *Portrait of a Decade* (1964), survey the course of black protest in the late 1950s and early 1960s. Important statements by black spokesmen include James Baldwin, *The Fire Next Time* (1963); and Martin Luther King, Jr., *Why We Can't Wait* (1964). C. Eric Lincoln, ed., *Martin Luther King, Jr., A Profile* (1970), is useful. The rise of militancy is reflected in the popularity of books such as Malcolm X's *Autobiography* (1965); Eldridge Cleaver's *Soul on Ice* (1967); and Huey P. Newton, *To Die for the People* (1972). Two

148

useful books on the movement away from integrationist ideas are Stokely Carmichael and Charles V. Hamilton, *Black Power* (1967); and J. H. Bracey, Jr., et al., *Black Nationalism in America* (1969). Howard Zinn, *SNCC: The New Abolitionists* (1965); and August Meier and Elliot Rudwick, *CORE* (1972), trace the emergence of two leading organizations. Anthony Platt, *The Politics of Riot Commissions* (1971), contains important material on the "official" versus the "unofficial" interpretation of black protests. Robert Fogelson, *Violence as Protest* (1969), is a controversial study which challenges the "official" view.

New Aid Programs

Republican irresolution annoyed the men of John Kennedy's New Frontier. They charted a new policy in which the negativity of deterrence and the totality of massive retaliation would not be the only choices. General Maxwell Taylor, army chief of staff, told Kennedy, "We must show the Russians that wars of national liberation are not cheap, safe, and disavowable but costly, dangerous, and doomed to failure." Worried about the relevance of ground combat in the all-or-nothing arena of atomic brinksmanship, Taylor and his experts sketched a heady new mission for the army: "nation building." To checkmate guerrilla tactics, highly trained elite forces could teach local troops the techniques of counterinsurgency and instruct the natives in twentieth-century technology and liberal democracy. Air cavalry and special units like the green berets might fill the interstices of nuclear stalemate.

Others in the new administration relied more upon moral example or upon America's wealth than upon military cunning. Caught up in a fervor of "can-do" activism, such men moved to short-circuit the cycle of poverty, the sense of helplessness which fueled communist appeals in the underdeveloped, nonwhite world. Ironically, though Kennedy found it difficult to secure congressional approval for reform at home, Capitol Hill enthusiastically funded Taylor's experiments along with new departures in foreign aid such as the Alliance for Progress and the Peace Corps. Just five months after the new president proposed "a ten-year plan for the Americas," all the nations of the Western hemisphere except Canada and Cuba signed the Charter of Punta del Este in

6

The perils of power: Foreign policy in the 1960s

August 1961. The United States promised $10 million over the next decade to finance social programs such as health care, housing and education, and economic credits to stabilize commodity prices and boost local rates of growth by 2.5 percent annually. Generosity in Latin America, the New Frontiersmen calculated, would thwart radicalism and ensure compliance: they talked of "judicious grants" which could encourage moderate, reformist leaders, while breaking oligarchic or anti-American regimes. The Agency for International Development (AID) operated on a smaller scale in all third-world areas. An even more imaginative program, the Peace Corps, sent volunteers to willing nations throughout the world. Functioning primarily in rural areas, the Peace Corps worked to improve health, education, and economic efficiency. Director R. Sargent Shriver expected no dramatic results, only "cumulative years of goodwill among the common folk." By 1963 volunteers worked in over forty countries as teachers, crop specialists, and construction supervisors.

Cuba: Need and Opportunity

A curious constellation of events made policy innovation not only feasible but almost mandatory. Everywhere, it seemed, Eisenhower-Dulles tactics prompted perverse results during the early 1960s. Despite his usual skepticism about unlikely schemes, Kennedy continued a Central Intelligence Agency (CIA) project to invade Cuba with a small force of anti-Castro expatriates. The disgruntled population, America's spies predicted, would welcome these rebels as liberators. On April 17, two days after CIA mercenaries had attacked Cuba's air bases with B-26 bombers, approximately 1,400 Cuban exiles waded ashore at the Bay of Pigs. Local peasants ignored the unlikely army, most of them pro-Batista urbanites, and Castro's forces soon surrounded them. Though some in the State Department urged full-scale intervention, Kennedy eloquently accepted the fact of disaster. "Victory has a hundred fathers," he said, "but defeat is an orphan." The episode only tightened Castro's control in Cuba, reinforced his dependence upon the Soviet Union, and loosed yet another round of Yankeephobia throughout most of Latin America.

Before Washington officials could recover from this setback, another element in Eisenhower's legacy threatened to spin away. Khrushchev thwarted Kennedy's anxious hopes for continuing detente. Unwilling to freeze a strategic balance which would solidify America's great lead in weaponry and industrial development, the Russians hoped first to gain easy concessions from an inexperienced president. At an informal summit meeting in Vienna during June 1961,

151

Khrushchev hinted at war unless NATO abandoned West Berlin. If the United States did not agree, the premier explained that he could secure the same result by signing a separate peace with his East German ally, Walter Ulbricht. Determined to uphold America's credibility, Kennedy mobilized the national guard, accelerated arms production, and tripled draft calls. Khrushchev blustered about "thermonuclear holocaust" but acted much more cautiously. Barbed wire and then a wall of cement blocks sealed off East Berlin from the Western sectors, ending an embarrassing flow of defectors (some three million since 1945) and cauterizing a black market in goods and currencies. Kennedy gracefully accepted this compromise, realizing the substance of victory.

Stung by rebukes from domestic critics for his poor showing, Khrushchev greedily took up a fortuitous opportunity for a major strategic victory. Frightened of America's aggressiveness, Castro apparently asked the Soviet Union for military hardware. Moscow replied with massive shipments of sophisticated weapons, including medium-range ballistic missiles armed with atomic warheads. Kennedy responded with a week of crisis diplomacy, a calculated vagueness keeping his opponents off-guard. During a televised address on October 22, he vowed, "The United States will not compromise its safety," and ordered the Strategic Air Command to full alert. Two days later, the navy had quarantined the island, its destroyers ready to turn away any Soviet merchant ships carrying missiles. But Kennedy also began searching for compromise: if Russia removed its weapons, the United States would not attack Cuba again. While public prodding continued—United Nations Ambassador Adlai Stevenson hounded the Soviets "to save the peace"—secret messages between Kremlin and White House soon confirmed Kennedy's offer. Then on Saturday, October 26, amid near-hysterical headlines warning of imminent nuclear war, Khrushchev tried an exchange: Soviet withdrawal from Cuba for the dismantling of American bases in Turkey. Not an unreasonable request, Kennedy nevertheless ignored it and the Soviet premier, no doubt shocked by America's grim tenacity, backed off. On Sunday morning, he accepted Kennedy's terms. Russian missiles were crated and sent home, over Castro's protests, within three weeks.

The Cuban missile crisis eclipsed the attitude and method of cold-war diplomacy. The swiftness of nuclear escalation frightened both sides; mutual blackmail, if miscalculated, could easily get out of control. Then, too, both powers had other concerns. In late 1962, China overran Tibet and ostentatiously began atomic tests in Sinkiang, near Russia's border. Mao Tse-tung openly challenged Moscow for leadership of the communist bloc. The Americans, on the brink of a whirlpool involvement in Vietnam, wanted to experiment not only with counterinsurgency, but also with other devices such as the Peace Corps and the Alliance for Progress. Superpower rhetoric mellowed, Khrushchev admitting, "If the United States is now a paper tiger, it has atomic teeth," and Kennedy calling for "mutual tolerance." During the summer of 1963, the two countries set up a "hot line" linking their capitals with teletype machines. And on July 25, America, Britain, and Russia initialed a nuclear test ban treaty which ended all except underground atomic explosions. (Russian fears that on-site inspections might reveal too much about its industrial potential made a total ban impossible.) Such gestures did little to ease rivalry between the two superpowers, but they did indicate a mutual desire to harness that competition into non-nuclear—and therefore more predictable—channels. Both Kennedy and Khrushchev wanted a stable world, free of dangerous uncertainties.

If Cuba daily reminded Washington officials of their free-world mistake, peaceful coexistence allowed them to act elsewhere in the third world. The Peace Corps won some friends, particularly during the early sixties, but its quiet humanitarianism could not change the larger picture. The Alliance for Progress proved ill-conceived: its loans only put Latin American nations deeper in debt without stimulating the expected economic "take-off." But most Americans, proud of their ingenuity, did not easily recognize signs of failure. Surely, with such riches, such power, such determination, the United States could build nations in the third world like itself: prosperous, democratic, and pro-West.

STRUGGLE IN VIETNAM

The End of Diem

Hoping to sharpen the nation's credibility while pushing back communism's most recent advance, the Kennedy administration tested its new approach in Southeast Asia. Diem still vetoed reform, despite pressure from American ambassadors, so the Democrats undertook the only other alternative, a military defeat of the Viet Cong. Billions of dollars, tons of sophisticated weapons, and 16,000 American combat troops inundated the Vietnamese countryside by 1963. The communist effort waivered, justifying the Pentagon's tactics, but Asian paradoxes soon diluted Washington's optimism. Hanoi increased its aid to the insurgents; Kennedy widened intervention to include a covert war against North Vietnam. More discouraging, Diem's regime came apart at the seams. Apparently limitless treasure from Washington had brought jolting corruption in Saigon. The scramble for loot hindered normal operations of state. Land reform collapsed. Conscripted soldiers seemed more bent on plunder than on winning popular support away from the Viet Cong.

At this point, Diem issued a series of Catholic moral laws in an attempt to discredit Buddhists, now forced either to abandon their religion or to face charges of treason. Their leaders organized massive demonstrations which culminated on June 16, 1963, when a priest martyred himself by setting fire to his gasoline-soaked robes. As if finally convinced of Diem's turpitude, city people paraded in the streets and prayed at pagodas for his downfall. For nearly two months, the regime waited for animosities to abate, but more self-immolations and the growing violence of student strikes convinced Diem and his brother, Ngo Dinh Nhu, that only strong measures could restore order. On August 21, detachments from American-trained special-forces units attacked Buddhist sanctuaries in Saigon, Hue, and most provincial capitals. This terrorism coupled with political arrests prompted another, even more violent cycle of protest and repression. Intellectuals and the urban middle class abandoned the Diem regime, now consumed in a near orgy of self-destruction.

No one knew what to do, least of all the surprised bureaucrats in Washington watching television reports from Saigon. One obvious reaction was to excise the cancer: Diem must go. The internal chaos of his regime enervated the war effort against the communists and mocked hopes for a democratic example for the third world. Religious persecution sickened Americans, including the president, himself a Catholic. During the fall of 1963 several Vietnamese generals suggested plans for a coup to the ambassador, Henry Cabot Lodge, receiving the reply that his country would not intervene in "an internal matter." Such vagueness apparently scared the plotters, for nothing happened, much to Lodge's disgust. In October the Kennedy administration ostentatiously canceled the commercial import program which financed Diem's government and publicly disavowed the rest of his family. Reassured, the generals wheeled into action, and on November 1 Vietnamese battalions near Saigon captured administrative centers and surrounded Diem's palace. The "George Washington of Vietnam" died that night, murdered while trying to escape his country.

American Goals and Vietnamese Realities

That same month an era also ended in the United States. On November 22, 1963, President Kennedy died in Dallas, Texas, an assassin's victim. Anxious to maintain continuity, successor Lyndon B. Johnson did not challenge the policy of slow engagement in Vietnam despite Attorney General Robert Kennedy's advice that a second Geneva conference might neutralize all Indochina. The new president wanted to help "those little people." Although Johnson's justification for war later became more sophisticated, the Texan never really forgot the Alamo and the brave men who defied everything there in their will to victory. White House advisers fleshed out this emotionalism with new variations on cold war themes. The United States must repel communist aggression now or face repeated nibbling elsewhere. If Washington faltered, many third world leaders would question America's willingness, even its ability, to protect their countries against subversion. Russia must understand Yankee determination to contain communism. Walt Whitman Rostow, the president's special adviser on foreign affairs, speculated that American pressure in Vietnam would divert Chinese expansion away from the Pacific toward central Asia, thus aggravating the Sino-Soviet split. Vietnamese problems thus became absorbed into global strategy: a Pentagon expert explained in 1968 that to repel communist aggression there was "only 10 percent" of America's purpose; in addition, the war must reassure allies and frighten enemies elsewhere.

Seeking larger goals, bureaucrats lost sight of their tool, Vietnam, since the tenth century a Confucian state. Ritual emperors symbolized universal order for thousands of economically self-sufficient villages. Individuals molded themselves into a historical process that emphasized continuity with the past, not progress toward a different future. The Vietnamese valued harmony and unanimity more than personal freedom or abstract principles. Rigid adherence to authority, they believed, insured the day-to-day functioning of society. Such communal certainty provided psychological security for its members and great tenacity for its primary institution, the village. Then French colonialism ripped away the emperor's "mandate of Heaven"—popular confidence in his right to rule—and warped the agrarian economy. The new masters demanded surplus, not self-sufficiency, so they herded Vietnamese together on rice or rubber plantations. Saigon and Hanoi became parasitic pleasure spas for these *colons* and their mandarin servants. Although ethnocentric French teachers tried for decades to "civilize" the natives, they educated only a class of intellectuals alienated from the rest of the people. Despite such changes, the villages remained, their timeless agrarianism the basis for both society and ethics.

The first Indochina War, followed by Diem's ruthless centralism, aggravated this rural-urban split, the tension between old and new, familiar and foreign. Westerners valued development, but the National

Liberation Front easily accepted the communal basis of life in Vietnamese villages. Red cadres talked of traditional ways and enacted land reforms immediately. Round-eyes too often exploited national resources or pursued irrelevant political theories while the communists deferred ultimate goals as they pursued popular changes. In contrast, rulers in Saigon tried to impose forms of democracy, but not its substance, upon an uninterested people. Peasants feared the city as a hostile place with novel, disruptive ideas.

Americans never realized that their revolution from above—their effort to replace Confucian unanimity with Western pluralism—could never compete with the Viet Cong's restoration from below. In one sense, however, Lyndon Johnson had few, if any, options. Only a strong American presence could stave off internal collapse in South Vietnam, now without a leader or even a government. The new president's old advisers did not readily abandon apparently successful tactics. Johnson accepted their theories about credibility as much as he had earlier theories about dominoes: "The United States must take a strong stand," he said, "or else no one will believe our promises." The lure of big gains at reasonable cost still bewitched Washington. After a month-long inspection tour, Secretary of Defense Robert S. McNamara and Chief of Staff Maxwell Taylor reported on October 2, 1963, that the United States could begin pulling out its troops by early 1964. But one thing escaped these computations: the nature of Vietnam itself. This was the tragic flaw which wrecked the careful calculations of computers and the estimates of Washington's most talented prognosticators.

A Vigorous Beginning, 1964–65

America began the second Indochina War during the winter of 1964–65, by pursuing its own national interests while responding to growing chaos in South Vietnam. A revolving door of military juntas undermined the anticommunist effort on the battlefield and only aggravated Diem's legacy of corruption and malaise. The Viet Cong rapidly filled the political vacuum in the countryside, appealing to many Vietnamese frustrated by years of indecisive warfare. By the middle of 1964, they had recaptured many villages and begun preparations for a major assault on provincial capitals, always supported by military aid from Hanoi. Considerably frightened at this prospect, Pentagon officials drew up plans for an air war against North Vietnam. Though only a substitute for the accelerating stalemate of counterinsurgency in the South, no other option seemed feasible, short of an embarrassing disengagement or total war. But escalation required legal, if not moral, justification. The White House drafted a congressional resolution authorizing such an attack and waited for an opportunity.

It came almost too quickly. During his 1964 presidential campaign, Johnson presented himself as a peace candidate, firmly rejecting prescriptions from critics like former Air Force Chief of Staff Curtis Lemay for "bombing Hanoi back into the Stone Age." Then in early August came reports of a naval encounter in the Gulf of Tonkin. Just after Vietnamese special forces and their American advisers raided two small islands on August 2, the United States spy-ship *Maddox* violated Hanoi's self-proclaimed twelve-mile territorial sea limit. Assuming that the destroyer was part of a larger operation, Ho Chi Minh ordered several PT boats into the area. As these ships closed in, both sides exchanged several volleys. Two days later, the *Maddox* and another destroyer, the *C. Turner Joy*, returned to the Gulf of Tonkin. Anxious naval captains and malfunctioning sonar equipment soon reported—perhaps created—a second "attack."

Denouncing such "unprovoked aggression" during a nationally televised speech, President Johnson ordered reprisal raids against North Vietnamese naval bases. The temporary feeling of crisis prompted Congress to pass the so-called Gulf of Tonkin resolution. Its open-ended phraseology authorized Johnson "to take all necessary measures" to repulse communist advances. Unaware of the dubious nature of Hanoi's attacks and, like the chief executive, innocent of Vietnamese complexities, the Senate adopted the de facto declaration of war, 88 to 2. Only two senators, Wayne Morse and Ernest Gruening, questioned the feasibility of this potentially unlimited commitment.

After the 1964 presidential election, United States officials generalized reprisal into a sustained air assault. Pentagon bureaucrats argued that the Saigon clique could not reform itself as long as the Viet Cong rebellion continued. Guerrilla attacks would go on as long as North Vietnam supplied them. Bombing strikes against the North and elite counterinsurgency operations in the South would defeat this national war of liberation, Washington's best and brightest told each other, and restore America's global credibility. But analysis could not alter reality. Angry discontent with the Saigon regime, together with carefully cultivated affinities between communist propaganda and Vietnamese traditionalism, fueled the Viet Cong rebellion. Forcing North Vietnam out of the war would only weaken, not defeat, guerrilla tactics in the South. The deepening morass of Vietnam frightened other nations. More and more, the immediate problem of destroying insurgents preoccupied Washington's planners. Because no one knew exactly what such

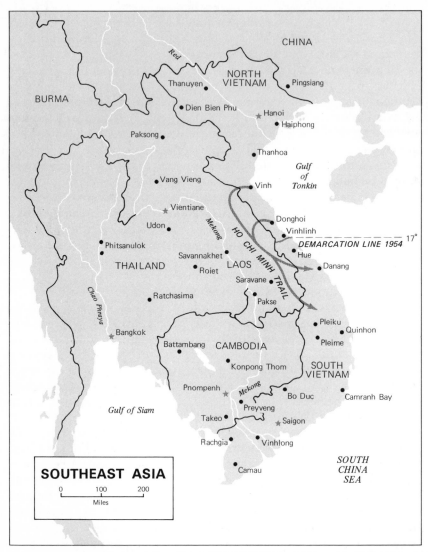

Map "Southeast Asia" (p. 998) in THE AMERICAN NATION: A History of the United States, 2nd Edition by John A. Garraty. Maps and Captions Copyright © 1966, 1971 by Harper & Row, Publishers, Inc. By permission of the publisher.

a mission required, the treadmill of escalation ground forward. It seemed reasonable: just a little more aid, just a few more soldiers would break the rebellion. Victory remained always so close. Johnson himself believed that a steady, predictable escalation would avoid intervention from China or Russia and at the same time convince the Viet Cong and Hanoi that they would not win.

Determination Becomes Self-delusion, 1965–67

The war slowly intensified. Sustained bombing of North Vietnam began on February 15, 1965, ostensibly in reprisal for a Viet Cong mortar attack against a Marine Corps base at Pleiku. That spring, American combat troops began to aid Vietnamese army units under fire. Johnson authorized the first "search and destroy" mission—independent sweeps involving large numbers of GIs—for June 27–30, 1965, several miles northwest of Saigon. Assumptions of American omnipotence soon withered, however, because Washington's overconfident planners underestimated the enemy. Guerrilla methods confused soldiers trained for large-scale wars of maneuver. Most military experts guessed that victory required a ten-to-one numerical advantage over Viet Cong–North Vietnamese troops. But the enemy, recruiting the bulk of their manpower within South Vietnam itself, more than matched, at this ratio, Pentagon escalations.

Washington ingenuity, now thoroughly intrigued by immediate problems, tried to cope with this depressing situation in two ways. Against a backdrop of Johnsonian rhetoric about "winning the hearts and minds of the Vietnamese people," a plethora of bureaucrats inundated the countryside with experiments. AID officials taught the villagers useful skills, health care, and modern agricultural techniques. Combat units built hospitals, schools, orphanages. Government schemes assured the farmer of high prices for his crop but low prices for the consumer. The junta in Saigon periodically deployed urban volunteers to countermand the work of communist cadres. Either because of Viet Cong terror or because of its own irrelevance, however, nation-building barely touched communist strength in rural areas. By 1967 frustrated officials adopted still another device for rural pacification: the strategic hamlet program. To protect villagers from Viet Cong attack and ensure their loyalties to Saigon, American soldiers garrisoned the bamboo towns, often erecting makeshift forts. Herded into barbed-wire enclosures, living under American machine guns, the peasants were expected to continue their agrarian way of life. Such concentration camps did achieve their military purpose, but they permanently alienated farmers, now isolated from land and tradition.

Bewildered and angered by the failure of their good intentions, Americans came to rely upon more direct and even savage tactics. Computer printouts in Washington explained that improved "kill ratios" could substitute for the elusive ten-to-one formula. Bombs, artillery, and rifles could kill so many enemy soldiers that, eventually, the Viet Cong and North Vietnamese could not replace them, given their relatively small population base. If such thinking skirted genocide, the nature of guerrilla war made it almost inevitable. The Viet Cong did not wear uniforms. They infiltrated villages using a combination of terror and appealing propaganda. Taking Mao Tse-tung's advice, the insurgents "swam like fishes in a sea of people." Confronted with American firepower, pajama-clad Viet Cong fought a war of stealth: ambush, booby-trap, sabotage, quick mortar barrage.

To many American soldiers, both enthusiastic volunteers and scared draftees, the war became one against the Vietnamese themselves. Murder became at once hideously personal and clinically remote. Search-and-destroy missions created a misconception that "body count" alone mattered. Some West Pointers, realizing that careers depended upon numbers, brutalized villagers for information and lied to superiors about enemy dead; GIs often tortured Viet Cong suspects, imitating the grotesque tactics of their foe. The United States command in Saigon charted "free-fire zones," huge areas in which helicopter gunships strafed anything alive. Chemicals defoliated the earth, and bombers pulverized North Vietnam's industry and South Vietnam's farms. Such devices may have limited communist freedom of movement, but they also destroyed American prestige. In a traditional society whose members valued their ties to ancestral lands and to village communities, terror, free-fire zones, and wholesale murder hopelessly discredited the round-eyes.

The Americans miscalculated badly, but no one admitted it. Middle-level civilians and field colonels reported what higher officials in Saigon wanted to hear, not the actuality of stagnation. America's ambassadors and generals further refined the stylized ritual; we are winning the war, they wired Washington, but send us more money, more men. For many Kennedy Democrats still in the administration, tough-mindedness became not a style but an end. A militant stand ensured approval as a "realistic appraisal" and garnered points in bureaucratic in-fighting. The Russians and Chinese, bickering over their 4,500-mile frontier, carefully refrained from any cold war challenge or diplomatic aid that might release their most dangerous rival from the quicksands of Southeast Asia. Such quiescence, in turn, freed America to act in Indochina and convinced its officials that the war somehow promoted communist mellowing. Having shoehorned the conflict into America's global strategy, Johnson isolated himself completely from Vietnamese realities and vowed that "I will not be the first president to lose a war."

United Press International

Mangrove forests in Vietnam before and after defoliation.

Neither Diplomacy nor Reform

Unrealistic calculations scuttled early opportunities for compromise. Johnson and his advisers used diplomacy either to justify further escalation or to secure an American victory. When U Thant, secretary-general of the United Nations, suggested in July 1964 that the Geneva conference reconvene, Johnson righteously refused: "We do not believe in conferences called to ratify terror." But nine months later, the war firmly escalated, the president told an audience at Johns Hopkins University that the United States would discuss peace. He even offered American capital to rebuild "a peaceful Southeast Asia," almost a bribe for surcease. Yet his continued demand for a noncommunist regime in Saigon was unrealistic, tantamount to a Hanoi-NLF capitulation. The enemy routinely rejected such transparent efforts to achieve at the bargaining table what American soldiers had not won in the field. Every rebuff, the president reminded his critics, proved communist perfidy.

Johnson used diplomacy more for warmaking than for peacemaking. During a thirty-seven-day period in December 1965 and January 1966, he halted the Rolling Thunder bombing raids against North Vietnam and ostentatiously sponsored a far-flung peace initiative. His closest friends applauded his cleverness. The air war had not materially impaired Hanoi's war production, and anyway, few military targets remained. Ho Chi Minh had simply decentralized, then camouflaged his industry in the countryside. Although Ho responded to Johnson's pause with hints about a coalition or neutralist government for South Vietnam, Johnson rejected further talks. Instead he pointed to enemy "truculence" and unleashed a new air war, this one directed against Hanoi's supply routes through Indochinese mountains and jungles. At the same time, Johnson vigorously escalated the ground war. Troop levels jumped from 150,000 in February 1966 to 550,000 at their peak in 1968. For nearly twenty-four months, America saved Vietnam from communism by destroying its land, its people, and even its society.

Unable to escape their misconceptions either by diplomacy or by force, Washington bureaucrats next tried to reform Saigon's government. Absorbed in its coups and intrigues but assured of American money, the military junta became not only dictatorial but also useless. Johnson summoned the two most recently installed generals, Nguyen Van Thieu and Nguyen Cao Ky, to a meeting at Honolulu during February 1966. He extracted promises from the quiet Thieu and the more flamboyant Ky that they would redistribute land, end corruption, and rule more liberally. Like Kennedy before him, the president had few levers to enforce the glib assurances from Vietnamese leaders who were his last option. The junta could always cash in its profits, leaving the country to the Viet Cong. Although the young generals did permit nationwide elections for a Constituent Assembly during 1966, no communist delegates and few neutralists participated in this "constitutional convention." The pair, elected President Thieu and Vice President Ky by suspiciously lopsided victories in 1967, easily took personal control over the new government apparatus. Shielded under America's massive military buildup, they "postponed" reforms and ruled through fiat and secret police. This facade of democracy in Saigon only aggravated discontent in the countryside, lending credence to communist propaganda about capitalist lackeys.

Protest

Although the ugliness of brutal, unending war in Vietnam did not repulse America's government, it soon repulsed many of its citizens. The televised conflict frustrated patriots, angry because a strange, unseen army had apparently stymied American GIs, the best soldiers in the world. Such people did not understand finely-spun theories about dominoes and third-world credibility, only the war's distressing inconclusiveness. Though fears of Russian or Chinese reactions sensibly restrained the administration, even military critics slowly realized that a major assault against Haiphong or Hanoi would not destroy the Viet Cong insurgency. Air Force navigators could seldom find, let alone interdict, supplies flowing south along the Ho Chi Minh Trail. Most enemy war materiel moved in small vehicles or on human backs along pathways, not cement highways. Bomb craters were simply avoided. The ground war against the Viet Cong also stalemated, despite the half-million troops which guarded major cities and rural outposts. Hanoi's regulars avoided combat with American units, while Viet Cong guerrillas easily hid among the peasant population. News broadcasts, with repetitious uniformity, mouthed what many dimly perceived: the United States was not winning the war.

As war-weariness withered public support, an unprecedented protest movement questioned the country's purposes. Although he had guided the Gulf of Tonkin resolution through the Senate, J. William Fulbright lashed out against what he called "the arrogance of power." "Power," the chairman of the Foreign Relations Committee observed, "tends to confuse itself with virtue." Many thought dangerous the Pentagon's sense of omnipotence and the president's voluble self-righteousness. Perhaps America could not, and should not, graft its domestic institutions onto alien societies. More and more people expressed their moral distaste against the Vietnam adventure. Months of teach-ins on college campuses and media coverage of generally peaceful protest marches culminated during October 1967. Nearly a quarter-million students, intellectuals, and ordinary Americans demonstrated against the war during a giant three-day rally at Washington. Thousands more marched in New York and San Francisco. The mushrooming antiwar movement deprived Johnson of his natural constituency among liberal Democrats. More ominous, the protests polarized many Americans into "hawks" or "doves"—those who favored victory or peace at any price—making impossible intelligent discussion of compromise solutions.

Tet and the President's Discontent, 1968

The year 1968 stripped away everyone's illusions. Many already doubted whether the United States could ever win in Vietnam at any reasonable cost. But a majority of Americans still did not believe that a motley assemblage of willful peasants, lacking air power, heavy artillery, and technology, might confound Yankee soldiers and their mechanical efficiency. Walt Rostow told reporters that captured documents showed a communist collapse to be "imminent." Then on January 29, 1968, during Vietnam's lunar new year celebrations, Viet Cong guerrillas and North Vietnamese armies coordinated a massive attack against Saigon and Hue, the imperial capital of Vietnam, and also against nine provincial capitals. The insurgents overran much of Cholon, the Chinese section of Saigon, and even penetrated the American embassy, killing several guards. In Hue, the rebels executed a reign of terror against their political opponents. The attacks on regional cities had the greatest military repercussions. To restore control, General Westmoreland had to shift troops from northern South Vietnam and from rural areas to take and then garrison places like Tay Ninh, Quang Tri, and Pleiku. Communist cadres quickly infiltrated the now unprotected countryside. The United States command, always able to extract theories, if not victory, from its struggle, saw silver in the lining of the Tet offensive cloud. Charlie had overextended himself, exhausting months of supplies in an unsuccessful effort to end the war. "The enemy is on the ropes," Westmoreland said. "Tet was his last gasp." If only he had 200,000 more men, the American commander promised he would crush the rural insurgency "once and for all."

But the masquerade could not go on much longer. Johnson asked Westmoreland whether the communists might not match another

American escalation. Yes, said the general. "Then where will it all end?" Johnson wondered. Several civilian advisers had for months counseled diplomatic compromise. McNamara added his columns of statistics, discovered their fabrications, and recommended a coalition government for South Vietnam. Then he resigned. George Ball, the under-secretary of state, repeatedly pointed out the folly of shooting a people into allegiance; the CIA for years had counseled against the effort. But Johnson had, until now, listened more to his generals, relying on their promises of easy victory. After the Tet offensive, the president asked an old friend and much-respected confidant of Democratic presidents, Clark Clifford, to chart a fresh course. The new secretary of defense soon discovered that the military numbers game was relatively straightforward. To send 200,000 men to Southeast Asia and still protect American commitments elsewhere, the president would have to call up the army reserves or triple already-high draft quotas. Only new taxes and wide-ranging controls on an overheated economy could ensure war production at a reasonable cost and temper an accelerating inflation. Yet senators privately told their former majority leader what many citizens knew instinctively: the country would reject such steps toward mobilization for war. Clifford urged Johnson to negotiate.

Events, not advice, finally shoved the president toward diplomacy. The Tet offensive had convinced many in Vietnam that the war could never end until the United States left. "Before the Americans came," an old man told a reporter in Saigon, "my home was on the land of my ancestors and my family was honorable. Now I live off my daughter's earnings as a hooch-girl." Morale cracked in the U.S. army. Helicopter pilots refused to fly during their last four weeks "in country." Some units sought escape in drugs or "fragging"—surreptitious assaults upon their officers. Others lost all restraint, as at My Lai where American soldiers bayoneted children and old men, apparently without thought or guilt. Both Vietnamese society and the army were coming apart under the strain of a stalemated war of continual and undecided conflict.

The adventure ended abruptly, at least in American politics. So chilling a cold warrior as Richard Nixon, the leading Republican candidate for the 1968 presidential nomination, advocated an end to the war, not necessarily a victory. Johnson gradually lost control of his party. On March 14, Senator Eugene J. McCarthy, an outspoken critic of Pentagon policy, nearly won New Hampshire's presidential primary. The next day, a much more potent challenge to Johnson emerged: Robert F. Kennedy. He announced his candidacy and pledged to stop the conflict. Such startling rebukes to an incumbent president matched the erosion of his constituency. Liberal Democrats abandoned the man they had praised lavishly so recently. Students and many intellectuals questioned Johnson's ethics, even his sanity. Yet the president, a great campaigner, could not defend himself publicly on the hustings: the Secret Service considered the security risk too great. Trapped in the White House, losing both nomination and popular respect, Johnson brooded about his nemesis, Vietnam.

On March 31, 1968, Johnson told a nationwide television audience that he had rejected Westmoreland's request for more troops. American escalation would stop. To signal his good intentions and lure Hanoi to the bargaining table, he halted bombing north of the nineteenth parallel. Then, almost as a postscript, Johnson announced that he would not run for reelection. Public sensation at this near-resignation clouded a diplomatic *tour de force:* negotiations would begin, thus defusing domestic demands for immediate disengagement. Yet the level of violence within South Vietnam actually increased. Thieu promised to conscript another 135,000 men, a figure which, together with 55,000 more Americans already in training camps, would almost fulfill Westmoreland's request. Proscribed from the North, American pilots intensified the air war in the South. The president was still attempting to "negotiate from strength." Moreover, he intentionally omitted any reference to a coalition government. Johnson still sought an American peace, a noncommunist South Vietnam.

Diplomatic Cobwebs

Ho Chi Minh, wanting to ensure the bombing halt, took up Johnson's offer for talks, hoping to use to good advantage the president's need for a negotiated peace. After several weeks of debate, the two governments began talks in Paris, each side anticipating that local feeling would promote its position. On May 10, 1968, Xuan Thuy, representing the Democratic Republic of Vietnam, and Averill Harriman, America's ambassador to Russia during World War II, walked into the Majestic Hotel, near the Arc de Triomphe. Publicly the pair deadlocked almost immediately, refusing to budge on the bombing issue. Hanoi insisted upon a prior, unilateral pledge from Washington not to resume the air war. Johnson wanted to include the question in a final settlement, thus preserving a club to encourage negotiation on other subjects. Privately, Harriman and Thuy gradually worked out a practical arrangement which reflected battlefield realities. Since nothing of much military value still existed, America would end all bombing if North Vietnam agreed "by its silence" not to escalate support for the Viet Cong. Both sides might then consider possible coalition governments for South Vietnam.

Though this compromise, however tentative, would have pleased most Americans and probably would have assured Hubert Humphrey's election in November, Johnson had reckoned without his obstreperous ally in Saigon. Thieu thought that the Republican candidate could arrange better terms: "I will win the peace," Nixon had vowed. So Saigon obstructed multilateral talks with the National Liberation Front (NLF), thus scuttling the Harriman-Thuy compromise. Johnson stopped bombing anyway, but he could not guarantee Saigon's good faith. If he cut off American aid, the communists would win by default. Thieu could always discipline Washington with threats that he would quit, bringing on chaos. Nixon's victory pleased Thieu immensely, but the new president required time to formulate specific policies. Diplomats marked time by haggling over the shape of the bargaining table. Behind closed chancery doors, Russia not surprisingly refused to rescue its rival from a Vietnamese swamp, thus capsizing Nixon's much-touted "secret plan" to end the war. By the beginning of 1969, the Republicans faced an extraordinarily difficult situation: stalemated war, ungovernable allies, domestic impatience with half-measures.

VIETNAM FALLOUT: THE ATROPHY OF AMERICAN RELATIONS ELSEWHERE

Russia and Europe

Washington's fixation with Southeast Asia distorted United States foreign policy. The lurking evolution toward detente with the Soviet Union halted in midstride. The war in Vietnam simultaneously pleased and worried the Russians; America's burgeoning armies flanked their Chinese rival while it consumed capitalist treasure. Yankee search-and-destroy missions in the Mekong Delta freed the Soviets for an unprecedented expansion of their influence in the Middle East. Yet Johnson's very willingness to use force convinced Khrushchev's successors, Leonid Brezhnev and Aleksei Kosygin, that the Americans respected only military strength. Then, too, many Russian scientists worried about the implications of NASA's mammoth space rockets and plans for orbiting platforms. So the Soviets mass-produced their most sophisticated missile, the SS-9, and accelerated atomic stockpiling. Unable to match this build-up weapon for weapon, given Vietnam's huge drain on available resources, the United States intensified the technology of nuclear war, developing Multiple Independent Re-entry Vehicles (MIRVs) which vastly increased the payload of a single rocket, and "smart bombs" which guided themselves to their target via television.

So another arms race and Russia's new role in the Arab world undercut the accommodation of the early sixties.

But neither power wanted to revert to the dangerous rivalry of cold war. During June 1967, Johnson and Kosygin conferred privately at Glassboro State College in New Jersey. Worried that the enormous success of Israel's just-completed Six Day War might somehow bring on a Soviet–American clash, each promised to respect his rival's vital interests in the crucial Middle East region. Rather than jeopardize the Nuclear Nonproliferation Treaty, finally signed in early 1969, Washington ignored Moscow's brutal repression of Czechoslovak reform efforts during 1968. Later, nervous shadowboxing gave way to detente directly as American troops departed from Vietnam during the early 1970s. Such trade-offs symbolized once again the high priority both nations attributed to avoiding atomic war.

Though consistently proclaimed as a crusade to reassure its allies, America's adventure in Southeast Asia further fragmented the Atlantic alliance. Western Europe's accelerating prosperity—itself a reflection of American spending overseas—eroded its sense of dependency. Arguments over strategy vitiated traditional comradeship. Determined to build a national nuclear force and, more grandiosely, to break out of "sterile bipolarity," Charles de Gaulle took France out of the NATO alliance, though he did not relinquish its protection. Many West Germans, wanting to normalize relations with their neighbors, chafed at Washington's rigid anticommunism. Even the "special relationship" between Great Britain and the United States withered. As economic obsolescence shoved the English toward the Common Market, they realized more and more their junior membership in the "atomic club." Prime ministers and many other Britons opposed America's policy in Vietnam. If Johnson felt somehow betrayed, England, no less than the rest of NATO, worried that its powerful protector had lost a sense of proportion. Far from thwarting a communist menace, the United States seemed bent upon self-destruction. Vietnam became the most visible wedge that drove the Atlantic community apart, Europe's regional interests clashing with America's global visions.

Old Puzzlements in the Third World

The conflict in Southeast Asia resuscitated old devices in American diplomacy throughout the third world. Determined to create an Asian consensus for his policy, Johnson did not challenge oppressive regimes in the Philippines, South Korea, and eventually in Cambodia, as long as they mollified his sensibilities about Vietnam. All three countries sent troops to Vietnam, the Koreans' savage fighting noted for its brutal effectiveness. American money once again supported a military oligarchy in Indonesia after General Suharto ousted the increasingly pro-Chinese Sukarno in 1965. Only Japan resisted Johnson's embrace, but regardless of politics, the tendrils of a vast commerce clamped the two nations together. During the late sixties, then, the United States forced everyone into a nexus of free world leader or communist dupe, ignoring throughout Asia, as in Vietnam, both nationalism and native culture.

Such tactics culminated in Latin America. Once again Washington honored dictators, as in Brazil where a cabal of generals supported by the United States in 1965 toppled the popular leftist João Goulart, who was showing growing interest in the nationalization of foreign businesses. Panicked by fears of "another Cuba," Johnson's men even tried to reimpose a clumsy overlordship in the Caribbean. In the Dominican Republic, a right-wing coup had ousted the constitutionally elected reformist government of Juan Bosch. But when Bosch's supporters attempted to regain control, American representatives on the island reported that communists had infiltrated Bosch's movement and requested Johnson to send the marines. Some 20,000 troops landed in mid-1965, and despite the quickly discovered inaccuracy of American reports, Johnson left the troops there until September 1966, when carefully supervised elections installed another pro-American leader, Joaquin Balaguer, as president. American gunboat diplomacy compounded the slow strangulation of the Alliance for Progress by a penurious Congress and a geyser of private investment from American corporations anxious for a quick profit. Preoccupied by Vietnam, Johnson either ignored change elsewhere or woodenly enforced a status quo stability. In this way, the Southeast Asian war blinded America to the future, distorting its foreign policies, pushing others into a ready-made mold. The tensions could not be checked for long, but Johnson contained them for the moment.

If complex, the Democrats' legacy was not unmanageable. Peace talks in Paris provided a continuing structure for negotiation, should one side or the other finally forgo its prescription for Indochina's future. If not, native troops, presumably more motivated than America's dispirited soldiers, and sophisticated firepower could "Vietnamize" the war while winning it. However plausible in the short run, such tactics could not remedy the flaw of American involvement. Searching for global credibility, Washington bureaucrats still ignored Vietnamese society, its peoples and possibilities. The United States could never impose a solution, either by force or by diplomacy. More years would pass before the nation's leaders abandoned this goal. By then, Johnson's war had become Nixon's.

169

But the Vietnam conflict was more than a tragic mistake for Asians and Americans. It symbolized the bankruptcy of worldwide anti-communist crusading, of "tough-minded" over-responses. The United States had overextended itself by 1968, but zealous bureaucrats could not find a route back. Instead they sacrificed more and more of America's strength elsewhere to justify their rashness. Most people did not immediately recognize another casualty of war, the American economy. To pay for the most expensive war in the country's history, the White House loosed an inflation at home and a dollar crisis abroad which developed their own momentum. By the 1970s America's wealth and self-confidence had visibly atrophied. The adventure in Vietnam, far from protecting domestic institutions, almost destroyed them.

BIBLIOGRAPHY

Though observers have hotly debated America's experience overseas during the sixties, most clues to foreign policymaking remain locked in scattered archives. Kennedy left no memoirs, of course, but see two "official histories" written by close friends: Arthur M. Schlesinger, Jr., *A Thousand Days* (1965); and Theodore Sorenson, *Kennedy* (1965). Often more tantalizing than informative, Lyndon Johnson's personal record, *The Vantage Point* (1971), is frankly argumentative. In addition to those sources mentioned at the end of chapter 4, see the results of Daniel Ellsberg's famous robbery in *The Pentagon Papers, The Defense Department History of United States Decision-Making on Vietnam, The Senator Gravel Edition* (5 vols., 1971). For the dangerous confrontation between Washington and Moscow in 1962, see David L. Larson, *The Cuban Crisis of 1962, Selected Documents and Chronology* (1963); and Robert F. Kennedy, *Thirteen Days: A Memoir of the Cuban Missile Crisis* (1967).

Scholars have concentrated especially on the process of decision-making during the Kennedy-Johnson years, largely to discover the reasons for America's disastrous intervention in Southeast Asia. Roger Hilsman, a former assistant secretary of state, gives his views in *To Move a Nation: The Politics of Foreign Policy in the Administration of John F. Kennedy* (1964). See also Richard E. Neustadt, *Alliance Politics* (1970); I. M. Destler, *Presidents, Bureaucrats and Foreign Policy: The Politics of Organizational Reform* (1972); Henry F. Graff, *The Tuesday Cabinet: Deliberation and Decision on Peace and War under Lyndon B. Johnson* (1970); and Thomas Halper, *Foreign Policy Crises: Appearance and Reality in Decision Making* (1971). Townsend Hoopes, assistant secretary of defense under Johnson, argues in *The Limits of Intervention: An Inside Account of How the Johnson Policy of Escalation in Vietnam Was Reversed* (1969) that only the imminence of debacle convinced America's leaders to stop an open-ended war. A most provocative book by David Halberstam, *The Best and the Brightest* (1972), insists that a failure of men—their lack of proportion and respect for others—not a weakness in institutions, misled the country into the maze of Vietnam. For a broader view, see Richard J. Barnet, *The Roots of War* (1972).

For its dispassionate summary, George McTurnan Kahin and John W. Lewis, *The United States in Vietnam* (rev. ed., 1969), remains a valuable chronology. Bernard Fall, especially in *Two Vietnams: A Political and Military Analysis* (1967), and *Vietnam Witness, 1953–1966* (1968), argues that French and American miscalculations grew from their ethnocentricity which hopelessly distorted realities in Southeast Asia. After the war had almost run its course, Frances Fitz Gerald returned to this theme in *Fire in the Lake: The Vietnamese and the Americans in Vietnam* (1972). The best writings in English about Vietnam are the works by Joseph Buttinger, *Vietnam: A Political History* (1968), and *Vietnam: A Dragon Embattled* (2 vols., 1967). Some excellent analysis appeared during the Nixon years. See John Galloway, *The Gulf of Tonkin Resolution* (1971); two excellent books by John T. McAlister, *Vietnam: Origins of Revolution* (1969), and *The Vietnamese and Their Revolution* (1970); William Standard, *Aggression: Our Asian Disaster* (1971); Don Oberdorfer, *Tet!* (1971); and Richard A. Falk, *The Six Legal Dimensions of the Vietnam War* (1968), a good, brief guide to an explosive topic.

On standard foreign policy, see Richard J. Walton, *Cold War and Counterrevolution: The Foreign Policy of John F. Kennedy* (1972); Elie Abel, *The Missile Crisis* (1966); and Jack M. Schick, *The Berlin Crisis 1958–1962* (1971). See also John Newhouse, *De Gaulle and the Anglo-Saxons* (1970); Robert S. Walters, *American and Soviet Aid: A Comparative Analysis* (1970); Jerome Slater, *Intervention and Negotiation: The United States and the Dominican Revolution* (1970); and Harland B. Moulton, *From Superiority to Parity: The United States and the Strategic Arms Race, 1961–1971* (1972). The relationship between American foreign policy and world economic conditions is discussed in David P. Calleo and Benjamin M. Rowland, *America and the World Political Economy* (1973); and Sidney E. Rolfe and James L. Burtle, *The Great Wheel: The World Monetary System* (1973).

The postwar era was a time of giantism and excess. Lyndon Johnson, the extravagant Texan who dominated the middle of the 1960s, provided an appropriate symbol: he drove too fast, threw gargantuan barbecue parties, and in one well-publicized incident, pulled his dog's ears until the puppy yelped. Restraint seemed a quality of the past. The era throbbed with raw power and extremes. American involvement in Vietnam escalated uncontrollably; the president and his critics roared at each other; the economy raced ahead; huge business conglomerates formed; rock singers grew old before they turned thirty; football replaced baseball as the national sport. By 1970 nearly three of every ten homes had more than one television set, and only three of a hundred had no TV at all. The post office, assisted by new zip code numbers and electronic eyes, delivered a yearly average of four hundred pieces of mail to every man, woman, and child. The Gross National Product approached one trillion dollars. Book publishers issued more than thirty-five thousand titles a year, double the number put out just ten years earlier. But growth did not necessarily bring satisfaction. The scale of American life had become nearly incomprehensible. Who could understand a trillion-dollar economy, trace lines of responsibility through the sprawling federal bureaucracy, or gain redress from an impersonal, computerized corporation?

THE ECONOMY: A GATHERING OF GIANTS

The Military-Industrial Complex

In his famous farewell speech of 1961, outgoing President Dwight D. Eisenhower described one of the most important trends affecting

7
The oversized society

American life: a permanent government-supported weapons industry. No longer, he explained, did Americans mobilize civilian industries for war and reconvert them after the peace. Cold-war pressures had kept the economy on a perpetual war footing and created "a permanent armaments industry of vast proportions." The old general warned that "we annually spend on military security more than the net income of all United States corporations," and he expressed fear that the resultant military-industrial complex held the "potential for the disastrous rise of misplaced power."

The military-industrial complex grew even larger during the Vietnam War. This national defense structure consisted, at the top, of politicians, military men, business contractors, and university researchers, and, at the bottom, of workers in defense industries. All of these groups were mutually dependent. Government grants for research and development comprised a significant portion of many university budgets; huge corporations such as General Dynamics and Lockheed depended almost exclusively on government contracts; in 1967 experts estimated that the salaries of nearly three million people came from defense-related work. But the government was beneficiary as well as benefactor: without this complex of research, industry, and manpower, policymakers could not have pursued their idea of national security which, in postwar years, required large-scale military capabilities.

The interests of the military-industrial complex cohered perfectly; the system demanded ever larger expenditures, always rationalized in patriotic language. If the air force wanted a new plane, Boeing wanted a lucrative contract, and the people of the Pacific Northwest wanted more jobs. Taxpayers who shouldered the bill had little control over spiraling costs, for few could evaluate the need for a new weapons system. Sophisticated weaponry made the concept of democratic policymaking increasingly obsolete. America's defense complex ran counter to other old values as well. How could Americans honestly extol the virtues of free enterprise and a free market economy when the Pentagon directed the largest planned economic system outside the Soviet Union?

The electronics industry was one chief beneficiary of government research money. For America, the 1950s and 1960s marked a transition to what political scientist Zbigniew Brzezinski termed a "technetronic age," an age based upon computers and communications networks. In the technetronic era, science and technology, not haphazard experimentation, became the major agents of change: major discoveries seldom came from a lonely basement tinkerer but from the collective work of laboratories which often received government funds.

The American space program—which depended upon the interrelationship of university research, government funding, and industrial production—was also a child of this new age. Shortly after the Soviet

Union launched its Sputnik satellite in 1957, Congress created the National Aeronautics and Space Administration (NASA), and in 1961 President Kennedy committed the nation to landing a man on the moon by 1970. Commenting upon why America should set the moon as its goal, Kennedy explained, "Why climb the highest mountain? Why thirty-five years ago fly the Atlantic? Why does Rice play Texas?" The space program, often compared to the Manhattan Project which developed the atomic bomb during World War II, organized scientific and technical bureaucracies into a crash program to surpass the Soviet Union in manned space exploration.

NASA officials liked to compare their feats to the popular solo flight of Charles Lindbergh in 1927. (Lindbergh celebrated his achievement as a union of man and machine in a book entitled *We*; the astronauts issued a ghost-written account of their adventure called *We Seven*.) But Lindbergh's flight rested largely upon private discoveries and a few backers; the Mercury and Apollo programs, products of government-managed technology, relied upon thousands of people in aerospace industries, operations teams, and recovery forces. The small Mercury program alone required nearly two hundred managers.

The methods and costs of space exploration were beyond the comprehension of most Americans. Some people in the Appalachians refused to believe that moon walks were anything other than television-studio theatrics. Critics of the program's expense called it a moon-doggle and compared it to the pyramids—a feat of much grandeur but little practicality. To counter such charges, NASA tried to project a highly utilitarian image, stressing the civilian "spin-offs" of space research, such as heart pacemakers and miniature electronic parts. But despite its wide publicity, staggering costs, enormous pool of employees, and spectacular technical achievements, the space program seldom attracted wide public enthusiasm.

The Great Business Boom

The huge infusion of government money into the economy, together with a rising level of consumer spending, brought rapid business expansion and made the 1960s the greatest decade of business consolidation since the 1890s. Growth seemed to be the key to economic survival, and the fastest way to expand was to merge with or to purchase other firms. Large corporations acquired ten times greater assets in 1968 than the amount that had changed hands in 1960. This growth of huge enterprises further centralized economic power. By the late sixties, the two hundred largest United States companies controlled 58 percent of all manufacturing assets in the nation.

New companies most often were purchased not by competitors in the same field but absorbed by business empires which managed a wide variety of unrelated industries. Financial dare-devils could no longer legally corner the market in any one product (horizontal monopoly) or establish control over all the steps of production in the manufacture of any one item (vertical monopoly). Modern entrepreneurs, however, pioneered conglomerates, businesses which minimized overall risk by diversifying holdings. Gulf and Western and Transamerica Corporation, two of the wonderchildren of the age, acquired companies as fast as they could find them; they owned Hollywood studios, auto-parts distributorships, land-development corporations, insurance companies, and sports arenas.

The secret of conglomerate growth lay in the acquisition of investment institutions such as insurance companies. These businesses dealt in capital rather than in goods and could funnel a steady stream of investment money into the conglomerate's coffers. With one subsidiary borrowing from another, conglomerates could internally finance their expansion. International Telephone and Telegraph (ITT), in an out-of-court antitrust settlement in 1971, was willing to sell two of its well-known properties, Levitt Construction and Avis Rent-A-Car, in return for government permission to purchase Hartford Fire Insurance Company. The terms of this deal—the largest acquisition in the nation's history—would later enter the Watergate-associated investigations into corruption during the Nixon administration.

Under pressure for rapid growth, some businesses fell into shady dealings and unsound financial practices. The decade was spiced with the kinds of abuses associated with periods of full-throttle expansion: bribed officials, defective products, defrauded consumers, and ineffective government regulations. But Americans of the sixties did little on a small scale, and true to form, one of the most daring frauds of all time racked the business world. A relatively new California insurance company, Equity Funding Corporation, built a phenomenal growth record on the basis of more than $2 billion worth of phony insurance policies and more than $120 million in nonexistent assets. Caught up in the Southern California boom mentality, the company's officials systematically fabricated two-thirds of the firm's policies, sending its insurance in force soaring from $54 million in 1967 to $615 billion just five years later. Government auditors never caught the fraud because they did not check the computers; an associate finally exposed the scandal in 1973. The Equity Funding scandal, probably the biggest computer crime ever, was a "simple perversion of a simple computer system," one data processor at Equity Funding later commented. The *Wall Street Journal* headlined the revelations with a warning: "Crooks and Computers Are an

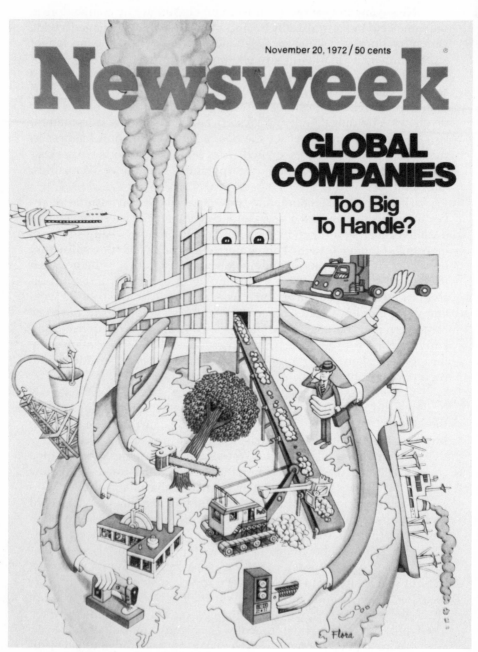

November 20, 1972 / 50 cents

Newsweek

GLOBAL COMPANIES
Too Big To Handle?

Artist James Flora (Agents Frank & Jeff Lavaty, N.Y.)

176

Effective Team." The staid financial daily forecast even greater electronic-assisted frauds in the future.

As American enterprise expanded at home, it also moved into other lands at a pace that astonished and alarmed many foreigners. A variety of motives led American businesspeople to establish operations in foreign lands: cheaper labor, lower interest rates, favorable tax laws, proximity to new markets and raw materials. Whatever the precise constellation of motives in particular cases, the net result was an outflow of American investment dollars which confirmed the nation's worldwide economic supremacy. IBM, for example, provided 70 percent of all computers in the noncommunist world and maintained research labs in most of the developed nations; Standard Oil of New Jersey drilled and distributed oil throughout the globe; Pepsi-Cola was a universal refreshment, admitted even behind the iron curtain.

The financial power of these multinational companies often exceeded that of the nation-states in which they operated. One official for the American Agency for International Development reported in the late 1960s that if the gross national products of nations were ranked with the gross annual sales of corporations, half of the top hundred would be corporations and two-thirds of these would be American-based. Devaluation of the dollar in 1971 slowed the flight of American enterprise abroad, and other multinational competitors—especially Japanese companies—began to challenge Americans in a few fields. Still, the spectre of American economic domination, raised so forcefully by French politician Jean-Jacques Servan-Schreiber in his *American Challenge* (1968), remained strong throughout the world.

Rapid business growth and new technological discoveries also changed the way Americans lived. Natural materials such as wood, wool, cotton, and natural rubber gave way to manmade substitutes— plastics, acrylic fibers, and synthetic rubber. By 1966 thirteen and a half million pounds of plastics were produced, used in everything from children's toys to surgical equipment. In 1968 the quantity of synthetic fibers surpassed the output of natural fibers, and doubleknit cloth soon revolutionized both the men's and women's clothing industries. Middle-class Americans could be distinguished anywhere in the world by the doubleknits they wore, and protesting youth of the 1960s adopted the natural cotton denim of blue jeans as a symbol of revolt against this age of synthetics.

All kinds of new products flooded the market. In 1968 alone almost one thousand new items entered the consumer package-goods field. The stiff competition for the buyer's dollar often made packaging and advertising more important than content. Critics of the highly competititve breakfast-food industry, for example, claimed that the quality of some products was so low that the flashy packages actually had more nutritional value than the overprocessed grain inside them. Fred Friendly, a prominent television executive, noted that "three soap companies account for about 15 percent of the nation's total television sales. This is one reason why Americans know more about detergents and bleaches than they do about Vietnam or Watts." The variety of new products grew so great that finding an unused brand name became a major problem. Large companies set computers to work providing print-outs of letter combinations which sounded attractive—"Exxon" and "Pringles" were just two of the results.

Businesspeople devised new methods to market these products. Throughout the 1960s, independently owned, locally operated shops found their customers turning to large chain or franchise operations which offered greater volume at lower prices. What MacDonalds did for hamburgers, Holiday Inn did for travel, K-Mart for retailing, and 7–11 Stores for neighborhood groceries. Every American city of any size had a "miracle mile" or a "strip" nearly identical to that of every other: a string of discount houses, supermarkets, and fast-food chains (Kentucky Fried Chicken, Arby's Roast Beef, half-a-dozen hamburger palaces). Shopping became easier when the California-based Bank of America introduced BankAmericard. This new kind of credit card, quickly imitated by New York banks, tempted consumers to spend and borrow more, channeled large amounts of consumer purchasing through a few large banks, and soon threatened to make currency nearly obsolete. These new forms of retailing and credit pushed Americans into higher levels of consumption and helped make their living standard the envy of the world.

Ecological Consequences

Galloping growth, however, came at the expense of the environment. To achieve a high living standard, Americans used the country's water, air, minerals, and timber as if they were unlimited, and they purchased more and more resources from foreign lands. In 1970, one expert calculated, Americans comprised less than 6 percent of the human race but used 40 percent of the resources consumed worldwide each year and produced 50 percent of the physical pollution.

Cheap energy was one basic ingredient in America's rapid industrial growth, and its use multiplied at an astonishing rate. Gasoline consumption rose from one billion barrels in 1950 to two and a quarter billion barrels in 1971; production of electricity increased 500 percent between 1950 and 1971. New products were partly to blame. Aluminum, for example, an excellent substitute for some uses of steel and tin, was dubbed "congealed electricity" because of the enormous amounts of energy required to produce it. Americans processed twenty times more aluminum in 1971 than they had before World War II, and each year production figures climbed higher. Aluminum beer cans, aluminum pipe, aluminum siding, all treasured for their light-weight and noncorrosive properties, contributed to the pressure on the environment.

Where would Americans find the energy required to fuel their economy in the future? Advocates of unrestricted development had some answers: strip-mining for coal, more oil drilling in offshore beds, development of atomic power plants, and construction of a pipeline to transport oil from the rich Alaskan slope.

But environmentalist groups, which began to gain strength in the late 1960s, opposed these plans. They argued that strip-mining, which had doubled between 1964 and 1972, destroyed the fertility of huge portions of land and upset the environmental equilibrium. Their outcries against offshore drilling reached a crescendo after spectacular oil spills washed onto shores in Louisiana and California, despoiling beaches and killing wildlife. Atomic power plants also caused alarm among some scientists and environmentalists. While industry and government assured the public that serious malfunctions in atomic reactors were nearly a statistical impossibility, consumer spokespersons such as Ralph Nader charged that near-catastrophes had already occurred and argued that the magnitude of any disaster involving radioactive material made even an infinitesimal risk absolutely unacceptable. Nader and others advocated crash programs to develop energy from safe and plentiful sources such as sun and wind.

Halting construction of the Alaskan pipeline became a cause célèbre among environmentalists, who claimed that the enterprise would upset the ecology of the frozen tundra and adversely affect plants and animals. For several years, groups such as the Sierra Club and Friends of the Earth successfully delayed the pipeline, but the "energy crisis" of 1973 brought rapid congressional approval. Construction of the Alaskan pipeline, along with relaxation of various environmental regulations, showed how quickly Americans would dismiss ecological considerations when faced with energy shortages.

Environmentalists and industrialists also clashed over the problem of pollution. The rising material standards which Americans thought would enhance their comfort bore a price tag of brownish skies, strangely colored rivers, dying lakes, odd-tasting water, and aggravated respiratory problems. Urban areas suffered most visibly; cities such as Los Angeles, New York, and Gary, Indiana, became positive health hazards. Breathing New York's air for a day, one study reported, was the equivalent of smoking four packs of cigarettes. Even areas of lesser population, however, had mounting pollution problems. The picturesque Rocky Mountain city of Missoula, Montana, for example, often lay shrouded in yellow smog; throughout the nation, once-sparkling trout streams turned into sickly trickles of industrial waste. Unrestricted dumping turned Lake Erie into a "dead" body of water and threatened the rest of the Great Lakes, a water network vital to sustaining population in the Northeastern, and Middle Western United States. In 1971 Congress passed a Clean Air Act setting standards for pollution emissions, but the bill was less stringent than environmentalists had desired.

Industrialists, of course, did not favor dead lakes and unhealthy air. But charged with running their companies at a profit, they could not afford to take the long view of many environmentalists. Most wished to postpone environmental concerns to keep their businesses profitable, and they often had the backing of their workers and anyone dependent upon their products. Industrialists and their supporters successfully diluted most efforts at pollution control by using two effective arguments: that regulation would put even greater stress on energy reserves by making it impossible to use high-pollution fuels such as coal, and that the cost of meeting stringent standards would make American industry uncompetitive with foreign enterprises and worsen the already critical balance of payments problem.

In April 1970 environmental groups held Earth Day, a carnival extravaganza of booths and speakers designed to spawn the same kind of nationwide concern that civil rights and antiwar causes had generated during the sixties. But environmentalism never really caught on. Instead, it frequently fell victim to theatrics or triviality. New York's mayor, John Lindsay, received wide publicity when he led a troupe of bicyclers through Manhattan to demonstrate how pleasant "Fun City" might be without traffic jams; first graders absorbed "ecology" lessons almost indistinguishable from the "don't be a litterbug" campaigns of the past; and utility companies passed out ecology tips, solemnly advising their patrons to conserve water by replacing the washers in leaky faucets. Nothing was intrinsically wrong with such actions, but they obscured the dimensions of the environmental problem and distorted Americans' understanding of the word *ecology*.

The science of ecology involved understanding the natural balance necessary to sustain life on this planet. Scientists such as Barry Commoner, author of *The Closing Circle*, were concerned less with unsightly beer cans on the lake shores than with the life-threatening imbalances which resulted when cities and industries dumped wastes into the water. Commoner toured college campuses, warning that severe damage to the ecological system was irreversible, after a point, and that we were rapidly approaching, if we had not already reached, that critical moment. The obsession with careless material growth, he argued, had strained the environment to the breaking point. But confronted with the choice of immediate radical change in living styles or a possible closing circle of disaster at a later time, Americans' decision seemed far from clear.

The Land Hustlers

The great land boom which began in the mid-sixties added to environmentalists' concerns. Huge land-development corporations began subdividing tracts at an alarming rate, focusing their efforts in the "sunshine states" of Florida, California, New Mexico, and Arizona, but also operating in Northern recreational states such as Colorado and Maine. The National Association of Home Builders estimated that Americans built ninety thousand *second* homes in 1971, although the *overall* number of homes constructed that year was lower than it had been a decade earlier. And the number of fishing huts, mountain cabins, seaside bungalows, and retirement villas represented only a fragment. Of the land which was cut into parcels and put up for sale as potential homesites, 97 percent remained close to its original state, with no improvements or structures. Americans of the late sixties, it seemed, just wanted to own a piece of land, whether they intended to build on it immediately or not.

What explained the obsession with land buying? Owning land has always held a special fascination for Americans. Cycles of feverish speculation and ensuing bust have laced American history, as each new generation proved itself as gullible as the last about real estate. In addition, Americans have always viewed open spaces as escape hatches: if life grew too discomforting, new land could bring a fresh start and the possiblity of success. The sixties provided a perfect climate for another land boom. The new affluence brought second homes within the reach of millions; faster automobiles and new interstate highways made distant vacation homes practical; increased leisure time and earlier retirement raised demand for recreation. And in a decade of fast economic growth, it was easy to appeal to people's spirit of adventure, to convince them that they could afford the monthly payments and that land was always a good investment. One company's sales pitch asked, "Do you know any big rich man who doesn't own real estate? . . . Wouldn't it be wise to buy land somewhere—anywhere—before prices get out of reach?" Land hustlers rolled out (and usually overstated) forecasts of population growth and made land ownership seem like a vanishing luxury.

While appealing to buyers' hopes for a quick buck, companies also capitalized on frustrations and fears. Had enough of crime in the street? Buy land in sparsely settled Maine. Had enough of shoveling snow?

181

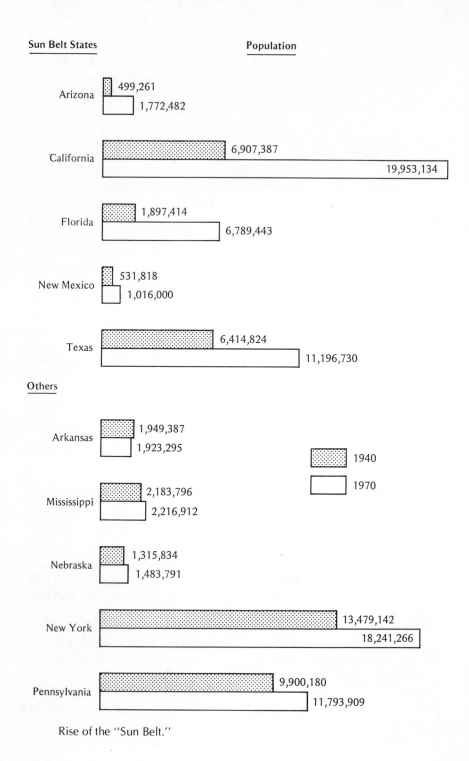

Rise of the "Sun Belt."

Buy land in Florida. Had enough of high-pressure jobs? Get away from it all in Colorado. Worried about growing old? Plan now for a healthy retirement in Arizona. To those who felt overwhelmed by modern life and feared that they had lost control of their existence, it was comforting to think that things could be scaled down on a little plot of land somewhere. Most people never built on their land; many never even saw it. Just knowing it was there, in many cases, provided escape enough.

As soon as businessmen discovered how easily they could sell land, "development" corporations sprang up everywhere. Some created attractive planned communities with good sanitary facilities, nearby employment opportunities, and luxurious recreation areas. But too many others simply bought large tracts of cheap land and resold it in expensive lot-sized packages. A development company in Florida, for example, purchased some swampy land for $180 an acre and quickly resold it for $640 an acre. For this enormous profit, the company did not drain the land, build roads, plan sanitation facilities, or construct major buildings. It merely hired a high-pressure sales force, ran advertisements in newspapers around the country, and gave the supposed community a fancy name. Word of such profits turned subdividing into a national craze, and most conglomerate enterprises quickly created land-development subsidiaries. By the early 1970s, developers in California were buying fifty thousand to one hundred thousand acres a year; subdivided land near Albuquerque, New Mexico, was slated to hold a population four times the size of Baltimore; and plots for sale in Colorado would have increased the state's population five times. In

Bill Wunsch, The Denver Post

An undeveloped development in Colorado.

North Carolina a real estate salesman and a former lawyer were charged with mail fraud after allegedly trying to sell over 60,000 acres of the Great Smoky Mountain National Park.

Most parcels were sold unimproved as "investments," though little of this land could ever be profitable. If families settled on all the subdivided lots in New Mexico, for example, there would be nowhere near enough water for survival. (In some areas southwest of Santa Fe the water table had already fallen a hundred feet.) Some companies sold lots in areas where the state refused to grant septic tank permits, and in developments which provided sewer service, the waste often drained into the same streams or lakes that had originally made the land attractive. Scientists studying popular recreational spots such as Lake Tahoe and the Pocono Mountains warned that pollution from excessive population threatened the areas' ecological viability. But if unhappy buyers decided to resell their land, they did not have high-pressure sales tactics to assist them, and many lost their money. Two-thirds of the thousand investors in one California development who responded to a poll said that they would not make the purchase again, and half of them already had their lots up for sale at a loss.

Land-development companies epitomized the big "catch-22" of modern America; the more people tried to escape bigness and discontent, the more they were trapped. By the early 1970s, concern mounted among government officials, consumer and environmentalist groups, and people who lived in afflicted states. Bumper stickers began to appear: "Our National Product Is Gross"; "Don't Californicate Colorado"; "Undevelop." But halting subdivision of land took more than slogans. If some local people tried to curb abuses, others had personal economic stakes in rising land values. In most states, boosterism continued to run so strongly that anything labeled "development" had a rhetorical advantage which outweighed its actual impact. Only the sluggish economy of the mid-seventies slowed the land boom.

THE SOCIETY: A MAGICAL MYSTERY TOUR

Visual Arts

At the Museum of Modern Art in New York on March 17, 1960, a Swiss artist, Jean Tinguely, displayed his *Homage to New York*. The 23-by 27-foot work of art was a tangle of junk which destroyed itself. Powered by fifteen motors, the creation beat, burned, and sawed itself to death as it produced music, abstract painting, and an offspring which moved about by itself for a time. Tinguely's contraption, part of a vogue of artistic "happenings," reflected one of the basic artistic trends of the 1960s and 1970s: concentration on action as well as on objects. It was not long before a young American artist, Chris Burden, took the next logical step. Wiring his body to an electrical outlet and placing a pail of water nearby, he unsuccessfully tempted visitors to the art gallery to electrocute him. This act of "art," like many others, involved the artist and the viewer as an integral part of the work. Presumably, the emotions aroused at the moment of execution, or even at the contemplation of it, were the preeminent artistic creation.

The art of the sixties surpassed earlier forms not only in scope and subject matter, but also in sheer size. Al Leslie, who went from abstract painting in the fifties to an interest in photography, began painting huge photo-like portraits often surpassing nine feet. Others could not contain their artistic visions in rooms at all and moved outside into natural settings. Plans for hanging curtains across canyons or placing ground markers miles (even continents) apart so that the completed work could be seen only from the air seemed appropriate artistic expressions for the space age.

Many older, established artists were still around, and although their work seemed almost conventional by standards of the late 1960s, it commanded fantastic prices. A set of bronze ale cans by Jasper Johns sold for $90,000. The works of Claes Oldenburg, Willem de Kooning, Robert Rauschenberg, Mark Rothko, Frank Stella, and the decade's most popular (and most traditional) painter, Andrew Wyeth, also brought high prices. The art world was stunned when an Australian museum bought the late Jackson Pollock's *Blue Poles* (1953) for $2 million, the highest price ever paid for a modern painting.

Like so much else during the 1960s, art became so big—both in definition and in profit—that it defied facile generalization. The abstract expressionism of Pollock and de Kooning survived, while new trends went in all directions: pop art, op art, earth art, performance art, process art, and more. Some artists abandoned worldly concerns to experiment

Photo by Paul Katz

Composition by graffiti aces.

with pure form and color; others, following the tradition of Ben Shahn, produced undisguised commentary on contemporary problems. As artists strove to break every convention and to explore every artistic dimension to its extremes, standards for defining "art" collapsed. To an age that accepted as art an artist making love in a public gallery or a replica of an IBM card, it seemed that nothing in life was *not* art. (Though if this was the real message of the decade, few Americans and few of the artists themselves felt comfortable with its implications.)

Americans interpreted the new artistic freedom in widely different ways. People on the political right often saw it as subversive, a movement encouraged by foreign enemies to demoralize youth. Others saw free-wheeling artistic standards and the proliferation of local galleries as ominous signs of artistic decay which pointed in two equally dismal directions. Artists might discover that publicity agents were more important than talent, and art would become the preserve of promoters, conmen, and exhibitionists. Or the sheer volume of all kinds of art would activate a variation of Gresham's law—bad taste would drive out good, and fad would replace substance. More optimistic observers, however, pointed out that American artists commanded worldwide respect and that artistic liberation might be producing a period of major cultural flowering.

Theater

Wild diversity and greater interaction between artist and viewer also entered the theater. Broadway, a street once virtually synonymous with theater, declined artistically and financially throughout the sixties. As its theaters showed a tedious fare of high-priced musicals to half-filled houses—seemingly limping along from one Neil Simon production to the next—cheaper and more experimental theaters sprang up, first "off" Broadway and then "off-off" Broadway. Producing plays that were often bad, frequently mediocre, and occasionally brilliant, these smaller houses attracted serious theatergoers throughout the decade.

The startling success of one "off-off" Broadway play, *Hair*, had a far-reaching impact. *Hair*, an irreverent "tribal-love-rock musical" inspired by the hippie movement of the mid-1960s, made a commercial success out of a protest against commercialism. Its attempt at audience involvement and its moment of nudity (when the cast briefly disrobed on a darkened stage) seemed mild by later standards but provoked heated disputes at the time. *Hair* moved to Broadway and subsequently toured America, spreading controversy throughout the country at the same time that the hippie life it portrayed became a cliché. *Hair* inevitably spawned imitators. Many theaters became preoccupied with rock music, audience-actor interaction, or nudity; few did well. *Oh! Calcutta!* was the only nude revue which really made money, and *Jesus Christ Superstar* the only other rock musical to duplicate *Hair*'s success.

Less commercial than *Hair* and more genuinely experimental was an avant garde company called the Living Theater. Begun as an artistically radical troupe in the 1950s, the Living Theater grew increasingly political, championing civil rights and antiwar causes. After the government closed it down, ostensibly for nonpayment of taxes, the group moved to Europe, where its members lived as a commune and concentrated on radical theater which would employ audience involvement to raise social consciousness. When the Living Theater returned to the United States in 1968, it spread its protest against drug laws, clothing conventions, sexual repression, and the establishment through unstructured plays which relied on audience reaction and response. To some critics, the Living Theater and other "guerrilla theater" groups symbolized the search for newer and more relevant forms of artistic expression; to others they represented self-indulgent exhibitionism, masquerading as art only because misguided critics had abandoned all standards and confused innovation with creativity.

A development more lasting than "guerrilla theater" was regional theater. New York had long been the country's tastemaker, but people in other cities began to recognize that artistic awareness was not bounded by the East River and the Hudson. One leader of a community-theater movement in Chicago commented, "The New York audience is like a marshmallow that's been in the fire a long time. It has a hard shell of sophistication and disdain, but underneath you'll find it soft and gooey." The Tyrone Guthrie Theater in Minneapolis, the Mark Taper Forum in Los Angeles, the Yale Repertory and Long Wharf Theaters in New Haven, Connecticut, and the Alley Theater in Houston were just a few of the thriving regional theaters. These community-sponsored efforts indicated that American theater had survived the 1960s and was alive and well in the 1970s.

Movies and Literature

Just as theater turned away from Broadway, the movie business abandoned Hollywood. For more than three decades, Hollywood and filmmaking had been synonymous. Using their sprawling back-lots and deploying armies of contract players and stars, the major studios nourished the dreams of moviegoers. Young men dueled alongside Errol Flynn or Clark Gable, while women floated through the glamorous world of Barbara Stanwyck or Lana Turner. But during the 1960s the giant studios and Hollywood hit bad days. Challenged by television and

187

victimized by urban decay, which frightened many people away from the old downtown movie palaces, Hollywood's film moguls watched box office receipts decline steadily. During the early 1960s, some producers tried to reverse the slide by making long-running extravaganzas, multimillion-dollar productions which dwarfed the penny-ante fare on television. A few of these films, such as *Spartacus*, made money and displayed some degree of cinematic style, but most were expensive duds—financial and artistic disasters. Seeking to reduce production costs and to bring new realism to the screen, many filmmakers completely abandoned the Hollywood sets and shot entirely on location, often outside the United States. At the same time, many of the old stars either died or retired; others, such as Rock Hudson and Elizabeth Taylor, suddenly discovered that their names alone no longer guaranteed a film's financial success. Increasingly, innovative young filmmakers cast relatively unknown performers in films which Hollywood's old guard would have considered off-beat losers.

Many of the successful films of the 1960s and early 1970s appealed to younger viewers, particularly to college-educated people. Stanley Kubrick—with the aid of Peter Sellers—lampooned the insanity of nuclear diplomacy in *Dr. Strangelove*, explored the mystical science fiction of Arthur C. Clarke in *2001: A Space Odyssey*, and examined the problems of violence and behavior modification in *A Clockwork Orange*. Young people flocked to these three films, which continued to draw big crowds whenever they were rerun in college communities. Another innovative director, Arthur Penn, penetrated the myths surrounding two young bandits of the 1930s—*Bonnie and Clyde*—and painted a sympathetic picture of the youth culture in *Alice's Restaurant*, a film based upon Arlo Guthrie's best-selling song. In one of the most surprising hits of recent years, Peter Fonda and Dennis Hopper updated the theme of the open road in *Easy Rider*. The story of two hippies who used a drug sale to finance a motorcycle trip across the Southwest to New Orleans, *Easy Rider* interwove all the themes of the new American cinema: social criticism, sex, and violence. Spokespersons for more traditional Hollywood films—in which stars stayed out of bed until they were married and then stayed discreetly covered—denounced the decline of old standards. But filmmakers recognized that only a handful of "family pictures" attracted as many viewers as the racier and more violent products. Producers rushed to sign new, young directorial "talents" and tried to pack more gore and naked flesh into their movies. Although some tastelessly exploited violence and sex, serious filmmakers also benefited from the lifting of old taboos.

By the early 1970s, most producers and directors abandoned the idea of general-audience films in favor of making special movies for special audiences. Before public boredom took its toll, X-rated films did a big business—not only in sleazy downtown houses but in many new suburban theaters and in small towns. At a more serious level, Robert Altman broke old molds with films such as *M.A.S.H.* (a kind of antiwar comedy), *McCabe and Mrs. Miller* (an anti-Western), and *The Long Goodbye* (an anti-detective film). In a series of loosely constructed but hilarious comedies, Woody Allen won the allegiance of people who appreciated anarchistic humor in the tradition of the Marx brothers. Those who liked the old shoot-'em-up genre found plenty of blood and action in *The Godfather, The French Connection,* and an endless series of police-detective-gunfighter films starring Clint Eastwood. Many of the best new films displayed a deep pessimism about American society, but nostalgia buffs could remember the 1920s in *The Great Gatsby,* the 1930s in *The Sting,* the 1940s and 1950s in *The Way We Were,* and the early 1960s in *American Graffiti.* Attempting to summarize recent trends, one critic described the film industry as in a state of "creative anarchy."

Most serious literary critics might have borrowed the term *chaos,* but they would have been very stingy with the term *creative.* The lack of outstanding literature, according to most observers, did not indicate a shortage of budding authors. By the early 1970s, one leading literary magazine received an average of ten manuscripts every hour, and one novelist estimated that the United States had more people writing fiction than reading it. Almost everyone with a typewriter, it seemed, had something to say about his or her personal problems and the turmoil of postwar society. Inevitably, critical acclaim oftentimes depended upon whether reviewers and writers shared the same frustrations. There were few Faulkners or Fitzgeralds—writers whom most critics considered great literary talents. In 1974 the Pulitzer Prize for fiction went begging: the jurors chose Thomas Pynchon's *Gravity's Rainbow,* but the Pulitzer advisory board dismissed the book as "unreadable," "turgid," "overwritten," and "obscene."

Like film producers, book publishers had difficulty finding works which might at least win popular acceptance, if not universal critical acclaim. Even picking a winning "potboiler" proved difficult, and many publishers conceded their confusion. Publishers and reviewers generally praised the works of Pynchon, John Barth, Grace Paley, and William Gass. Some other writers sold great numbers of books, particularly in paperback editions, but people like Jacqueline Susann *(The Love Machine)* and Richard Bach *(Johnathan Livingston Seagull)* hardly qualified as serious authors. Perhaps Kurt Vonnegut, in his best efforts, came closest to satisfying both critics and massive numbers of readers: his books *Slaughterhouse Five* and *Cat's Cradle* combined an impish sense of humor with a deep moral outrage against the state of American society.

Popular Entertainment: Sports and Music

The trends in professional sports reflected the giantism and violence in American society after 1960. There were more leagues, more teams, more fans, and more television coverage; players' salaries increased, and ticket prices rose. In 1960 big-league baseball still dominated the sports scene, and the two major leagues continued to expand into new cities during the 1960s and 1970s. But despite its growth, the national pastime lost ground to other spectator sports, particularly to the faster-moving and generally more violent games of football, basketball (a noncontact sport only in theory), and ice hockey. Pro football's much balleyhooed Super Bowl replaced the World Series as sports' most talked-about annual attraction. Cities competed vigorously for almost any type of professional franchise, with lucrative television contracts and generous tax writeoffs making the lure of a team even more attractive. Supported by pacts with ABC and then NBC, the American Football League successfully challenged the older National Football League. Threatened by a potentially ruinous bidding war for top players, the two leagues finally merged in 1970. Even though similar financial problems troubled basketball and hockey, new "major" leagues and more teams were organized. Always seeking new forms of competitive products to sell, promoters marketed golf tournaments, imported European-style soccer, and even team competition in tennis. Only professional boxing, beset by the persistent taint of fixed matches and a declining supply of hungry fighters, really lost ground in the 1960s. Still, a contest for the heavyweight championship, especially one involving Muhammed Ali, could reap more money than any other single sports event.

Sports became bigger and bigger business, even at the college level. Top players began to hire specialized "sports agents," to seek investment opportunities or tax shelters, and to sign lucrative contracts endorsing products. One shrewd agent maneuvered the rival pro hockey leagues into paying his client, a very ordinary player, $1 million to avoid complicated legal problems. When fast-food chains became hot investments during the 1960s, sports celebrities like Joe Namath and Muhammed Ali challenged Colonel Sanders and McDonalds for the drive-in trade. Namath, the sometimes brilliant but mostly injured quarterback of the New York Jets, used his reputation as a swinging bachelor to give sex appeal to products as diverse as shaving cream, popcorn poppers, and pantyhose. After breaking Babe Ruth's lifetime home run record, Henry Aaron signed a $5 million contract with Magnavox. And with the rising popularity and profitability of women's sports, girls could dream of duplicating the athletic and financial feats of tennis star Billie Jean King.

190

Boston
Foxboro
New York City
Jersey City
Philadelphia
Baltimore
Washington, D.C.
Quebec
Montreal
Ottawa
Toronto
Rochester
Buffalo
Pittsburgh
Capital City
Norfolk
Greensboro
Jacksonville
Miami
Hamilton
Cleveland
Cincinnati
Atlanta
Detroit
Louisville
Birmingham
New Orleans
Indianapolis
Memphis
Chicago
Green Bay
Milwaukee
St. Louis
Minneapolis
Kansas City
Houston
Omaha
Dallas
San Antonio
Arlington
Winnipeg
CANADA
Regina
UNITED STATES
Denver
Calgary
Salt Lake City
Phoenix
Edmonton
Vancouver
Seattle
Anaheim
Portland
Los Angeles
San Diego
Oakland
San Jose
San Francisco

• home of a professional sports team, 1974

191

Sports figures continued to be society's heroes. Some players, like football's Jim Brown, retired in favor of full-time filmmaking, but others, such as O. J. Simpson and the ubiquitous Namath, found it more profitable to hop back and forth between stadium and sound stage. Inevitably, politicians tried to use the glamor which surrounded bigtime sports. Richard Nixon assiduously cultivated his image as the nation's number one sports fan. (He even contributed his own "trick" play to the 1972 Super Bowl; perhaps an evil omen, the play lost thirteen yards.) During the 1968 and 1972 presidential races, candidates rushed to sign up prominent athletes for their campaign teams.

Many rock and roll stars surpassed sports figures as popular heroes and financial entrepreneurs. Leading performers received huge fees for concert appearances and staggering royalties from album sales. Some superstars, like Janis Joplin, Jimi Hendrix, and Jim Morrison, lived at a frenetic pace, spending money wildly while killing their talent and ultimately themselves on drugs and alcohol. When Morrison succumbed to a heart attack at twenty-seven, physicians reported that his internal organs resembled those of a person in his fifties. Other stars displayed more concern about their health and their financial balance sheets. Bob Dylan, the Beatles, and James Brown became multimillionaires; even the Grateful Dead, a group closely associated with the hippie movement, eventually concentrated upon cash flows and tax writeoffs as much as upon music. In 1973 *Forbes*, a business magazine, estimated that at least fifty rock superstars earned between $2 million and $6 million a year. "The idea all along," admitted Alice Cooper, "was to make $1 million. Otherwise the struggle wouldn't have been worth it. . . . Look at me. I'm twenty-four, but I look thirty."

In addition to obtaining great financial rewards, rock musicians slowly gained serious critical attention. The success of the Beatles and Dylan helped rock music escape the be-bop-a-lula image of the "greasy '50s," and many talented musicians turned to rock or to folk-rock as serious forms of artistic expression. The poetic lyrics of Dylan and Paul Simon interpreted the frustrated dreams of restless youth, their concern about the "sounds of silence" ("people talking without listening"), and their outrage against the persistence of social injustice. Young composers blended various types of musical styles into the rock idiom: traditional folk music, jazz, black blues, and country-Western music all influenced post-1960 trends. *Tommy*, a rock opera by The Who, won wide acclaim, and filmmakers ultimately made a movie version. Rock aficionados studied various forms of rock—the "Motown sound" of the Supremes and the Four Tops, the "Nashville sound" associated with the capital of country-Western music and such diverse performers as The Band and Kris Kristofferson; the "California sound" first popularized by the Beach Boys; the "bubble-gum music" of Donny Osmond and the Jackson Five; and the sadistic "freak rock" of Alice Cooper and the bisexual-masochistic David Bowie.

By the 1970s, rock music enjoyed a secure place in the cultural spectrum. The Madison Square Garden wedding of Sly Stone, for example, attracted guests such as John Kennedy, Jr., and Andy Warhol. Following the successful pattern of *Rolling Stone*, rock magazines not only reported musical trends and peephole gossip, but they branched into film criticism and investigative political reporting. Even the *New York Times* hired a rock critic, who reviewed a Rolling Stones concert with the kind of attention once reserved exclusively for "serious" music. Initially considered an ear-splitting diversion for teeny-boppers, rock fulfilled the prophecy of one of its founding fathers, Chuck Berry: "Roll over Beethoven, tell Tchaikovsky the news."

The Educational Labyrinth

The pressure of the baby-boom generation, the demands of a rapidly expanding economy, and the concern with minority groups brought enormous changes to America's educational establishment in the postwar era. Thousands of new schools had to be built and equipped, and many corporations stood ready to sell the latest in instructional devices. Under Lyndon Johnson's Great Society programs, federal funds became available for expanding and upgrading education. Almost every suburban classroom had its arsenal of audiovisual equipment: projectors, tape recorders, television sets, record players, and overhead projectors. Some instructors began to use "teaching packages" containing all kinds of material to help students understand a particular topic or concept. Most of the new techniques sought to involve students as active participants rather than as passive listeners. In some schools, architects eliminated walls, creating an open and airy environment in which students would, hopefully, become more expressive.

The educational revolution affected course content as well as teaching techniques. The "new math" and the "new English" substituted analysis and understanding for traditional categories and extensive memorization; the "new social studies" emphasized personal evaluation of documents rather than regurgitation of names and dates. Under pressure from women's organizations and minority groups, most schools replaced the stereotyped middle-class characters of Dick and Jane. At its best, the educational revolution promised to produce people who could think, evaluate, and make critical judgments. At its worst, it could degenerate into multimedia entertainment with little intellectual substance. Undoubtedly, changes in method outstripped changes in educational personnel, and many older teachers found themselves confused and resentful. New approaches which worked in a laboratory school did not automatically succeed in the average classroom. Brighter pupils easily adapted to the "new math," but slower students graduated without the basic skills needed to balance a checkbook. After more than a decade of experimentation, critics of the new techniques contended that "Johnny still can't read, and he can't · add, either."

One answer to the failure of traditional classrooms was to offer education outside the school system. Some parents who disliked the "authoritarianism" of traditional public schools sent their children to experimental "free schools." In response to criticism of education for minority children (such as Jonathan Kozol's *Death at an Early Age*), some reformers attempted to use the free-school concept in ghetto areas. Head Start, originally a Great Society program, attempted to provide educational experiences for poor and minority preschoolers so that they would enter kindergarten on a par with more "privileged" middle-class children. Educational television also helped preschoolers and reached dropouts, adults, and school-aged youngsters as well. Anyone with a television could view an array of educational material ranging from American history to language instruction to guitar playing.

In the mid-sixties Congress appropriated funds for a Public Broadcasting System, a pilot project emphasizing educational and public-affairs programming. Among other things, public television developed the most successful venture in children's shows—"Sesame Street." Colorful and fast-moving, "Sesame Street" had its viewers reciting numbers, letters, and difficult words (some in Spanish) before they entered kindergarten. Although "Sesame Street" captivated both parents and children, traditionalists disliked the program's flashy style while some innovators criticized its emphasis on repetition. By the early 1970s, the national government's commitment to educational television had waned, largely because of controversial programs (especially politically-oriented news broadcasts) and opposition from the commercial broadcasting networks. Some of the more popular programs, such as "Sesame Street," continued under a variety of foundation grants, but by the mid-seventies government-supported educational television seemed in trouble.

Many schools experienced rapid changes in their student bodies during the 1960s. Especially in rural areas, public officials worked to consolidate small schools into better-equipped large ones. As a result, the size of educational institutions increased dramatically. In 1950 there were over eighty-six thousand school systems in the country, averaging about three hundred students each; by 1965 there were fewer than 30,000 systems, averaging 1,400 students each. Most children no longer knew all their classmates or teachers, and many students rode buses to school. The undoubted educational gains of consolidation came at the expense of nearby facilities and a feeling of community.

As long as school buses assisted consolidation of small schools, they were generally welcomed as symbols of educational progress, but when courts began to order busing to fulfill another educational function—racial integration—many white people began to view them as part of a sinister plot. In Pontiac, Michigan, vigilantes destroyed a whole fleet of school buses in an attempt to stop racial integration (a policy which, despite the protests, was eventually carried out with fair success). In the late 1960s and particularly in the political campaigns of 1970 and 1972, busing provided the focus of discussion on civil rights questions. Using buses to achieve "racial balance" raised complicated social, legal, and educational problems. Even some minority-group parents denounced forced integration, fearing that their children would lose traditional cultural values in white-dominated schools. They called for "community control" rather than desegregation. Debates over issues such as these, perhaps more than the actual mixture of races itself, kept many school systems in a state of turmoil into the seventies.

The baby-boom generation also strained institutions of higher education. Universities contended not only with the natural population increase but also with a rising percentage of youth who chose to go to college. In 1955 only 27 percent of college-aged people attended school; by 1965 the figure had risen to 40 percent. The flood of new students stemmed from private affluence, government assistance programs, and the desire of many young men to avoid the draft by staying in school. Graduate schools also boomed. By the mid-1960s there were about a quarter of a million full-time graduate students, three of five receiving some form of financial support. Half of all the Ph.D. degrees granted in the United States between 1861 and 1970 were earned in the sixties. A researcher, writing in 1971, commented that "we have created a graduate education and research establishment in American universities that is about 30 to 50 percent larger than we shall effectively use in the 1970s and early 1980s."

Large numbers of students gave university life the appearance of a business (or a factory, some students said). During the mid-1960s, most state universities computerized registration and recordkeeping, an innovation which increased both the efficiency and the impersonality of college life. As universities expanded their physical plants, administrators had to devote more time to land purchases, financial arrangements, and construction problems. Even feeding and housing so many students required bureaucracies of substantial size. Sometimes, it seemed, education was purely incidental. In this business atmosphere, teachers' unions inevitably developed. Such organizations helped instructors obtain job security, fringe benefits, and retirement plans. But the growing adversary relationship between faculty and administration further fragmented the university community and sometimes distracted attention from the primary goal of education. Caught in the middle of rapidly growing institutions, students reacted in various ways. Some found the expansion and disruption exciting; some found it demoralizing. Some chose to go to small liberal arts colleges; some spent four years protesting and demonstrating. The vast majority quietly muddled through.

Give Me That Big-time Religion

During the 1950s some observers happily noticed that Americans were becoming an increasingly religious people. Church membership climbed steadily; President Eisenhower spread "piety along the Potomac"; and the Reverend Norman Vincent Peale's popular *Power of Positive Thinking* seemed to spread faith and optimism throughout the land. In 1955 sociologist Will Herberg noted that the Judeo-Christian religious tradition was merging with American ideals to produce a consensus on deep-seated values among Protestants, Catholics, and Jews. A few skeptics reminded Americans that church attendance did not necessarily measure religious commitment and charged that churches emphasized form over substance, fund-raising over worship. But if the religious messages were vacuous, at least the sanctuaries were full. Most churchgoers seemed content with the way things were.

Churches, however, mirrored the society at large, and they did not escape the turmoil of the 1960s; the bureaucratization, the split over social issues, and the disenchantment of the young. By the end of the decade, established churches had been wracked by factionalism, had lost membership, and were threatened by an array of newer sects and evangelical movements.

The merger movement during the sixties became almost as fashionable in religion as in business. Mainstream Protestant denominations seemed preoccupied with consolidation and centralization. Lutherans, Methodists, and Congregationalists each approved important mergers arranged by their national decisionmaking bodies and accepted by most local congregations. Greater centralization crept into other functions as well. More and more, national church boards set church policy, raised funds, budgeted money, and directed missionary and social efforts. The

196

umbrella organization for Protestant churches, the National Council of Churches, revamped its structure in mid-decade to further centralize direction of its affairs. But the interjection of national-level decisions into affairs of individual churches often created dissension within congregations.

When national church bodies, which were fairly liberal politically, began to express themselves on controversial issues such as civil rights or the war in Vietnam, factional disputes in local congregations became severe. Many Americans wanted their church to remain detached from social issues, as it had in the 1950s; others pressed for the church to be even more active in protest against injustice and inhumanity. The split over the role of the church was basic, and it was bitter. Many pastors walked a tightrope, fearing that a lean toward either side might lose half their congregation. The lack of a clear identity drove many people out of the church and into agnosticism or uninstitutionalized, personal religion.

The Catholic church had to contend not only with social issues—Catholics were bitterly divided between blue-collar conservatism and the "Catholic Left radicalism" of priests such as Daniel and Phillip Berrigan—but Catholics faced even more explosive matters of church policy. The Second Vatican Council of 1962–65 ushered in a reformist period by substituting English for Latin in the liturgy. After this, demands accelerated for greater changes. While religious traditionalists looked on in horror, some Catholics pressed for liberalization of rules on priestly celibacy and birth control, and others endorsed folk-rock masses.

American Jews confronted a problem even more baffling than divisions over doctrine and social policy: how to maintain an ethnic and religious identity. Greater numbers of Jewish young people failed to understand or follow their Hebrew school lessons; many married gentiles. In fact, the majority of American Jews, while still identifying themselves as part of a Jewish ethnic group, belonged to no synagogue or temple. Economic success and the decline of anti-Semitism seemed to pose a greater threat to the Jewish faith than old-style persecutions.

Discontent within established churches and general social turmoil helped produce new movements and faiths. Evangelism swept the country, turning such luminaries as Billy Graham, Oral Roberts, and Billy James Hargis into millionaires. Although their religious organizations were often huge bureaucracies relying upon mass media and the latest advertising techniques, their evangelism attracted people through its appeal to personal religion and past virtues. Evangelical fundamentalism provided an anchor for many Americans who felt buffeted by uncontrolled change.

Some popular preachers, such as Carl McIntire and Billy James Hargis, closely linked Christianity, anticommunism, and ultra-right-wing politics. Hargis charged that the Equal Rights Amendment would bring the nation to the brink of hell, and his organization carried on a well-funded campaign against women's liberation. In early 1970 he adopted the slogan "soap and water, haircuts and dresses." He challenged the "degenerate idea abroad today that Jesus was a welfare case looking like a shiftless 'hippie,'" and suggested, "If anyone can find any Biblical evidence that Jesus had long hair, please send it along." McIntire joined Hargis in an attack on the environmentalist movement. He charged, "It has been thought that the great emphasis upon ecology was a diversionary tactic to turn people's minds away from . . . what the Communists are doing throughout the world to take over. But now it is seen to be even deeper than that; it involved the rejection of Christianity."

While Hargis and McIntire occupied the far right, Oral Roberts and Billy Graham became important establishment figures. Roberts financed his own university in Oklahoma and used the school's successful basketball team as a promotional device. (During one stretch the squad lost only 19 of 134 games.) He also built a huge television empire which rivaled that of the acknowledged king of evangelists, Billy Graham. Still, Graham continued to be the most revered fundamentalist leader. He took his crusades around the world, preaching to crowds of over a hundred thousand people, and he became an important spiritual counselor to President Nixon, often leading prayer breakfasts at the White House. Year after year he stayed near the top of the list of "most admired Americans."

During the 1960s wholly new religious movements sprang up, particularly among the young. The Bahá'i faith built several breathtaking and expensive structures in the United States and gained numerous converts; members of the Hare Krishna sect, with their shaved heads and robes, appeared on the streets of larger cities; "Jesus freaks" replaced political agitators on some college campuses; the Children of God and other communal groups attracted middle-class youth who were willing to renounce their families and adopt a new life and loyalty; and the "Perfect Master," Guru Maharaj Ji, gained a wide following, including ex-political radical Rennie Davis. Religion took on other dimensions as well. Americans became fascinated with spiritualism, mysticism, and transcendental meditation. Bookstores expanded their sections on religion and the occult, and the success of *Rosemary's Baby* and *The Exorcist* indicated that such subjects had wide appeal to moviegoers. Many people of all ages and political persuasions, it seemed, looked to religion for escape from a bureaucratic, centralized, and oversized society.

By the middle of the 1970s, the idea became commonplace that sheer size, in and of itself, was a major social problem. The Watergate affair and other illegal activities by the Nixon administration highlighted the consequences of giantism in the executive branch of the national government; congressional committees and political economists warned of the dangerous machinations of multinational corporations; and in a surprising move, the Department of Justice filed an antitrust action against the giant telephone monopoly, American Telephone and Telegraph. Yet neither denunciations of bigness nor actions such as these provided any real solutions. For example, could the national government ever catch up with the operations of multinational giants? Would a lengthy legal battle (experts predicted that it would drag on until the 1980s) between an army of lawyers from the Justice Department and Ma Bell's corps of attorneys really serve the public interest? Only incautious social seers volunteered easy answers and quick solutions. Perhaps the most popular means for dealing with the dilemma of an oversized society was to attend one of the numerous disaster movies. People flocked to theaters to see the sinking of a giant ocean liner *(The Poseidon Adventure)*, the destruction of the sprawling city of Los Angeles *(Earthquake)*, the toppling of a majestic skyscraper *(The Towering Inferno)*, and the undoing of the overblown Nixon Administration *(All the President's Men)*. This type of exorcism, however, proved much more difficult away from the silver screen.

BIBLIOGRAPHY

The best introduction to the growth in scale of American social and economic institutions in the postwar period is W. Lloyd Warner's extensive, though now somewhat outdated, *The Emergent American Society: Large Scale Organizations* (1967).

The changes in government–business economic relations in postwar America are effectively presented in John Kenneth Galbraith, *The New Industrial State* (1971); Seymour Melman, *Pentagon Capitalism* (1970); and James L. Clayton, ed., *The Economic Impact of the Cold War* (1970). An excellent study of the multinational corporation is Raymond Vernon, *Sovereignty at Bay* (1970). Harry M. Trebing, ed., *The Corporation in the American Economy* (1970); and Robert Sobel, *The Age of Giant Corporations* (1972), cover other developments in business. Issues of land use and environmental concern are covered in the wide variety of articles in Garrett De Bell, ed., *The Environmental Handbook* (1970). Rachel Carson, *Silent Spring* (1962); Barry Commoner, *The Closing Circle* (1971); and Paul Ehrlich, *The Population Bomb* (1968), were instrumental in stimulating environmental concern.

Trends in education are analyzed in great detail in Daniel Bell, *Post-Industrial Society* (1973). Two influential critiques of mass education are Charles Silberman, *Crisis in the Classroom* (1970); and Jonathan Kozol, *Death at an Early Age* (1967).

Trends in culture and entertainment are best followed by referring to contemporary periodicals, but Richard Kostelanetz, ed., *The New American Arts* (1965), provides a good introduction. Stephen Stepanchev, *American Poetry Since 1945* (1965); Alvin B. Kernan, ed., *The Modern American Theater* (1967); and Barbara Rose, *American Art Since 1900* (1967), are useful. On rock music see Carl Belz, *The Story of Rock* (1969); on consolidation in sports see Joseph Durso, *The All-American Dollar* (1971). William O'Neill, *Coming Apart* (1969) has several chapters on the arts and culture. For religious developments, Sydney Ahlstrom, *A Religious History of the American People* (1972), is standard; James Morris, *The Preachers* (1973), is highly interesting and readable.

Already historians and social scientists have begun fierce debates over the nature of society and politics during the middle and late 1960s. A few writers have taken the viewpoint, expressed in a popular work by Ben J. Wattenburg *(The Real America),* that the period was one of broadly distributed material growth, marred only by "the Cause People, the Movement, the Failure and Guilt complex and their assorted camp followers." Other interpreters have posed the opposite extreme, seeing the 1960s as a time of glorious revolt followed by a harsh, if usually bloodless, repression. Predictably, most scholars have staked out positions somewhere between these extremes. Yet even critics like Wattenburg, who praise the decade's tremendous economic and physical growth and who denigrate the radical "Movement," concede that the outpouring of political and cultural radicalism, particularly among well-educated young people, constituted one of the crucial developments in the history of the 1960s.

"The Movement," the term radicals applied to a loose collection of disparate groups, brought together many different styles of political and cultural radicalism. Members of the New Left urged political solutions for the failures of liberalism; they believed that through radical political action idealistic organizers could change "the system" and bring "power to the people." In contrast, the young cultural radicals displayed little interest in politics. Even more deeply estranged from American society than most political radicals, devotees of the eclectic counter-culture advocated a more natural, more relaxed, more sensual style of life as the best antidote for what they saw as the commercialism, sterility, and puritanicalism of American society. While the New Left hoped to outflank liberal politicians by attracting people to new, radical

8

The years of protest

organizations, cultural radicals preferred to shock middle-class citizens by flaunting "far-out" life styles. And both the cultural and the political radicals, initially mostly white and male, had difficulty forming alliances with nonwhite militants or with women's groups. "The Movement" gradually became as much at odds with itself as with liberalism.

Most important, none of the radical groups ever discovered any workable strategy for changing the direction of American life. Members of the New Left did gain some broader support on specific issues—American withdrawal from South Vietnam became their most popular cause—but they quickly found that few Americans shared their disillusionment with basic institutions and that even fewer were prepared to embrace radical political solutions. As a result, radical politics often meant ineffectual gestures—demonstrations, manifestos, and random acts of violence—against "the system." Similarly, young cultural radicals attracted only a minority of the baby-boom generation. Many young people did adopt the trappings of revolt, such as patched Levis and long hair, but most retained a desire to find some place within the existing social and economic structure. Still, the revolt against liberalism was one of the most important phenomena of the 1960s and early 1970s; the loosely structured political and social radicalism touched almost every area of American life.

THE REVOLT OF "YOUTH"

Young people's enthusiasm for John Kennedy led most supporters of the New Frontier to expect that the 1960s would be a decade of dramatic reform. These young Americans, liberals believed, could help raise both the quantity and the quality of life; a new generation of liberal reformers could cure old economic injustices and then turn their attention to improvement of the arts and educational facilities. But even before JFK's death, some young people were becoming disillusioned with his administration and with liberalism itself. These young radicals, almost all of whom were white and from relatively affluent middle-class homes, began to denounce American institutions and values, trying to frame their own alternatives to big-government liberalism. The potpourri of sources from which dissatisfied young people sought insight and inspiration reflected the diversity of the new radicalism. Unlike the "Old Left" of the 1920s and 1930s, which looked primarily to Marxism, radicals of the 1960s sampled a variety of social theories. "Beat" writers, Eastern mystics, academic dissenters, and even folk-rock songwriters helped provide the movement's intellectual base.

Radicals of the 1950s

While the middle-class protesters of the 1960s were still opening their school day by saluting the flag, the Beat poets and novelists of the 1950s had already dismissed American society as an "air-conditioned nightmare." Jack Kerouac's novel *On the Road* (1957) glorified the drifter, the ever-searching rebel who resisted the temptations of materialistic America. The poems of Allen Ginsberg denounced materialism and middle-class morality and celebrated the satisfactions of marijuana, Eastern mystical religions, and homosexual love. In their best works, Beat poets such as Ginsberg and Gary Snyder displayed a free-flowing style which epitomized their rejection of restrictive forms and too-orderly ideas. Part hipster and part huckster, Ginsberg kept alive the spirit of the Beat movement, becoming a revered elder-in-residence to the radicals of the 1960s. His appearances on college campuses helped pass on the Beats' distaste for materialism, their rejection of middle-class morality, and their search for new modes of artistic expression.

While the Beats protested America's supposed cultural sterility, the radical sociologist C. Wright Mills attacked its liberal political system. Although Mills taught at Columbia University, his personal life style—he would roar up to his office on a motorcycle—and his political ideas clashed with the urbane liberalism which dominated leading colleges. Mills's writings helped popularize theories that became the New Left's central tenets: that an undemocratic "power elite" dominated American society; that liberalism had lost its social consciousness and become an ideology of the status quo; and that most liberal intellectuals merely offered scholarly-sounding rationalizations for an illiberal society. Mills also condemned United States foreign policy as an extension of the same undemocratic values; he warned that a small group of politicians, military officials, and business leaders enjoyed virtually unchecked power. An activist as well as a scholar, Mills visited Cuba and wrote a short book praising Fidel Castro's social experiments. After his death in 1962, Mills became one of the radical movement's most popular intellectuals. Many radical graduate students began theses on Mills, and some people in the movement even named their babies C. Wright.

The critique of American liberalism received greater philosophical development in the works of Herbert Marcuse. A German-born radical whose American disciples included black activist Angela Davis, Marcuse attacked the sophisticated technology and economic prosperity which liberals praised so highly. The United States, according to Marcuse, was a quasi-totalitarian "technocracy." Real power lay with the "technocrats"—the experts in government, business, science, and

203

other dominant institutions who ultimately determined social policies and priorities. In such a "one-dimensional society," people became slaves to the technological imperative. The economic system must continue; progress, as defined by the technocrats, must march forward; rationality and order must reign supreme. The political process offered no choice: voters could choose only among candidates who endorsed the same social and economic policies and who ultimately relied upon the same group of technocrats. Freedom was an illusion. In reality, people had become enslaved to a mass-production, mass-consumption economic system which satisfied only "false needs"—new-model automobiles, electronic gadgets, and thousands of other products which gave no real sense of happiness or personal fulfillment.

Marcuse's tone was uncompromisingly pessimistic; in the early 1960s the old radical saw little chance that Americans could throw off the yoke of the technocracy. Nevertheless, disaffected young people borrowed from Marcuse and his many popularizers. Terms such as *false consciousness* and *technocracy* became part of the radical vocabulary. From Marcuse and other writers, young critics could find reasoned doubts about the social impact of technological development. And like C. Wright Mills, Marcuse endorsed the idea that the liberal "good guys"—including the people who ran the big universities and the big government in Washington—really were the villains. Some young people came to see liberalism as a new form of conservatism; others saw it as a suave totalitarianism which enslaved people with images and illusions rather than with guns or concentration camps.

Even more than Marcuse, Paul Goodman helped popularize the theory that supposedly liberal institutions actually repressed Americans. In *Growing Up Absurd* and a variety of essays, Goodman argued that educational institutions stifled children's healthy natural instincts and subtly indoctrinated them with the values and skills of a badly flawed society. Order and regularity, he claimed, took precedence over spontaneity and creativity; memorization of meaningless data became more important than critical thought; the interests of teachers and administrators outweighed the needs of students. Goodman applied this same critique to all of American society. He contended that large bureaucratic institutions, run by technocratic "experts," worked against essential human needs and desires. Just as large educational complexes miseducated children, large government ignored the welfare of the governed. Centralized institutions, whether public or private, always sought more power; Goodman considered this usurpation dangerous to individual liberty and the general welfare. Experience and common sense, he claimed, showed that large centralized institutions rarely performed their appointed tasks. By bringing ever more things under control of inefficient and ineffective bureaucrats, Americans only magnified the consequences of centralized bungling. Goodman did not see technology as an uncontrollable demon; the problem, he argued, lay in the way centralized institutions applied technology to society. He proposed radical decentralization and a return to small communities as the solution to the absurdities and potential terrors of technocratic America.

Goodman's hopefulness and enthusiasm for change contrasted with Marcuse's pessimism. Goodman claimed that his seemingly utopian schemes—small, volunteer-run radio stations, for example—actually offered highly practical alternatives to centralized structures. In the early 1960s he expressed faith that young people could remake society by forming decentralized institutions, and he demonstrated his commitment by taking an active role in almost every phase of the radical movement. He picketed his publisher, participated in campus demonstrations, and taught at decentralized "free universities." As much as any other writer or older radical, Paul Goodman understood the younger dissidents' search for greater personal involvement and closer community with others. Efforts by some young people to establish communal institutions owed much to Goodman's influence.

Their experience in the civil rights movement of the late fifties and early sixties also propelled some young people, white as well as black, toward an open break with liberalism. Lacking great financial resources, the early civil rights movement relied upon youthful volunteers who could perform time-consuming jobs: preparing leaflets, running mimeograph machines, and marching in demonstrations. All these activities brought young people together in a common cause. Often traveling long distances and sleeping in makeshift accommodations, civil rights workers discovered a camaraderie and commitment that seemed to be missing elsewhere in America. Working together, young people found personal fulfillment in a crusade which they hoped would change the entire society.

At the same time, many of these young activists began to claim that the American political system was hopelessly corrupt and that the liberal political leaders were hypocritical about their commitment to reform. Attending school during the era of the cold war, young volunteers had been brought up on textbook descriptions of American democracy, and the realization that black people suffered all types of legal discrimination and racist harassment proved disquieting. Seeking immediate solutions, civil rights workers inevitably confronted hostile political leaders, the people whom reformers called "the establishment" or the "white power structure." Segregationists in Alabama and Georgia would make no concessions, and even liberal politicians such as John Kennedy stressed the need to "go slow" and to avoid sudden changes in race relations. On many occasions Southern crowds beat up civil rights workers while FBI agents simply looked on and took notes. After confronting the racial hatred of Oxford, Mississippi, or Cicero, Illinois, many young activists charged that liberals offered band-aid solutions for deep national wounds. Segregation and racism, young civil rights workers charged, were evils which no decent society would tolerate.

Social and Psychological Sources of Radicalism

Not all young people protested, and the new radicals represented only a minority of those between eighteen and twenty-five. Others remained true to the liberal spirit of John Kennedy, voting for Lyndon Johnson and going off to fight a war for "democracy and freedom" in Vietnam. Many bitterly resented long-haired hippie protesters, and they desperately wanted the suburban homes, electric kitchens, and nine-to-five jobs rejected by the young radicals. The talk of a generation gap obscured the equally large fissure within the youth generation itself. But the protesters seemed to dominate their peers as they dominated the newspaper headlines. Deeply disturbed about the direction of American society and convinced that they could find better alternatives, the youthful rebels became the symbols of their generation.

What distinguished the young radicals from others of their age? Drawing upon several studies of college students, psychologist Kenneth Keniston argued that the rebels were "psychological adults" but "sociological adolescents." Contrary to conventional wisdom, Keniston found that protesters tended to be excellent students and psychologically healthy individuals who sincerely believed that university life and liberal society in general needed a radical reformation. Keniston suggested that these dissidents were passing through a stage of life which he called "youth," a kind of limbo between adolescence and adulthood. Unlike young people who accepted their parents' society, most "youths" tried to avoid any commitment to a final "adult role"; they glorified a life of "openness" and identified adulthood with stagnation and even death. A young student radical of the mid-1960s gave this feeling a popular slogan: "Don't trust anyone over thirty!" According to Keniston, "youth" represented a new stage of life peculiar to advanced technological societies. Only in an affluent nation could young people enjoy a prolonged educational experience and avoid settling into a workaday routine. Instead of wanting the executive suit and tie or the split-level home, young radicals saw their role as one of protest and agitation for social change.

206

Of course, not everyone in the stage of life called "youth" rebelled openly. But it was middle-class white youth—the people whom their parents expected would find a secure niche in American life—who provided the core of the opposition to bureaucratic liberalism during the 1960s. To these young people, liberalism's failures seemed much more important than its considerable successes. Liberals *had* produced greater material affluence, but at a price: work seemed boring; life lacked adventure and excitement; racial discrimination oppressed millions of people; and personal relationships seemed as "plastic" as the products by which "straight" people measured success. The cool, rational, orderly world of John Kennedy appeared to lack genuine feeling and to substitute eloquent rhetoric for meaningful change. In contrast, "the Movement" seemed to offer hope of immediate personal fulfillment as well as the chance for basic social change. Through the new radicalism young people could instantly complete Paul Simon's "dangling conversations" or explore Bob Dylan's "smoke rings of the mind." Brought up in comfortable affluence with the instantaneous medium of television, young radicals became accustomed to having even the most baffling problems resolved quickly, within the period of a thirty- or a sixty-minute TV show.

Despite the movement's internal contradictions and opposition from most Americans, many young people joined with a small number of aging radicals like pacifist David Dellinger and lawyer William Kunstler in an effort to build a new political coalition in the United States. Although radical politics remained more a style than a real movement, the left-wing opponents of liberalism became increasingly visible during the 1960s.

Radical Politics: The New Left

Young people began to show new interest in radical politics during the late fifties and early sixties. Students at various universities—particularly the University of Wisconsin, the University of California at Berkeley, and the University of Michigan—debated the relationship between "radical scholarship" and social activism. How could university professors avoid the kind of "scholarly dispassion" which radicals considered a means of justifying a repressive status quo? How could intellectuals create a new theoretical structure for a broad-based radical movement? In time, many young graduate students came to see themselves as prototypes for a new breed of university professors: in the style of C. Wright Mills they would awaken campus life and bring new vitality to radical thought. Some university students took more direct action. Dissident young people in the San Francisco Bay Area began to demonstrate in the late fifties on behalf of such causes as dissolution of the House Un-American Activities Committee, abolition of capital punishment, and elimination of racial discrimination. Young radicals were also active in the South, helping unemployed miners fight the large coal companies in Hazard County, Kentucky, and working for various civil rights organizations. In 1961 a group of college students in North Carolina founded the Student Nonviolent Coordinating Committee; SNCC (pronounced "snick") quickly became the most militant civil rights organization in the nation. SNCC's young activists registered black voters, desegregated public facilities, and organized black communities throughout the South. In SNCC, unlike most other radical groups of the early 1960s, blacks played a prominent role.

The white-dominated Students for a Democratic Society (SDS), which began as an arm of the Old Left's League for Industrial Democracy, shared SNCC's activism. SDS's Port Huron Statement, largely written by Tom Hayden, was one of the New Left's most thoughtful documents. Paralleling the ideas of Herbert Marcuse, the Port Huron Statement argued that America's highly organized, highly bureaucratic, supertechnological society had created a sense of loneliness, a blind obsession with material possessions, and a widespread feeling of hopelessness. The United States "rests in national stalemate . . . its democratic system apathetic and manipulated rather than of, by, and for the people." What America needed, Hayden suggested, was a dramatically new social and political system in which people "share in those social decisions determining the quality and direction" of life. SDS preached the virtues of "participatory democracy," a decentralized political, economic, and social system which would return "power to the people." As well as anyone, Tom Hayden captured the feeling of powerlessness and the search for authentic relationships which characterized much of the opposition to liberalism during the 1960s.

In its early years SDS viewed community organization as the key to the social and political revolution. Poor people fell victim to the power elite of corporate liberalism, SDS argued, because they could not exert political pressure commensurate with their numbers. SDS branched out from the college campuses—many of its early members came from the University of Michigan—and launched grass-roots projects among the urban poor. By moving into the ghettos SDS hoped to stimulate formation of counter-organizations and counter-governments and to channel poor people's discontent into radical political activities. In cities such as Newark, New Jersey, SDS mounted drives against urban renewal and in support of better housing, more jobs, and school lunch programs. The first SDSers displayed a missionary zeal. While some young radicals were already sprouting long hair and smoking dope, the SDSers bragged that they were turned on to political organizing. But despite their commitment, they quickly discovered the difficulties of organizing poor people, especially for a group committed to participatory democracy. Drawn mostly from white middle-class families, young SDS members, unlike veteran organizers such as Saul Alinsky, were too impatient. Seeking a more congenial environment, SDS shifted its emphasis back to the college campus, the heart of the youth revolt in the 1960s.

Campus Protests

The first serious campus protests occurred at the University of California at Berkeley in the fall of 1964 after university officials tried to limit political activities by students. Dissident students charged that the university administration was bowing to pressures from right-wing businessmen in the Bay area and destroying free speech on campus. As protests against the new university regulations escalated and a temporary truce collapsed, rallies, takeovers of university buildings, and police raids highlighted what became known as the Berkeley Student Revolt. A number of campus groups joined under the banner of the Free Speech Movement, but radicals gathered most of the headlines. In early December 1964 student protesters began wearing IBM cards as name tags; the radicals soon called a campuswide strike. Although critical newspapers pronounced the action a failure, student leaders claimed that almost three-quarters of the student body supported the three-day walkout. Many graduate teaching assistants and some professors gave at least tacit support. The Free Speech Movement later took a different turn, becoming the "Filthy Speech Movement." A young New Yorker who had drifted West to "make the scene" at Berkeley arrived with a simple protest sign: "FUCK." (Some people claimed that the letters stood for "Freedom Under Clark Kerr," the president of the University of California.) This example inspired a group of imitators, the "word-mongers," who gave Berkeley an even more lurid reputation among conservatives. By the spring of 1965 many of the basic issues which had precipitated the first student protests had been largely forgotten amid the diversions.

The revolt at Berkeley provided a scenario which repeated itself throughout the 1960s. In banding together to fight the administration or outside enemies—James Kunen, a clever observer of the 1968 disturbances at Columbia, called them "the biggies"—young people discovered a new sense of community. Like the civil rights workers in Mississippi, they developed a kind of garrison mentality, viewing themselves as victims of a faceless power structure. Elevated by their underdog status, student propagandists announced that they were the "new niggers."

The modern "multiversity" provided a perfect target. Big universities displayed what radicals considered the major sins of modern liberalism: an emphasis on competitiveness, reliance on bureaucratic structures, and an apparent feeling that bigger inevitably meant better. Sensitive young students, many of whom had been reared in families which stressed openness and concern for their children's feelings, felt especially frustrated by the impersonality and routine of universities such as Berkeley and Columbia. They complained that large, impersonal lectures and haphazard discussion sections exemplified the multiversity's assembly-line approach to education. Many students felt reduced to IBM numbers, subject to the whims of giant computers and dependent on faceless bureaucrats who ran the multimillion-dollar operations. Even the University of California's liberal President Clark Kerr considered himself primarily the administrator of a large "benevolent bureaucracy," a huge enterprise which produced knowledge instead of consumer goods. "The university and segments of industry are becoming more alike," Kerr observed in 1960. Finally, most students resented what they considered invasions of their personal freedoms by university officials. Women, even those who were legally of age, had to observe dress codes and dorm hours on most college campuses during the early 1960s; men at many state universities were required to take two years of ROTC; and faculty-dominated committees censored student publications. Dissidents began to demand that universities abandon or relax these restrictions, reduce the number of required courses, and offer programs "relevant" to mid-twentieth-century society.

When student muckrakers examined the multiversity's role in American society, they saw additional crimes. Professors conducted classified research for the Defense Department; Harvard chemists, not Dow Chemical, had developed napalm. Seeking additional space for new buildings, athletic stadiums, and parking lots, universities sometimes expanded into neighboring black ghettos and pushed out the residents. Some private universities, radicals also discovered, owned inner-city properties and qualified as genuine slum landlords. To make the indictment complete, big universities rarely admitted black students; when they did, recruitment efforts centered on talented athletes and a few top-flight students. Viewed from within, the multiversity seemed to offer mind-numbing courses and senseless regimentation. Seen as part of a corrupt liberal society, it appeared to aid war and racism.

Student and faculty pressures brought significant changes and a few strategic retreats by the old guard. Most colleges relaxed archaic restrictions, abolished compulsory ROTC, adjusted curriculum requirements, made special efforts to recruit minority students, and established separate minority studies programs. A few professors even encouraged social activism by permitting students to substitute "relevant" outside projects for more traditional assignments. Although a number of spectacular "busts" temporarily halted protest at some universities, most campuses continued to serve as staging areas for forays against the outside world. At many urban universities large groups of street people—dropouts, hangers-on, and runaway teenagers—provided additional troops for campus demonstrations and swelled the ranks of the "student" opposition. A radicalized university, many activists began to hope, would be an important tool for changing the larger society.

Teach-ins and Marches

The protests against American involvement in the war in Vietnam demonstrated the value as well as the limitations of the university in radical politics. The crusade against the Vietnam War did not begin on the campuses, but dissent within the academic community gave the antiwar movement an influential forum. During early 1965, after President Johnson mounted an all-out bombing campaign against North Vietnam, antiwar activists organized a nationwide series of teach-ins, meetings at which supporters and opponents of American participation in the war debated before largely student audiences. Initially some protesters hoped that the teach-ins would spark vigorous exchanges with government officials and that the confrontations might eventually change the policies of the Johnson administration. Such lofty expectations quickly vanished as the emphasis of the gatherings changed. Rather than providing a lever for ending American involvement, teach-ins became a means of opening a dialog to reach some broad consensus on war policy. By 1966 most militant opponents of the war charged that teach-ins only wasted precious time. Obviously, the meetings were having little effect on President Johnson's actions, and the novelty of the gatherings was wearing thin. Although teach-ins continued sporadically throughout the 1960s—and even into the seventies on some campuses—the antiwar movement began to desert the lecture platforms for the streets.

Antiwar demonstrations borrowed from the tactics of the civil rights movement and the techniques of the teach-in. Beginning with a mass march, demonstrations often concluded with a series of predictable speeches and entertainment by folk-rock musicians. Organizers claimed that by bringing large numbers of people into the streets, they could dramatize the strength of the movement, raise "radical consciousness" among undecided people, and pressure the national government to change its policies. Throughout the 1960s the movement's leaders tried to organize rallies for many different causes—black power, women's liberation, the rights of military prisoners—but only the antiwar cause continually attracted great numbers. Increasingly, the radical left found itself tied to one issue: American involvement in Southeast Asia. Energies that might have gone into community organizing or other grass-roots projects became channeled into a seemingly endless series of antiwar marches. Each new march had to outdo the last; organizers struggled to attract more people or to devise new strategems to goad the liberal establishment. During the October 1967 March on Washington, a group of what the *East Village Other* newspaper called "witches, warlocks, holymen, seers, prophets, mystics, saints, sorcerers, shamans, troubadours, minstrels, bards, roadmen, and madmen" tried to exorcise the Pentagon, hurling "mighty words of white light against the demon-controlled structure." Alas, the five-sided symbol of the military-industrial complex hardly budged, but such productions undoubtedly raised the spirits of the protesters.

The difficulties of organizing such demonstrations helped cover up differences over goals and tactics; negotiations with political leaders, police chiefs, rock entrepreneurs, and portable-toilet vendors sometimes seemed as complex as the government maneuvers to conduct the war itself. By collecting thousands of people at one demonstration, leaders of the movement could reassure themselves that all was going well. Even a fraction of a percent of the baby-boom generation, gathered in one spot, made a good-sized crowd, while a sprinkling of older people raised hopes that the movement was making converts outside its normal youth market. Such gatherings gradually became ritualized. Protesters sprawled on the grass, half-listening to familiar political rhetoric, and reminisced about previous demonstrations and "hassles." For many people, marches served much the same function as revival meetings: the faithful assembled from across the country, exchanged pleasantries, felt their faith renewed, and then went back to plan the next gathering.

The vast majority of the protesters strongly opposed the war and felt estranged from the liberal society, but many simply lacked interest in sustained political activity. In time, the antipathy which many disaffected young people felt toward the liberal establishment transferred to the "peace bureaucrats" in the New Left. Most cultural radicals, whom the mass media labeled hippies, preferred to "do their own thing." San

Francisco, the old home of the Beats, once again became the new mecca, as the Bay area sparked the cultural revolution of the 1960s.

Haight-Ashbury and the Hippies

Many political radicals received their first exposure to the cultural side of the youth revolt when novelist Ken Kesey and his band of "Merry Pranksters" showed up at a 1965 antiwar demonstration in Berkeley. An early convert to the glories of hallucinogenic drugs, Kesey attracted a group of "zonked-out" disciples to his farm near La Honda, California. Unlike Drs. Timothy Leary and Richard Alpert, two professors who had conducted serious experiments with LSD at Harvard during the early 1960s, Kesey and the Pranksters preferred a good "trip" to speculations about the deeper religious or mystical properties of drugs. The Pranksters, their faces painted with Day-Glo, jammed into an old bus, which Kesey outfitted with expensive stereo equipment and cameras, and roared off to "freak out the straights." At the Berkeley rally Kesey lampooned the ultra-serious political radicals. Between harmonica choruses of "Home on the Range," he compared one New Left guru's speaking style to Mussolini's and chided marchers for playing the warmakers' game. "There's only one thing to do," advised Kesey, "and that's everybody just look at it, look at the war, and turn your backs and say . . . Fuck it!" Such advice hardly ingratiated Kesey with most political radicals, but his pranks and espousal of hard drugs did increase his reputation in the San Francisco hippie communities.

In the mid-1960s San Francisco was the center of radical youth culture. Haight-Ashbury, a decaying neighborhood on the city's west side, became the hippies' mecca. Initially, life in Haight-Ashbury seemed "beautiful" (a favorite word of cultural radicals). "Hip" people from all over the country flocked to the Bay area, trying to escape the workaday cares of "corporate America" and hoping to enjoy the easy life styles of the "age of Aquarius." Many young people were excited by the hippies' communal living arrangements, their casual attitudes toward sex, their experimentation with all types of drugs, and their fascination with the electrified sound of folk-rock. Spokespersons for the hippies declared themselves liberated from "hang-ups" like work and clothing fashions. Attired in America's cast-offs, particularly old military uniforms, the new rebels embraced philosophies which stressed mystical experiences and universal love. Unlike members of the New Left, the hippies had little interest in political questions and no passion for new political organizations.

Like the earlier Beat writers, some began to study Eastern faiths such as Zen and Taoism; a few joined Dr. Timothy Leary's League for Spiritual Discovery or eclectically sampled all sorts of non-Western, psychedelic cults; many simply borrowed the slang of the hipsters or produced their own slogans. "Make love, not war" and "flower power" became part of the hippie litany. (Corporate merchandizers quickly discovered such profundities and emblazoned them upon T-shirts, Day-Glo buttons, and drinking mugs.) Sociologists eagerly studied the hippie phenomenon while anguished parents wrung their hands. How to avoid losing one's children to the hippies dominated cocktail conversation in fashionable suburbs, and a quick tour of Haight-Ashbury became an essential part of any middle-class tourist's visit to San Francisco.

But Haight-Ashbury soon turned from a haven for flower children into just another rundown slum. San Francisco's political establishment declared war on "this hippie thing" and the city's police chief condemned the flower children as people without "the courage to face the reality of life." Quickly taking their cue, many patrolmen on the beat ruthlessly searched for marijuana and other drugs or simply harassed any long-haired, unkempt young person. At the same time, Haight faced an invasion of petty criminals, drifters who discovered that the gentle hippies were easy prey for a few dollars or for free sex. Haight also developed internal strains. The radical Diggers, a group which tried to live without money and according to the Golden Rule, complained that corporate entrepreneurs had taken control of the community's economic life and that phony weekend hippies inundated the area. As dope became big business, pushers began to peddle stronger and stronger chemicals. The wiser "heads" warned about the dangers of barbiturates—"Speed Kills," proclaimed the posters—but many naive young people became hooked on harder drugs or experienced bad trips on powerful hallucinogens. A few died from overdoses. A handbill printed in August 1967 expressed the growing disillusionment with Haight-Ashbury.

> The trouble is that the hip shopkeepers probably believe their own bullshit lies. They believe that dope is the answer and neither know nor care what the question is.
>
> Have you been raped? Take acid and everything will be groovy. Are you cold, sleeping in doorways at night? Take acid and discover your inner warmth. Are you hungry? Take acid and transcend these mundane needs.
>
> You can't afford acid? Pardon me. I think I hear somebody calling me.
>
> They would never believe that they were guilty of monstrous crimes against humanity. They won't believe it this summer, when the street reeks of human agony, despair, and death death death.

Radical Youth Culture

Despite the rise and fall of Haight-Ashbury, more and more young people seemed to be joining the counter-culture. By 1966 groups such as the Beatles were revolutionizing rock music, and Bob Dylan had already augmented his acoustic guitar with the amplified sound of folk-rock. Initially, groups from San Francisco took the lead in exploring the possibilities of electronic rock. Using more amplifiers, mixers, and microphones than even the Rolling Stones dared assemble, Jerry Garcia and the Grateful Dead attracted a devoted following in the San Francisco area. The Dead gradually added various kinds of light shows, and Ken Kesey's Pranksters laced the whole show with LSD. ("Can you pass the acid test?" the Pranksters slyly asked concertgoers.) The result was "acid rock" and a whole new genre of drug-related, "mind-blowing" sounds. Acid rock became an instant success, financially as well as artistically. Promoter Bill Graham began staging weekly encores at San Francisco's Fillmore Auditorium. The popularity of San Francisco groups—particularly the Dead, the Jefferson Airplane, and Big Brother and the Holding Company (featuring Janis Joplin)—rapidly spread. With the unsuspecting cooperation of many disc jockeys, songs such as the Airplane's "White Rabbit" covertly extolled the benefits of drugs. Graham soon opened the Fillmore East in New York, and smaller clubs popped up almost anywhere there were young people.

The union of disaffected youth, rock music, and drugs—the combination which made the Woodstock Rock Festival of 1969 briefly appear to represent the real flowering of a cultural revolt—was consummated. By the late 1960s the hippies seemed to be everywhere. Aided by the wonders of modern technology—mass-produced books and magazines, stereo record albums, automobiles, airplanes, and psychedelic chemicals—the youthful cultural revolution became a nationwide phenomenon. The counter-culture was difficult to classify: it was variously a state of mind, a way of life, or sometimes just a style of dress. It even developed its own mass media. The success of the *Berkeley Barb* and the *Los Angeles Free Press* encouraged other underground newspapers, and radical young journalists soon formed the Liberation News Service. Although few of these enterprises survived for any length of time, the proliferation of the underground press helped bring together young people who felt estranged from American society. The growing population of counter-cultural students and street people created little Haight-Ashburys around major college campuses and in dilapidated districts of most large cities.

New York City's East Village, a run-down section near fashionably radical Greenwich Village, quickly became the East Coast's version of Haight-Ashbury. The East Village attracted young rebels and spawned a group of counter-culture celebrities. Ed Sanders, one of the East Village's most enterprising residents, published a small underground periodical with an unprintable title and formed the Fugs, a kind of anti-rock group whose most famous songs were "What Are You Doing After the Orgy" and "Kill for Peace." Together with Abbie Hoffman and Jerry Rubin, Sanders also conceived the spurious Youth International Party—the Yippies. A free-wheeling attempt to blend political and cultural radicalism and to gain attention from the media, the brief but exciting Yippie movement made Rubin and Hoffman important celebrities within both the New Left and the counter-culture.

Yippie radicalism owed more to Groucho, Harpo, and Chico than to Karl Marx. The Yippie program was theater in the streets, an updated drug-inspired vaudeville of the radical Left. With the Yippies, revolution and symbolic defiance became one and the same. In perhaps their most famous stunt, they invaded the New York Stock Exchange, hurling "real" money at brokers who were wildly trading their paper securities. Abbie Hoffman facetiously claimed that his brand of cultural revolution would eventually produce upheaval through a mystical process he called "cultural ju-jit-su." Confronted with the taunts of the Yippies in the streets, corporate America would eventually hack itself to pieces because of its innate contradictions. When they chose to be serious—which was not very often—Rubin and Hoffman could offer a fairly cogent critique of liberal institutions and values. But the Yippies' penchant for playing radicalism for laughs—Hoffman entitled his treatise *Revolution for the Hell of It*—oftentimes alienated more serious supporters of "the Movement."

The Meaning of the Counter-culture

Historian Theodore Roszak, who popularized the term *counter-culture*, viewed dissident young people as the vanguard of a reaction against technological society. Saturated with the meaningless trappings of misdirected affluence and frightened by the hubris of the techno-scientific mentality, "technocracy's children" sought a society and a level of consciousness which allowed for beauty, mystery, feeling, and love. Roszak sympathetically explored the counter-culture's interest in Eastern religions, Beat writers, anarchist philosophers, and mystic poets. Writing in 1968 (*The Making of a Counter-Culture*), he viewed the new opposition's search for alternative forms of personal liberation and its emphasis on the whole person as exciting alternatives to the "myth of objective consciousness"—the scientific world-view which had dominated Western thought for several centuries. But Roszak prophetically warned that the white middle-class rebels would have to avoid at least two dangers: losing touch with disadvantaged people, particularly non-whites, who had never enjoyed the temptations of technology; and becoming "an amusing side show" for the swingers of *Playboy* magazine's America.

Yale law professor Charles Reich, another sympathetic observer of the counter-culture, had few such misgivings. In *The Greening of America*, Reich argued that the United States was about to embark upon a new age of awareness—Consciousness III. Most Americans had already left behind Consciousness I, the robber-baron, dog-eat-dog mentality of the nineteenth century; many young people were abandoning Consciousness II, the philosophy of modern liberalism which emphasized the benefits of bureaucratic organizations and the benevolence of the capitalist welfare state. In contrast, Consciousness III envisioned an open society in which people renounced competition, stereotyped relationships, and subservience to formal institutions. Consciousness III was a state of openness and freedom. Even young people's favorite article of clothing, blue jeans, expressed their basic world-view: Levis provided one set of clothes for all occasions and offered freedom from the social constraints of expensive clothes. (To the charge that a sea of blue-jeaned youth meant conformity, Reich argued that, unlike pressed suits, jeans conformed to people's bodies and expressed their individuality.) Like grass peaking through sidewalks, the young rebels of Consciousness III would eventually break apart the concrete jungle of technocratic America.

Reich's book, based primarily upon his experiences with undergraduates at Yale, sparked much controversy. Some critics reminded Reich that the Consciousness III group comprised only a small segment of the total youth generation. Others suggested that the new opposition, as Roszak had feared, had already been exploited by the technocracy. Hippie-style clothes and a more relaxed view of sex became fashionable among some business and professional people, and the hippie life style often became a cliché devoid of any ideological substance.

Although the counter-culture had many defenders, even more writers denounced it as a dangerous and foolish revolt against modern life. Psychologist Bruno Bettelheim dismissed the outcries against technology as the babbling of "obsolete youth" in a technological society that required discipline, rationalism, and order. Political scientist Zbigniew Brzezinski adopted a somewhat similar attitude, suggesting that youthful protesters were twentieth-century Luddites. Noting that most dissidents were in the humanities rather than the sciences, Brzezinski claimed that the rebels were blindly attacking the new technological society which threatened their power and prestige. He dismissed the politics of the New Left as "only a reaction to the more basic fear that the times are against them, that a new world is emerging without either their assistance or leadership." The counter-culture, Brzezinski concluded, was the "death rattle" of the historically obsolete.

Ambitious politicians joined the attack upon "dirty hippies" and "permissiveness," although their analyses seldom rose above the level of the banal. Ronald Reagan, a fading movie and television actor, pledged to "straighten out things at Berkeley" during his successful campaign for the governorship of California in 1966. Reagan and other politicians also took an increasingly hard line against drug use, condemning the spread of marijuana as proof of young people's disrespect for law and order.

1968: THE POLITICS OF CONFRONTATION

By 1968 the protest against liberalism had become both a political and a cultural issue. The 1968 presidential campaign reflected the diverse tensions within American society and channeled them into the political arena. As events would show, however, the political process offered a poor forum for resolving the deep social and cultural divisions; few national contests have produced as much bitterness and political violence as the 1968 elections.

The Fall of Lyndon Johnson

Lyndon Johnson became the first casualty of the fierce political wars. After capturing more than 60 percent of the popular vote in 1964, Johnson had celebrated his "politics of consensus." Some Republicans even worried about their party's future. But trapped in an unpopular and unwinnable war, blamed for racial conflict, and assailed by enemies of Great Society liberalism, Johnson saw many of his old supporters desert him. The tall Texan, who had once thoroughly enjoyed his role as "the leader of the free world," now found himself the butt of innumerable jokes. (The Smothers brothers and their talented second banana, Pat Paulsen, used their popular television show to mount an imaginary campaign against a bumbling "President Johnston.") As his standing in opinion polls and his support in Congress steadily dropped, LBJ's enemies gleefully lampooned his outsized image.

Dissident Democrats organized a "Dump Johnson" movement to deny the president his party's nomination in 1968. At first considered hopeless, especially when Senator Robert Kennedy refused to run, the anti-Johnson campaign finally coalesced behind an unlikely hero, Senator Eugene McCarthy of Minnesota. After a slow start, Gene McCarthy became a political celebrity, a suave antipolitician who played very well against the bumptious Johnson. Introspective and aloof, McCarthy intensely disliked the kind of handshaking spectacle which Johnson called "pressing the flesh." The Minnesota senator also instinctively recoiled from the type of rhetorical overkill which Johnson displayed so often. He promised no great societies, and his whole campaign suggested a refreshing modesty about the nation's capability and his qualifications. "All we want is a moderate use of intelligence," he told his supporters at the Chicago convention.

Flanked by a few aides and a small group of supporters, McCarthy began to trudge through New Hampshire campaigning in the nation's first primary. Gradually his unorthodox campaign style caught on, and a small army of college students invaded the Granite State to support the only peace candidate in either major party. Johnson declined to campaign in New Hampshire, and reporters found McCarthy the most interesting candidate on the road. His "quixotic children's crusade," as the media called it, gained much free publicity on the evening news, and the communists' Tet offensive in Vietnam increased doubts about Johnson's war policy. McCarthy won about 43 percent of the Democratic vote and disproved conventional wisdom about the invincibility of an incumbent president, at least within his party. McCarthy also accomplished something else: he seized media coverage for the anti-Johnson movement. Even before the results in New Hampshire, Johnson's mounting problems in Vietnam and within the Democratic party convinced Senator Robert Kennedy to enter the race. Unfortunately for his image, Kennedy delayed a formal announcement until after the primary, and "anti-Bobby" liberals pilloried him as a political scavenger. But the new contender added to the president's problems.

Facing sure defeat by McCarthy in the Wisconsin primary, a physically exhausted Lyndon Johnson retired without a fight. On March 31, the president dramatically announced that he would not seek another term. Coupling his retirement with a serious offer to negotiate in Paris with North Vietnam and the National Liberation Front, he proclaimed that he would not let partisan politics stand in the way of his search for peace. About to be relieved of the responsibilities of the presidency, Johnson abandoned the spartan routine which his heart condition required. He resumed smoking and began to eat greater amounts of rich fried foods. Within two years he suffered a serious heart attack; within five years he was dead.

219

The "Politics of Joy" and the "New Politics"

Johnson's retreat brought forth a full-scale charge by Hubert Humphrey, LBJ's vice-president and an unsuccessful presidential contender in 1960. Humphrey enjoyed the full support of party chieftains—labor leaders such as George Meany, political bosses such as Chicago Mayor Daley and Texas Governor John Connally, and LBJ himself. With this backing, Humphrey could ignore the primaries and use his political muscle to line up delegates. But although he tried to gain support with the unlikely theme, "the politics of joy," even Humphrey came to recognize the foreboding political atmosphere of the 1968 election.

The unrelenting political violence of 1968 made a mockery of Humphrey's politics of joy. In April, Dr. Martin Luther King, Jr., was gunned down in Memphis; black ghettos erupted in anger. Disorders rocked more than one hundred towns; thirty-six people died; and public officials deployed more than fifty thousand national guardsmen and federal troops. Many black and white radicals refused to believe that another lone gunman, this one a none too bright ex-convict named James Earl Ray, could have killed still another national leader. To some, Dr. King's death seemed an additional sign that sinister forces were loose in the land. This would not be the last time Americans would gather around their TV sets to watch funerals and memorial tributes.

As Americans recovered from the shock of King's death, Gene McCarthy and Robert Kennedy attempted to use their campaigns to bring alienated Americans back into "the system." McCarthy's brand of "new politics"—a much-abused phrase which suggested no backroom deals with powerful interest groups, reliance on youthful volunteers, and straightforward political speeches—appealed to bright, politically aware college students. (Bobby Kennedy once joked that McCarthy had all the A students while he could attract only those who got B's and B−'s.) Shaving beards and donning skirts to "come clean for Gene," thousands of young men and women canvassed door-to-door and state-to-state with their hero. Kennedy's efforts also excited young people, but many idealists complained that his campaign smacked too much of the "old politics." Kennedy tried to make special appeals to a diverse coalition of white ethnic voters, blacks, chicanos, liberals, and even George Wallace supporters. As he vigorously stumped Indiana, assisted by plenty of Kennedy money, reporters dubbed his campaign train the "Ruthless Cannonball."

He has the Poles in Gary,
The Blacks will fill his hall,
There are no ethnic problems on the Ruthless Cannonball.

While Humphrey rested on his safe cushion of nonprimary delegates, Kennedy and McCarthy tried to impress party leaders with their vote-getting ability. McCarthy lost to Kennedy in Indiana and Nebraska, but in Oregon he became the first politician ever to defeat any Kennedy. The Kennedy mystique seemed broken; Bobby battled for his political life in preparing for the California primary. A Kennedy campaign was something special: an array of movie stars, folk singers, athletes, university professors, and even business executives dropped everything to follow Bobby. Ignoring threats against his life, Kennedy waded into crowds wherever he went. Many white politicians would not dare to walk into black and chicano neighborhoods; none could command the tumultuous reception which Bobby Kennedy received. Unlike another so-called people's candidate, George Wallace, Bobby surrounded himself with no special bodyguards. He allowed only a few burly friends to shield him from danger.

The night of the California primary, these same supporters stood helplessly nearby as Kennedy was shot at point-blank range in the kitchen of a Los Angeles hotel. Police immediately arrested Sirhan Sirhan, a Jordanian immigrant, whom a jury later convicted of Kennedy's murder. Minutes before the shooting Kennedy had accepted congratulations for a narrow victory over McCarthy in the climactic California primary; twenty-four hours later, he was dead. Although McCarthy said that he would continue to fight for the nomination, Kennedy's death took the heart out of his campaign. To novelist-reporter Norman Mailer, McCarthy looked like a punch-drunk fighter stumbling toward Chicago and his inevitable beating by Hubert Humphrey.

Miami and the Siege of Chicago

Republican delegates assembled first to choose their presidential candidate. Meeting amid racial violence and protest in Miami (four people were killed during racial disorder there), Republicans chose a face from the past—former Vice-President Richard Nixon. Although he had lost the 1960 presidential contest and had presumably retired from politics after his defeat in the California gubernatorial race of 1962, image-makers proclaimed a "new Nixon." (Early in the 1968 campaign, a critic complained that "there is no new Nixon. What we have here is the old Nixon, a little older.") In truth, the dogged campaigner, whose fellow law students at Duke had called him "Old Iron Butt," simply outlasted the field. Nominated on the first ballot, Nixon surprised the convention by selecting Spiro T. Agnew, the obscure governor of Maryland, as his running mate. Once considered relatively moderate on social issues, Agnew had recently gained an image as a hard-liner when he insulted a group of nonmilitant black leaders and endorsed the idea of shooting looters during ghetto disturbances. In his acceptance speech, the "new Nixon" suggested peaceful overtures to the Soviet Union and the People's Republic of China and pledged to give black Americans "a piece of the action in the exciting ventures of private enterprise." But the address also contained echoes of the old Nixon. He praised the "forgotten Americans, the nonshouters, the nondemonstraters"; he suggested that Americans had been "deluged" by government welfare progams which had only "reaped . . . an ugly harvest of frustrations, violence, and failure"; and he promised that his attorney general would "open a new front against crime."

The cry for "law and order" became stronger after the violence that accompanied the Democrats' Chicago convention. Mayor Richard Daley and various security agencies expected trouble. Several peace groups planned demonstrations and the Yippies promised to stage a "festival of life," an answer to what they called the Democrats' "festival of death." Abbie Hoffman talked about sending ten thousand nude Yippies wading into Lake Michigan, releasing greased pigs in Chicago's

United Press International

Riot-trained U.S. Army regulars carry their gear on arrival in Chicago, August 25, 1968.

crowded Loop area, and slipping LSD into the city's water supply. Mayor Daley took Hoffman's jokes seriously and, in the words of reporters from the London *Times*, prepared "security in the paranoid style." Although information indicated that the number of demonstrators would fall far below the Yippies' expectations, the mayor readied his twelve-thousand-man police force and had the Illinois national guard and the United States army waiting for action. "If you're going to Chicago, be sure to wear some armor in your hair," warned an underground newspaper editor.

After several days of skirmishes between youthful protesters and the Chicago police, serious violence erupted on the night delegates selected Humphrey as the Democratic nominee for president. As police beat demonstrators, nonprotesting bystanders, and even a few reporters, the bitterness invaded the convention, a gathering already torn by a fight over a peace plank in the platform and challenges to "boss control" of certain delegations. When Abraham Ribicoff denounced the "Gestapo tactics" of the Chicago police, Mayor Daley leaped to his feet, shouting obscenities at the senator from Connecticut. Ribicoff's statement eventually received support from a special commission which labeled the disorders a "police riot." Policemen, the commission concluded, had faced taunts and some stray missiles, but they responded out of all proportion to the provocations. According to one eye-witness,

> *Some police pursued individuals as far as a block and beat them. . . . In many cases it appeared to me that when the police had finished beating the protesters they were pursuing, they then attacked, indiscriminately, any civilian who happened to be standing nearby. Many of these were not involved in the demonstration.*

But many people saw events the other way: one poll revealed that almost 60 percent of the American public blamed the demonstrators and supported the police.

On the question of disorders at the convention and on the war issue, Hubert Humphrey found himself caught in the middle of squabbling Democrats. He dared not openly criticize either Mayor Daley's policemen or the antiwar forces. Humphrey tried to pretend that the Democratic party would pull together, but his early campaign efforts belied such optimism. Antiwar hecklers confronted the underfinanced and badly advised Humphrey at every stop, and his audiences remained small and generally unenthusiastic.

The Great Race of 1968

Initially George Wallace suffered none of these problems. Running on the American Independent ticket, the former governor of Alabama preached law and order, a slogan which black people and liberals denounced as code words for racism. Wallace's angry denials were, in a sense, correct. The black revolt was only one of the social issues which Wallace hoped to exploit. His standard address—bored reporters called it "The Speech"—contended that "there's not a dime's worth of difference" between the two major parties, denounced "pointy-headed professors" who "don't know how to park a bicycle straight," and predicted that all the "intellectual morons" and "theoreticians" were "going to get some of those liberal smiles knocked off their faces." Wallace cleverly linked distaste for big government with fears of the counterculture. "Our lives are being taken over by bureaucrats, and most of them have beards." Campaigning with a variety of country-Western singers, Wallace made good his promise to shake up the major parties. At one point, when Humphrey's effort was floundering, Wallace appeared to have a chance of finishing second in the electoral vote. By fall, however, his campaign had peaked. As election day neared, many Northern Democrats, primarily blue-collar workers and ethnic voters, who had been leaning toward Wallace began to return to the Democratic ranks. Aided by their desertion of Wallace, the vice-president nearly caught Nixon.

Richard Nixon and his army of strategists watched Humphrey draw closer until the last polls showed the race a toss-up. Finally deciding that he would have to untangle himself from Johnson's Vietnam policy, the vice-president announced in October that he would risk a bombing halt in hope of speeding the Paris peace talks. And several days before the November election, President Johnson ordered a temporary cessation of air raids over North Vietnam. These steps induced many antiwar people, including Gene McCarthy, to announce at least grudging support of Humphrey's candidacy. Despite his late surge, however, Humphrey fell about a hundred thousand votes short, and Nixon captured the presidency with only about 43 percent of the popular vote. The lonely long-distance runner, as Garry Wills called Nixon, had finally won the big race.

Although Nixon and Humphrey had tried to identify themselves with the younger generation, their nominations, and the election of the former vice-president, demonstrated the tenacity of traditional political habits and institutions. Careful studies of voting behavior revealed that people most likely to cast ballots were unyoung, unpoor, unblack, and largely unsympathetic to the exuberance of youthful radicalism. Most

224

voters identified cultural rebellion with ingratitude for the material abundance which they associated with "the American way"; they considered left-wing politics, with its stress upon demonstrations and direct participation, socially disruptive. Those who initially wanted to cast a protest vote supported McCarthy, Kennedy, or Wallace, believing that in their own unique ways they were different from conventional politicians. With Kennedy's death, some of his discontented working-class supporters switched their allegiance to George Wallace. And after McCarthy's virtual retirement from political life after the violence of Chicago, many supporters of the new politics stayed home. Others joined the vast majority of American voters in choosing between two familiar candidates who stood firmly in the center of the American political spectrum. By 1968, then, the youth-inspired rebellion had failed to bring participatory democracy, the age of Aquarius, or even the triumph of the new politics. Although shaken by the agitation of the New Left, the people who dominated the American political system remained committed to the liberalism of the Democratic party or the moderate Republicanism espoused by Richard Nixon.

The 1968 presidential election seemed to settle little except that Nixon rather than Humphrey would move into the White House. Fewer people voted than in 1964, and many Americans expressed little confidence in any of the candidates. Several polls revealed that most voters rated Senator Edmund Muskie, Humphrey's running mate, as the best person in the field. Through it all, the war went on, racial tensions remained high, and many college campuses continued under siege. Richard Nixon, the candidate who promised to "bring us together," faced a badly divided society and an uncertain political future.

THE SEARCH FOR "POWER"

Black Power, 1968–74

After 1968 the black revolution diverged in many different directions. No leader replaced Martin Luther King, and the SCLC lost most of its prestige when the much-publicized Poor People's March bogged down in the spring rains of Washington, D.C. Their waterlogged tent camp (Resurrection City) broke into squabbling factions, most protesters slowly deserted the capital, and the government finally expelled the few survivors. Only the Reverend Jesse Jackson, a dynamic young leader who later organized the Chicago-based Operation PUSH, gained much glory from the affair. Other groups suffered fates similar to that of the SCLC. CORE, the organization which had begun the freedom rides in 1961, gradually lost influence and visibility. H. Rap Brown, Stokely Carmichael's outspoken successor, kept SNCC in the headlines for a short time—he once defiantly proclaimed that "violence is as American as cherry pie"—but finally dropped from sight after a grand jury indictment. (In 1972, Brown was arrested in New York City after holding up a black social club in Harlem.) The fire seemed to go out even of the most militant black-power advocates; after 1968 there were no more major ghetto disturbances.

Many young blacks sought new opportunities in the business world and the professions. Business people's desire to head off further ghetto disorders and the government's requirement of affirmative action to hire minority workers meant new and better job opportunities for some black people. Colleges and professional schools also made special efforts to recruit ethnic-minority students (and women), a policy which many whites denounced as a quota system. The gap between black and white incomes narrowed somewhat in the late 1960s, and some people foresaw the gradual end of black militancy. But these gains turned into slight losses with the economic problems of the early 1970s. The median income for black families remained about $4,000 less than for whites; economists estimated that unemployment figures for blacks exceeded 10 percent, compared to about 5 percent for whites.

The Nixon administration moved cautiously and obliquely on racial questions. Gaining only five of every one hundred black votes in 1968, the president had much more political capital invested in the white South. "Watch what we do, not what we say," suggested John Mitchell, the man most closely identified with the "Southern strategy." But even Daniel Moynihan, a former Kennedy official and Nixon's most liberal domestic adviser, urged a policy of "benign neglect." If black groups expected little from the national government, Moynihan reasoned, disappointments over the lack of radical change would generate less frustration and violence. The administration gave greatest priority to finding jobs for black workers, and even Nixon's most severe critics expressed cautious praise for efforts to achieve equal employment opportunities.

On almost every other issue, however, spokespeople for black civil rights severely criticized what Nixon's men did as well as what they said. Bishop Stephen Spottswood, the NAACP's board chairman, accused the administration of deliberately adopting an anti-black posture; Father Theodore Hesburgh, president of Notre Dame and head of the United States Civil Rights Commission, denounced the president's reluctance to enforce existing civil rights measures; and Leon Panetta, head of the Civil Rights Division of the Department of Health, Education and Welfare, resigned in protest against Nixon's opposition to school busing as a means of integrating public schools. From the outset, the administration braked the drive toward school desegregation. In deference to Southern supporters, the White House initially ordered HEW to revise the Johnson administration's tough desegregation guidelines and exempt schools "with bona fide educational and legal problems." And in a dramatic sign of the administration's attitude, Nixon's Justice Department argued against implementation of a desegregation plan in Mississippi. (Traditionally, government attorneys had appeared in support of black litigants.) In March 1972 the president himself asked on national television for a moratorium on busing. The administration's record in other areas proved equally disappointing to the vast majority of blacks: the government did little to help register black voters in the South; despite the hopes of Housing and Urban Development Secretary George Romney, attempts to push integration in housing got almost nowhere; the president called for drastic cuts in the poverty program; and the administration even failed to provide adequate funding for its pet project, black capitalism.

With blacks receiving little from the national government, some young activists sought political control of county and local governments. Although black people continued to register and vote in smaller numbers than whites, black candidates started with a powerful base of support. By 1974 a number of large cities—Cleveland, Atlanta, Detroit, Los Angeles, Gary, Newark—had elected black mayors, and many blacks gained seats on city and county councils. By 1974 more than seven hundred black politicians held office. Even Bobby Seale, the erstwhile black revolutionary-turned-politician, ran a fairly close second in a race for mayor of Oakland. Militant black nationalists—and black officeholders who did not need white votes—often denounced black politicians who played "the white man's game." Conversely, most black candidates tried to keep their distance from the ultra-nationalists. When a black political caucus gathered in Little Rock in March 1974, a number of prominent politicians avoided the meeting, fearing identification with outspoken nationalists like LeRoi Jones. After almost ten years of struggle, black leaders still failed to settle on a common definition of black power.

Brown Power

Although the black power movement captured more attention, other ethnic groups also displayed new cultural pride and growing political militancy. Throughout the 1960s, Mexican-Americans and Indians emulated the tactics of the black movement to organize their supporters and to attract the attention of the national news media. "Brown power" and "red power" made white Americans increasingly aware of the nation's pluralistic culture; they also dramatized the price that nonwhite minorities had paid—in economic deprivation and loss of self-respect—for their cultural and racial differences.

Mexican-Americans often confronted the type of discrimination with which black people were too familiar. Especially among migrant farm laborers, wages were low, housing inadequate, and education virtually nonexistent. The language barrier and the proximity of Mexican culture kept many Mexican-Americans far outside the mainstream of American life. During the 1960s the average *chicano* child had only a seventh-grade education; nearly nine of every ten *chicanos* dropped out of Texas high schools before graduation. Yet the problem was not inadequate motivation or low intelligence. As one teacher put it, "Our kids don't drop out, they are pushed out by poverty." Children could not concentrate on their studies if they were hungry, and many young people left school to help support their families.

Even if poverty did not force *chicanos* out of school, the attitudes of officials often did. In some California school districts, students could be expelled for speaking Spanish, even on the playground. Bilingualism, a quality highly valued among middle-class white children, was a badge of inferiority among Mexican-Americans. Standing on the edge of two cultures, many *chicano* youths had severe identity problems which contributed to high dropout rates and low scholastic achievement. Advancement for Mexican-Americans, it seemed, had to proceed along two fronts—lifting their economic status and creating a positive cultural identity.

Cesar Chavez launched the drive to raise wages among Mexican-American farm workers. Chavez, who had grown up in California migrant camps during the late 1930s, recalled his family's first grape-picking job. "Each payday the contractor said he couldn't pay us because the winery hadn't paid him yet. At the end of the seventh week we went to the contractor's house and it was empty—he owed us for seven weeks' pay. . . . We were desperate." Chavez never forgot his people's poverty, and when the *bracero* program ended in 1964 he began to unionize workers in the grape fields. With the source of new, cheap labor from Mexico diminished, unionization had a chance. The outlook grew even brighter when Chavez's United Farm Workers Union (UFW) attracted support from the powerful American Federation of Labor. During the grape-pickers' strike in Delano, California, in 1965, Walter Reuther of the United Auto Workers joined Chavez on the picket lines, carrying a sign reading *"HUELGA"* (Strike) and reminiscing about his

228

own organizing fights during the 1930s. Robert Kennedy also visited the scene and became the UFW's most influential political supporter. But the growers held out, always finding enough hungry and jobless people to replace the strikers. Finally, Chavez adopted the technique that would bring the UFW some success and make him famous—the nationwide boycott. Dramatizing his personal commitment, Chavez went on a lengthy fast, an act which damaged his frail health.

Chavez's appeal to boycott California grapes captured the sympathy of liberals and radicals during the mid-sixties. For over a year, millions of Americans refused to buy grapes (the army bought them in great quantities to send to Vietnam, however), and growers finally signed with the UFW. Chavez, always a favorite of the media, became the first Mexican-American to receive sympathetic national coverage, and many reporters hailed him as a Spanish-speaking Martin Luther King. When lettuce growers signed what Chavez considered "sweetheart contracts" with the Teamsters Union, he appealed to Americans to boycott lettuce. By the early seventies, however, the novelty of boycotts had worn off, and Chavez's victories grew fewer and fewer. As other events and other individuals monopolized the headlines, his cause received less national attention, and the UFW's power waned proportionately. The union not only failed to repeat the great Delano victory, but when the first UFW contracts came up for renewal, many grape growers switched and signed with the less militant Teamsters. In 1973 the UFW urged people to boycott certain California grapes and wines (in addition to Teamster lettuce), but popular response was limited. Still, the UFW again made gains in union elections held throughout California fields during 1975.

While Chavez worked to improve economic conditions among field workers, a charismatic minister in New Mexico, Reies Lopez Tijerina, attempted to organize a separatist movement and reopen the Mexican-American War of 1846–48. His organization, the Federal Alliance of Land Grants, reclaimed Southwestern land, water, and grazing rights which whites had usurped over the last hundred years. In 1967, he declared the area an independent republic. Guerrilla bands supporting Tijerina formed in Northern New Mexico in the late sixties and seized control of a portion of Kit Carson National Forest. When authorities arrested some of his followers, other disciples of Tijerina raided the courthouse in Tierra Amarilla to free them. The desperate action, which killed one deputy, catapulted Tijerina into the national news and caused widespread fear among Anglos in the area. Rumors swept New Mexico that Cuban-trained guerrillas were hiding in the mountains, and the national guard patrolled the area for a time. But Tijerina seemed to be fighting for an idealized and unretrievable past of small, independent peasant communities untouched by modern America. More practical leaders and organizations, not the Federal Alliance of Land Grants, appealed to most *chicano* militants.

The Brown Berets, a group initially patterned after the Black Panthers, attracted some followers. Like the early Panthers, young Brown Berets tried to provide social services in the *barrios* and to run programs which raised ethnic pride and consciousness. Jose Angel Gutierrez's political party, La Raza Unida, also gained support. In 1970 La Raza captured a majority of seats on the school board in Crystal City, Texas, and began to remold the educational system according to the needs of the Spanish-speaking population. Soon La Raza gained control of all other political offices in Crystal and turned the town into a showcase of *chicano* government, hoping to spread the party's popularity into *barrios* throughout the Southwest. Whether La Raza would remain an independent political party (with limited appeal in Anglo-dominated areas) or become more a political pressure group, forming alliances with major parties, remained unclear.

Despite the rising level of *chicano* militancy, national officials devoted little serious attention to the problems of Mexican-Americans. Some Southwestern school systems did begin to teach some basic skills in Spanish while at the same time trying to improve children's use of English; "*chicano* studies" programs quickly followed creation of black studies on some college campuses. But *chicano* problems remained largely invisible on the national level. In 1969 Senator Joseph Montoya of New Mexico introduced a bill to extend the life of the President's Inter-Agency Committee on Mexican-American Affairs, a group which studied *chicano* problems. The bill passed the Senate and went to the House, where it was "lost." After months of delay, searchers finally found the bill, misfiled in the Foreign Affairs Committee.

Red Power

"Red power" did not really break into the national news until a cold November morning in 1969 when a group of militant Indians seized Alcatraz Island in San Francisco Bay. On the basis of an 1868 Sioux treaty that gave Indians possession of any unused federal land, the group argued that they could legitimately claim the abandoned prison on Alcatraz. Hundreds of Indian supporters soon joined them, demanding that the government convert the island into an Indian cultural center and appropriate funds for a "Thunderbird University." Few white people took the Indians' proposals seriously. News reporters played up the announcement that the Indians would create a Bureau of

230

Caucasian Affairs and would pay the government twenty-four dollars in glass beads for the property, but they largely ignored the more serious issues. Although the government refused the Indians' demands, it wished to avoid a confrontation which might provide the Indian movement with martyrs, and authorities did not move onto the island. Officials simply waited until the austere conditions on Alcatraz and the lack of publicity thinned the Indians' ranks. Finally in the summer of 1971 federal marshals evicted the fifteen Indians who remained and closed the incident.

For many Indians, the occupation had a symbolic significance. "Not just on Alcatraz, but every place else, the Indian is in his last stand for cultural survival," explained Richard Oakes, one of the elected spokesmen for the Alcatraz community. Many leaders saw Alcatraz as an important step in the formation of a pan-Indian cultural consciousness which would preserve the native American heritage. The Indians on Alcatraz represented tribes throughout the United States. They hoped that Indians could begin to use their separation from white society to instill pride rather than breed inferiority. And Alcatraz provided a particularly apt location for protest; the Indians claimed that its uninhabitable buildings, bad water and sanitation, and certain unemployment resembled conditions on most Indian reservations.

Although seizure of Alcatraz gave the "Indian problem" brief national headlines, white injustice and Indian protests were hardly new. The vast majority of Indians missed out on the great affluence of postwar America. After two and a half decades of tremendous national "progress," the per capita income of Indians was 60 percent less than that of whites; Indian life expectancy was only forty-seven years; half of all Indian children never completed high school; and the unemployment rate for Indians was 40 percent (on most reservations it exceeded 50 percent). But statistics told only a small part of what it meant to be a native of America. The Indian was the arch-villain of western movies, the embodiment of a cruel stereotype of sloth and incompetence, the obstacle to "civilization" in history textbooks. (Indian leader Russell Means said that historians "have to realize that Columbus was a honkie half a world off-course, and that *we* discovered *him*.") Discrimination against Indians was everywhere. La Nada Means, one of the original occupiers of Alcatraz, remembered the "meanness of the small towns around the reservation. Blackfoot, Pocatello—they all had signs in the store windows to keep Indians out. . . . There were Indian stalls in the public bathrooms; Indians weren't served in a lot of the restaurants; and we just naturally all sat in the balcony of the theaters." What were the effects of such treatment? "It becomes part of the way you look at yourself," she explained.

231

In response to these conditions, Indians tried to organize throughout the sixties. In 1961 a few young Indians formed the National Indian Youth Council and announced that Indians should "rise up, in unison, and take what is ours by force." Three years later, Indian militants conducted a "fish-in" in Washington State, protesting the government's attempt to force Indians to buy expensive fishing licenses when treaties guaranteed them perpetual fishing rights. Some young Indian leaders began to promote ethnic consciousness in other ways. Folksinger Buffy Sainte-Marie captivated white, as well as Indian, audiences. Her songs, such as "Now That the Buffalo's Gone," publicized injustices done to native Americans. Lehman Brightman, militant organizer of the United Native Americans, edited *Warpath*, a publication focusing on Indian conditions. Vine Deloria's *Custer Died for Your Sins: An Indian Manifesto* (1969) and other works advocated a "cultural leave-us-alone agreement" between whites and Indians.

After Alcatraz, taking a cue from the tactics of other activist minorities, Indian militancy increased. Chippewas in the Minneapolis-St. Paul area organized the American Indian Movement (AIM). In 1973 two AIM leaders, Russell Means and Dennis Banks, began protesting the disparity in law enforcement for Indians and whites. In Custer, South Dakota, officials charged a white with second-degree manslaughter for fatally stabbing an Indian, while in nearby Rapid City an Indian accused of killing a white woman was held for murder without bail. Means and Banks led protests in both cities, and the hundreds of Indian demonstrators eventually clashed with police. AIM then seized a trading post at Wounded Knee, South Dakota, the place where the Seventh Cavalry had brutally crushed the last substantial pan-Indian resistance movement in the 1890s. AIM leaders believed that this small community on the Pine Ridge Reservation offered an appropriate place for launching a revival of "Indianness."

The occupation of Wounded Knee, highly publicized by the media, shattered the image of the passive, downtrodden Indian. It also became a focal point for the lagging radical cause in general: before authorities barred entry to the settlement, Angela Davis, William Kunstler, and other veterans of radical movements visited Wounded Knee. The militants' demands demonstrated their dislike of both the national government and the older tribal leaders. AIM members vowed to hold the town until the Senate Foreign Relations Committee reviewed broken treaties with Indians, until the government investigated corruption in the Bureau of Indian Affairs, and until the Ogallala Sioux tribal chairman, Dick Wilson, was removed from office.

AIM's bold tactics split the Indian community. Some Indians condemned AIM's members as outside agitators who wreaked physical destruction on an Indian town and repudiated Indian ways by attacking tribal elders. Others, including many older traditionalists, sympathized with AIM's opposition to Dick Wilson, criticizing him for corruption and for his cozy relationship with the Bureau of Indian Affairs. After federal marshals cleared Wounded Knee, the next tribal election reflected the division. Although Wilson was reelected, Russell Means received only several fewer votes, which indicated the hollowness of the outside-agitator theme.

The siege of Wounded Knee did not end Indian militancy: AIM then shifted its focus into the courts. Indicted on various counts, Banks and Means began a spectacular trial in St. Paul, first trying to have United States treaties with Indians (which had subsequently been violated) admitted into evidence on their behalf. After a nine-month trial, the presiding judge dismissed the indictments and charged the government prosecutors with serious misconduct. By the mid-seventies other Indians throughout the country were also launching legal challenges and threatening direct action to redress grievances. Although militant tactics did not gain automatic support from all the Indian community, red power, like black power, had a far-reaching impact. It promoted a new pride in Indian culture, a fresh concern with preserving an ancient heritage, and a stronger determination to make whites live up to past promises.

Woman Power

In 1955 Adlai Stevenson told graduates of Smith College that their job in politics should be to use the "humble role of housewife" to influence their husbands and sons. The advice neatly fit the then-current emphasis on domesticity. A woman's discontent, eminent psychologists of the 1950s reported, stemmed not from her dull and un-challenging life but from a psychological disorder resulting from a failure to accept her feminine character. These "experts" believed that ad-vocates of women's rights were maladjusted and neurotic, that their frustrations derived from unfulfilled sexual desires or unsatisfactory relationships with their fathers. The stereotype of the feminist who "just needed a good man" to cure her anxieties remained firmly implanted in the minds of many American males.

Most psychologists recommended individual therapy to "re-adjust" discontented women to their "natural," passive, home-centered roles. Some advocated programs that would channel the need for self-expression into "proper" areas such as cooking, childbearing and in-terior decorating. Mass-circulation women's magazines responded with a repetitious array of articles which pictured cookery, decoration, and crafts as truly challenging and creative pursuits. Despite the subsequent women's liberation movement and the growing numbers of working women, articles on home-centered women's activities remained the standard fare of women's magazines.

Some women, however, began to argue that the answer to female discontent lay not in molding errant women into the female stereotype but in reforming society so women could escape the traditional female role without feeling guilty. These spokeswomen presented evidence that wives who worked felt greater self-esteem and related better to their husbands and children than did women who lost their personal identity amid the confines of homelife. It followed that women should have the choice, without suffering any social stigma, to pursue careers outside the home. This view found some acceptance in high places. In 1961 John Kennedy established a presidential commission on the status of women, a group which eventually reported that widespread sex discrimination—in both occupation and salary—made it difficult for women to find well-paid jobs which matched their capabilities. Although the report advanced only moderate solutions to inequality, it did focus serious attention on women's employment problems. It also regarded working women as positive contributors to society, not as instruments of family breakdown.

The same year in which the commission issued its report (1963), a far more influential analysis appeared—Betty Friedan's book *The Feminine Mystique*. The book launched a new feminist movement. Going far beyond the simple issue of job discrimination, Friedan presented a full-blown critique of the sex-role conditioning which, from birth, channeled women into a position of inferiority. From dolls and dainty ruffles through teenage dating conventions to myths of married bliss, women were caught in a mystique which prevented them from developing their full potential as human beings. Women had to break through the social conditioning to gain true equality and self-esteem.

Friedan's book appeared at a propitious time. Concern with civil rights for blacks was at a high point, and women began to realize that issues of equal opportunity, equal pay, and full acceptance applied to them as well as to blacks. In addition, the stereotype which white society had of blacks—childlike, irresponsible, emotional, and intellectually inferior—became a mirror in which women also saw themselves. Too many white males expected both women and blacks to be docile and to "know their place."

The black people's struggle also provided organizational and tactical models for the women's rights movement. In 1966 Betty Friedan and other women founded the National Organization for Women (NOW).

Similar to black civil rights organizations, NOW campaigned against institutions which practiced sex discrimination, lobbied for creation of child-care centers, and publicized the cause of women through the media. NOW created local chapters and encouraged "consciousness-raising sessions," small groups of women who would discuss their lives, vent their grievances, and come to recognize their inferior status. Consciousness-raising would, feminists hoped, enable women to lead fuller, more satisfying lives.

The black movement also fought legal battles which ultimately benefited women. The Civil Rights Act of 1964, passed mainly in response to racial inequality, prohibited discrimination on the basis of sex as well as color. (Southern congressmen inserted the provision hoping that the spectre of female equality would quash the bill.) The Civil Rights Act provided the principal legal tool which women's groups used to force government and business to stop sex discrimination. By the late sixties, the government required corporations receiving federal funds to adopt nondiscriminatory hiring practices and equal pay scales; in the early seventies, the government additionally required affirmative action to recruit more women and minority-group applicants.

The antiwar and radical movements of the late 1960s also contributed to the feminist upsurge. Demonstrating against injustice made antiwar women more conscious of their second-class roles; men dominated the podiums and the news while women typed circulars and brewed coffee. The development of a radical critique of American society provided some women with a full-blown explanation of injustice. Capitalism, according to the radical view, lay at the heart of women's oppression; it was a more basic problem than simple male chauvinism. Capitalism encouraged competitiveness and the desire to dominate others; it fostered a female consumer class to keep mass production at a high level; it conditioned women to think that a lifetime of work in the home was "natural," thereby creating millions of unpaid workers. Dominated and exploited, housewives provided slave labor. The social conditioning and economic imperatives of capitalism ran so deep that change would not come easily. Communist Chinese society, which displayed sexual equality, became a model for many radicals who concluded that women's liberation required thoroughgoing social revolution.

The development of a radical feminist position splintered the women's movement. NOW, consisting largely of middle-class professionals, sought to obtain equality through legislatures and courts. Political radicals, such as Weatherwoman Bernardine Dohrn, who joined the FBI's "ten most-wanted list" after her alleged connection with bombing incidents, attacked the same capitalist system in which members of

NOW wanted to work. Cultural radicals sought to abolish marriage, which they considered a sexist institution; some rejected male companionship in favor of lesbianism. As all these feminist groups received publicity, women who recoiled at their philosophies began to organize as well. Movements of contented housewives who resented the feminists' implications that they were ignorant, useless, and discontented rallied in support of the old values. These women believed that passivity, motherhood, and devotion to their husbands should continue to be the hallmarks of virtuous women.

Some observers believed that disagreement weakened the women's movements, but such divisions may have been healthy. Together, these groups publicized all conceivable positions which women might take, and young women could now choose from widely varying life styles. In this sense, women could have more alternatives than men, most of whom continued to be bound by a rigid workaday "male mystique."

"You've Got a Long Way to Go, Baby"

By 1974 the women's movement had a record of mixed success. Its greatest victory probably came in government efforts to halt discrimination in hiring and pay. But President Nixon vetoed free day-care for children of working mothers, a measure essential to achieving true equality of pay. Women's-rights activists applauded a 1973 Supreme Court decision that abortion during the first three months of pregnancy was a matter of personal privacy. The decision opened the way to abortion virtually on demand during early pregnancy; however, it also reinvigorated the foes of abortion. A "Right to Life" group, championing the rights of the unborn, conducted a massive campaign against abortion, and President Nixon also strongly criticized the court's decision.

The greatest battle came over the Equal Rights Amendment to the Constitution. The amendment, granting equal rights specifically to women, passed Congress in early 1972 and was ratified by about half the states. But the necessary approval from three-fourths of the states did not come, and the amendment's progress stalled. NOW lobbied in its behalf, but vigorous opposition from people such as conservative commentator Phyllis Schlafly and organizations such as the Christian Crusade more than counterbalanced NOW's efforts. Opponents charged that the amendment's effect on military service, alimony, and protective-labor laws would work against most women's best interests.

If legal victories came slowly, women found that changes in social mores were even more difficult to achieve. By 1970 over 40 percent of all women held full-time jobs, a figure which reflected the growing number of women who had entered the traditional "male" sphere over the last two decades. But women also continued to occupy the traditional home-centered female role as well. Women were changing, but men were not. True sexual equality seemed as far away as ever. One study showed that when a wife took on full-time employment, most husbands assumed only a few domestic chores. Husbands of working wives did about one-fourth of all work around the house, but women still did three times that much. And men continued to expect certain supposedly male prerogatives. One study revealed that among husbands with wives who worked full-time, 38 percent still believed that women should be paid less than men for the same work; 32 percent still felt that sexual intercourse should occur whenever they desired it (regardless of the woman's feelings); 71 percent thought that men had no obligation to help around the house "all the time"; and 80 percent said they would be unwilling to make sacrifices for their wife's career. (Husbands of nonworking women expressed these attitudes of inequality even more frequently.) The study showed that although a wife's employment might increase her self-esteem, it by no means brought her equality, even in her husband's eyes.

By the seventies, it was clear that men, much more than women, needed their consciousness raised if sexual equality were to be achieved. The women's movement began trying to broaden its appeal to reach the male half of society, and "men's liberation" or "human liberation" gained a few supporters. Some men, usually husbands of feminist activists, began organizing consciousness-raising sessions patterned after NOW's, and two radical heroes of the 1960s, Abbie Hoffman and Jerry Rubin, contritely apologized for the male chauvinism of their old movement.

But gains for women depended upon economics as much as attitudes, and the declining job market of the seventies limited alternatives for women faster than government pressure or male acquiescence could open them. Then too, as radical politics slipped out of fashion in the mid-seventies, militant feminism also receded. As in other areas, the protesters of the sixties had their impact, but how thoroughgoing a change came about remained unclear.

BIBLIOGRAPHY

The controversial ideas of Paul Goodman and Herbert Marcuse can be traced in their works. *One-Dimensional Man* (1964) and *An Essay on Liberation* (1969) were Marcuse's most important books published in the 1960s. Among Goodman's many works are *Growing Up Absurd* (1960), *People and Personnel* (1963), and *The New Reformation* (1971).

237

Charles Reich, *The Greening of America* (1970), is an effort to interpret the nature of the youthful revolt. A more insightful analysis is Theodore Roszak, *The Making of a Counter-Culture* (1969); his later work, *Where the Wasteland Ends* (1972), is also valuable. William Braden, *The Age of Aquarius* (1970), is a useful analysis by a journalist. And three studies by Kenneth Keniston—*The Uncommitted* (1965), *The Young Radicals* (1968), and *Youth and Dissent* (1971)—have been extremely influential. An entertaining example of the "new journalism"—*The Electric Kool-Aid Acid Test* by Tom Wolfe (1968)—traces the rise and fall of Ken Kesey.

Introductions to the political left include Paul Jacobs and Saul Landau, eds., *The New Radicals* (1966); and Jack Newfield, *A Prophetic Minority* (rev. ed., 1970). Later interpretations include Peter Clecak, *Radical Paradoxes: Dilemmas of the American Left, 1945–70* (1973); Edward J. Bacciocco, Jr., *The New Left in America, 1956–1970* (1974); Irwin Unger, *The New Left* (1974); and Kirkpatric Sale, *S.D.S.* (1973). A critical perspective from the Old Left is Irving Howe's *Beyond the New Left* (1970). See also Michael Miles, *The Radical Probe* (1971); and Robert A. Dahl, *After the Revolution?* (1970). Daniel Yankelovich, *The New Morality* (1974), is a preliminary assessment of the impact of the 1960s upon youth.

The turbulent 1968 presidential campaign is best followed in Lewis Chester, et al., *An American Melodrama* (1969). Other good reminiscences of the year of the new politics include Norman Mailer, *Miami and the Siege of Chicago* (1968); Jeremy Larner, *Nobody Knows: Reflections on the McCarthy Campaign of 1968* (1970); and David Halberstam, *The Unfinished Odyssey of Robert Kennedy* (1968).

A good introduction to the youthful dissent of the late 1960s is The Editors of Rolling Stone, *The Age of Paranoia* (1972). I. F. Stone, *The Killings at Kent State* (1971), is a preliminary investigation of a still untold tale. The Chicago Seven trial is discussed in Jason Epstein, *Conspiracy* (1970).

Indian militancy is discussed in Stan Steiner, *The New Indians* (1968); and Donald T. Berthrong, *The American Indian: From Pacifism to Activism* (1973). Vine Deloria, *Custer Died for Your Sins* (1969), is an important manifesto by an Indian spokesman. *Chicano* activism is treated in Stan Steiner, *La Raza* (1970); Edward Simmen, ed., *Pain and Promise: The Chicano Today* (1972); and Matt Meier and Feliciano Rivera, *The Chicanos* (1972). The most important statements from the women's liberation movement include Betty Friedan, *The Feminine Mystique* (1963); and Robin Morgan, ed., *Sisterhood is Powerful* (1970). William Chafe, *The American Woman: Her Changing Social, Economic, and Political Role, 1920–1970* (1972), is an excellent historical analysis.

238

The problems of blue-collar workers are sympathetically analyzed in Richard Sennett and Jonathan Cobb, *The Hidden Injuries of Class* (1972). Sar A. Levitan, ed., *Blue-Collar Workers* (1972); and Michael Novak, *The Rise of the Unmeltable Ethnics* (1972), are also useful.

Finally, Alvin Toffler, *Future Shock* (1970); Victor C. Ferkiss, *Technological Man* (1969); Arthur Schlesinger, Jr., *The Crisis of Confidence* (1969); and Andrew Hacker, *End of the American Era* (1970), are four of the stimulating books which tried to assess the state—and the future—of American society during the late 1960s.

Violence in Vietnam

Despite the years of antiwar protest and Richard Nixon's talk of a secret peace plan, the war in Vietnam continued. By nature, Nixon was cautious and methodical; in 1968–69 the new commander-in-chief seemed to enjoy the luxury of time, time enough to plan a careful withdrawal from the war. Nixon's approach reflected the influence of Henry Kissinger, a Harvard professor who became the president's special adviser on foreign affairs. After a thorough review of war policy, Nixon and Kissinger made several crucial decisions: as quickly as possible, the United States would turn the ground war over to the South Vietnamese, begin a gradual withdrawal of American forces, and continue to press Hanoi for some type of "honorable" end to the conflict. In July 1969 the president placed his Vietnam policy within a grander design—the so-called Nixon Doctrine—pledging that the United States would continue giving military assistance to anticommunist governments in Asia but would have Asians, not Americans, do the fighting. In later statements, Nixon made it "perfectly clear" that the United States would not "bug out" on its commitment to Saigon or allow North Vietnam to gain a quick victory. The president rejected Secretary of Defense Melvin Laird's suggestion of a more rapid pullout; instead, Nixon tried to ensure that he would leave behind a viable anticommunist government.

9

The ecstasy and the agony: The Nixon years

To achieve his aims, Nixon stepped up the violence in Vietnam. The total commitment of American forces declined very little at first, and the Pentagon actually drafted more men during Nixon's first months than under Johnson in 1968. The United States also increased the number of offensive operations on the ground. The president honored Johnson's bombing halt over North Vietnam, but the air force sent its squadrons of B-52s against targets in the South as well as in Cambodia and Laos. Hoping to play down the amount of activity, military briefing officers revised the English language: attacks on the enemy became "accelerated pacification" efforts and "protective reaction strikes."

Antiwar forces severely criticized the apparently widening war. Public revelations of the My Lai massacre (which had occurred in March 1968) intensified revulsion against American involvement. The unfolding story of My Lai was shocking. American servicemen testified to the killing of unarmed civilians, women, and children by a company under the command of an ineffectual lieutenant named William Calley. After bungling an attempt at a coverup, the army finally prosecuted several officers, but only Lieutenant Calley was convicted. A member of another unit testified to similar murders by his outfit. "I used to think my company was a bad-ass one until I started seeing others," he said. "Sometimes you thought it was just my platoon, my company that was committing atrocious acts. . . . But what we were doing was being done all over."

The seemingly endless violence and stories of atrocities intensified the drive to get out of Vietnam. Long supine before the White House, even Congress came alive. In September 1969, New York Senator Charles Goodell introduced a bill to cut off all funds for the war after December 1, 1970. Two months later, in November 1969, an estimated crowd of one million people marched through Washington, singing "Give Peace a Chance" and calling for an immediate end to the conflict. The quiet, dignified mood of the vast majority of demonstrators failed to impress the president, who pointedly announced that he would spend the crisp fall afternoon watching a televised football game. Maddened by Nixon's attitude and saddened by their failure to influence policy, many veteran antiwar organizers began to close up shop. The days of massive demonstrations in Washington, they concluded, were over.

In May 1970 Nixon temporarily escalated the war by ordering an American-led invasion of neutral Cambodia. North Vietnamese forces had been using various parts of Cambodia as staging areas, and Pentagon strategists had long pressed the White House to "clear out the sanctuaries." As long as neutralist Prince Norodom Sihanouk controlled the Cambodian government, the Johnson administration resisted this pressure; but when a right-wing military regime overthrew the prince in March, Nixon finally approved the project. A quick strike, it was hoped, would throw the enemy off balance and capture valuable supplies. Rejecting Kissinger's advice that the Pentagon routinely announce the invasion (which the White House called an "incursion"), Nixon went on national television to defend his action. His overblown rhetoric and self-pitying tone made the speech a disaster in public relations.

> *We will not be humiliated. . . . If when the chips are down, the world's most powerful nation . . . acts like a pitiful, helpless giant, the forces of totalitarianism and anarchy will threaten free nations and free institutions throughout the world. . . . I would rather be a one-term president and do what I believe was right than be a two-term president at the cost of seeing America become a second-rate power.*

From any perspective, the Cambodian operation marked an important turning point in the United States' withdrawal from Vietnam. Although American troops encountered surprisingly little resistance and grabbed relatively few North Vietnamese supplies, the president's defenders considered the "incursion" a great success. They claimed that it upset North Vietnam's plans and allowed the United States more time to beef up Saigon's forces. But the invasion also produced an uproar in the United States, especially on college campuses. Student strikes, protest marches, and some destruction raised havoc at more than four hundred schools; outbreaks at Kent State (Ohio) led to the killing of four students. Many colleges abruptly ended the spring semester early and closed their doors. Shaken, Nixon made an unannounced pre-dawn visit to young antiwar protestors at the Lincoln Memorial; seeking a common ground with the bewildered students, he talked about football and surfing rather than the new escalation in the war. The reaction to the invasion of Cambodia indicated that Vietnam had become "Nixon's war" and that the president could not prolong American involvement much longer.

The New Left: Factionalism and Violence

Paralleling the violence in Vietnam (or growing out of it, according to some social scientists) was a violent new direction in the radical antiwar movement. Political radicals, such as members of SDS, realized that neither rock music festivals like Woodstock nor even campus protests constituted a revolution. Most students probably opposed the war, and many remained dissatisfied with college life. Activists could tap this student alienation and channel it into demonstrations against the war or against the still expanding multiversity. But as radicals gained student converts, their coalition became more unstable. If embattled university officials simply outwaited the less committed protesters or conceded some campus grievances, most confrontations ended.

Increasingly, radical leaders fought among themselves over tactics and long-range goals. Frustrated by a renewed emphasis on revolutionary theories, Jerry Rubin proclaimed that "ideology is the brain disease of the left" and that "the revolution is for seven-year-olds." Meanwhile, the Weathermen—later called the Weatherpeople or the Weatherfolks in deference to the feminist movement—pledged to "bring the war home to Amerika" to help groups such as the Viet Cong. To the tune of the Beatles' "Nowhere Man," this small but highly publicized faction of SDS sang,

He's a real Weatherman/Ripping up the mother land,
Making all his Weatherplans/For everyone;
Knows just what he's fighting for/Victory for the people's war,
Trashes, bombs, kills pigs and more/The Weatherman.

Predictably, the Weatherpeople met limited success. Their much-publicized "Four Days of Rage," an invasion of Chicago, proved a disaster. After smashing some windows, almost all the helmeted Weatherpeople were overwhelmed, beaten bloody, and arrested by Mayor Daley's police.

After the fiasco most prominent Weatherpeople went underground; some joined other radicals in a bombing campaign against the symbols of "Kapitalist oppression." Between September 1969 and June 1970 there were more than 174 bombings and attempted bombings on college campuses. An explosion in a University of Wisconsin science building killed a graduate student, and radicals at Columbia burned one professor's research notes. Universities gradually adjusted to the almost daily bomb scares which plagued some schools, and cautious scholars began keeping valuable materials and manuscripts at home. Bombers also struck off-campus, hitting targets such as the Bank of America, Chase Manhattan Bank, and finally the United States Congress. At least three Weatherpeople blew themselves apart when their "bomb factory" in New York's fashionable Greenwich Village exploded in 1970. Few of the attacks did major damage—corporation bathrooms in which explosives were hidden endured the brunt of the onslaught—but they contributed to an increasingly ugly mood throughout the country.

Even without the bombings, politics in the streets was becoming more violent. Young dissidents sometimes went beyond peaceful protest; burning a few small buildings, destroying a handful of police cars, and "trashing" all kinds of facilities. President Nixon and Vice-President Agnew sanctimoniously upheld the rule of law. "You see these bums, you know, blowing up the campuses," the president grumbled after students protested (in most cases nonviolently) the invasion of Cambodia in May 1970. "We cannot afford to be divided or deceived by the decadent thinking of a few young people," mused Agnew. But we could "afford to separate them from our society—with no more regret than we should feel over discarding rotten apples from a barrel."

Some law enforcement people shared these sentiments. More violence came from the upholders of law and order than from outgunned students and radicals. In early 1968 state troopers killed three protesting

Wide World Photos

Jackson State College, Mississippi, May 15, 1970: a women's dormitory hit by police bullets.

black students at Orangeburg State College in South Carolina. During a 1969 confrontation at Berkeley, a protest against destruction of a "people's park" near campus, state patrolmen indiscriminately dropped tear gas from helicopters and fatally shot one long-haired bystander in the back. In December 1969 Chicago police stormed the Illinois headquarters of the Black Panthers and killed two people, including Panther leader Fred Hampton. In May 1970 white policemen and highway patrolmen opened fire on a women's dormitory at Mississippi's Jackson State College, murdering two unarmed students. And in the most celebrated incident—probably because the victims were middle-class and white—Ohio national guardsmen shot 15 students, four of whom died, at Kent State.

Along with an apparently rising crime rate, the political disorders encouraged the administration's drive for "law and order." To most Americans, the young radicals remained an unpopular band of troublemakers. After the killings at Kent State, where none of the victims had belonged to any radical organization, most Americans believed that the national guard had fired in self-defense. A state grand jury indicted several student leaders but no guardsmen; ignoring requests from Kent State students and parents of the slain young people, the Nixon administration refused to reopen the case. (Finally in 1974, after Nixon's third attorney general, Elliot Richardson, had ordered a new investigation, a federal grand jury indicted eight guardsmen for conspiring to violate the civil rights of the dead and injured students. Ruling that the government had failed to prove a conspiracy, a district judge threw out the indictments.)

Even after the bloodshed at Kent State, Nixon and Agnew continued their tough talk, and Attorney General Mitchell strengthened the Justice Department's internal security division. Failing to obtain full cooperation from feisty old J. Edgar Hoover, the administration authorized a sweeping plan for clandestine, and illegal, intelligence gathering outside the FBI. The scope of the activity against radicals during the early years of the Nixon administration still remains unclear. (The White House later claimed that the top-secret plan, first revealed during the Senate's hearings on Watergate, was withdrawn four days after President Nixon's initial approval. Skeptics expressed doubts, and evidence made public in 1975 revealed that the CIA had engaged in some illegal activities against suspected subversives. Supporters of the CIA conceded that some domestic surveillance had occurred but claimed that the agency had limited its spying to radicals with ties to foreign nations. After these revelations President Ford ordered an investigation of the CIA, and Democrats in the Senate sponsored a probe into antiradical activities by all government agencies.) But there was no doubt that the Nixon administration and some state officials mobilized the judicial system against radical dissidents during the late 1960s and early 1970s.

In the most celebrated case, the Chicago Seven conspiracy trial of 1969, the American legal system appeared at its worst. The Nixon administration, particularly Attorney General Mitchell, pressed indictments against eight leading radicals, charging them with conspiracy and with crossing state lines to encourage the riots at the 1968 Democratic convention. (Mitchell's predecessor, Ramsey Clark, had refused to prosecute because of insufficient evidence.) Several of the defendants had never even met before the trial; they considered the indictments a blatant attempt to cripple the radical movement through specious charges. But if they agreed that they were being railroaded, the "conspiracy" (as they facetiously came to call themselves) disagreed on almost everything else. "We couldn't even agree on where to go to lunch," joked Yippie Abbie Hoffman. The defense team, led by radical attorney William Kunstler, hoped to make a serious constitutional challenge, but some of the defendants viewed the affair as a counter-cultural "happening." Goaded by Judge Julius Hoffman's obviously prejudicial rulings, the defense never put together a coherent strategy. At the end of the trial, Judge Hoffman, a balding little man whom the defendants lampooned as "Mr. Magoo" and "Julius the Just," unexpectedly cited all the defendants for various actions in contempt of court. Concluding the affair, the twelve jurors rendered an obvious "compromise verdict": they acquitted all defendants of the conspiracy charge but convicted the most famous of crossing state lines to incite a riot. The result satisfied no one—appeals courts overturned these convictions along with Hoffman's contempt citations—but the trial was at least over. (The Nixon administration later declined to retry the case; another federal judge convicted several defendants of contempt, but gave them suspended sentences.)

Such trials—including prosecutions of black militant Angela Davis, Bobby Seale of the Black Panthers, antiwar priests Philip and Daniel Berrigan, twenty-one members of the Black Panthers of New York, and various lesser-known radicals—produced few convictions, but they did cost the radical movement precious time, energy, money, and support. The defense of Angela Davis, for example, cost several million dollars and required a tremendous legal effort by a group of young attorneys. Meanwhile, all the unsuccessful prosecutions still helped to focus public attention on the "criminals" who were trying to overthrow the American system. Simply by filing charges, the government encouraged public fears of the radical "menace" and greatly harmed all leftist political organizations.

246

The Blue-Collar Protest

President Nixon's policies, especially his actions in Vietnam and his crusade for "law and order," apparently gained solid support from blue-collar workers; certainly he enjoyed vocal backing from prominent persons, such as country-Western singers, who claimed to speak for "common working people." Spokesmen for American workers often condemned "scruffy" hippies as cowards who were afraid to defend the country and even as traitors who wore the flag on the seat of their pants. Old Glory became a symbol of the cultural and political clash: police sewed flag emblems on their uniforms, workers pasted flag decals on their windshields, the president prominently displayed a flag pin in his lapel, and the star of the television show "Hee-Haw" painted his guitar red, white, and blue. Another country-Western singer expressed his contempt for the cultural revolution in two best-selling ballads. "I'm proud to be an Okie from Muskogee," and "When you're runnin' down our country, man, you're walkin' on the fightin' side of me," sang Merle Haggard. Some construction workers translated Haggard's lyrics into action: in May 1970 a group of pipe-wielding "hard-hats" attacked peaceful antiwar protesters in New York. Apparently endorsing this kind of support, Nixon welcomed a delegation of construction workers to the White House and posed for pictures in his own hard hat, appropriately adorned with an American flag.

Some sociologists viewed the hard-hat phenomenon as evidence of "working-class authoritarianism" and decried American workers' alleged affinity for repressive right-wing ideas. Unable to comprehend the complex issues of modern society, these commentators argued, workers unthinkingly embraced supporters of traditional values and attacked those who symbolized change. The popular television character, Archie Bunker, exemplified this view of working-class know-nothingism. Sprawling in front of his "boob tube," Archie announced his love for the president, policemen, and white sports heroes; he openly denounced hippies, "spades," and "bleeding-heart liberals." Creators of the series claimed to be satirizing "Bunkerism," but critics contended that by showing such attitudes, the program only validated and strengthened prejudices. Many working-class Americans, the program's detractors claimed, did not laugh *at* Archie; they laughed *with* him.

Although blue-collar America certainly contained its share of Archies, people in all walks of life shared his prejudices. Singling out one group as latent fascists seemed unfair. One study of the attitudes of manual laborers, for example, revealed that they opposed the Vietnam war more strongly than suburban businessmen. And examinations of racial views indicated that a good many white workers supported the movement for black equality. The working-class discontent of the late 1960s defied simple explanation.

One thing, however, seemed clear: despite generally rising real wages, most blue-collar workers felt that they were not doing as well as they should be. Blue-collar families saw their neighborhoods "invaded" by blacks and destroyed by urban renewal projects, their streets "overrun" by criminals, their savings and paychecks undermined by inflation, their take-home pay cut by rising taxes, and their sons shipped to Vietnam. Some of these grievances were overstated, but many were authentic. The small increase in real income, for example, never quite covered all the new expenses. In 1968 an urban worker with two children, according to figures from the Bureau of Labor Statistics, needed almost $10,000 a year to live at "a moderate but adequate standard of living." Yet even well-paid workers made less than $8,000, and more than 60 percent of white middle-class families required two or more breadwinners to boost their living standard into the "moderate" range. Only through the miracle of installment buying could most families afford new appliances and late-model cars; in 1969 the total installment debt reached almost $90 billion.

In addition to concern about money, many American workers expressed dislike for their jobs and their lives. (A government study revealed that lower-status white-collar workers—file clerks, salespeople, and computer programmers, for example—shared most of the complaints of blue-collar workers.) Trying to escape the tedium of factory work or the boredom of manual labor, growing numbers of workers turned to alcohol and drugs; most told interviewers that daydreaming provided the best way to make the work day pass less painfully. Employers and labor leaders began to warn that low morale and high absenteeism threatened to undermine American industry. But workers themselves voiced more concern about the declining quality of their lives. Labor-union officials, many rank-and-filers claimed, cared little about lax safety standards or bad working conditions.

Workers complained that home life offered little escape from the rigors of their jobs. Rising early in the morning or working the last shift at night, they returned home exhausted, lacking both the energy and the money for leisure activities which business and professional people took for granted. For a blue-collar family, dinner at a good restaurant and an evening at the movies were rare treats. The plant bowling league and television were the most common types of recreation; going out to dinner usually meant wolfing down the standardized fare at the nearest fast-food chain. And vacations rarely involved two-week rests at a Holiday Inn. Blue-collar families generally visited nearby relatives or jammed into a small trailer or camper, their answer to lakeside cottages and deluxe mobile homes.

Many blue-collar workers felt that other people looked down on them. While many workers had no use for hippies, dissident young people generally expressed the same type of contempt for the Archie Bunkers. Similarly, workers felt uncomfortable with better-educated business leaders or professional people. Talking to a sociologist, a house painter complained that "whenever I'm with educated people, you know, or people who aren't my own kind . . . um . . . I feel like I'm making a fool of myself." When he went to a social gathering, "there were all these people in suits and I had on a jacket. . . . Somehow people were introducing themselves to each other all over the place, but nobody was introducing themselves to *me*. So that's how it is," he concluded.

Richard Nixon posed as the president who would listen to the "forgotten American." He hoped to turn blue-collar discontent to political advantage. But he and his vice-president discovered that they could not simply stampede workers into voting Republican on the basis of an anti-hippie, law-and-order campaign. Neither blue-collar workers nor the issues were that simple.

The End of Anger

In the 1970 elections, Nixon and Vice-President Agnew plied blue-collar voters and other "middle Americans" with one theme: a small group of New Left hooligans, aided and abetted by "radical liberals" within the Democratic party, threatened the country's stability. For two years, Agnew had been assailing the "biased liberal" media which "slandered" the president, the gnawing spirit of permissiveness which originated with Dr. Spock, the "nattering nabobs of negativism" who scorned traditional American values, the "curled-lip boys in the Eastern ivory towers" who thumbed their noses at ordinary people, and the crime in the streets which threatened the lives and property of decent citizens. As election day neared, Agnew stepped up his attacks on the New Left and "radical liberals," announcing that it was "time to sweep that kind of garbage out of our society." Charging into the campaign late, Nixon claimed that a climate of permissiveness threatened American life and that a new Congress of law-and-order Republicans would help restore decency and morality. In a radical departure from his normal practice of addressing only carefully scrutinized audiences, Nixon borrowed a tactic from George Wallace: he allowed long-haired demonstrators into his rallies and then used them as foils.

Despite Nixon's energetic campaigning, the Republicans failed to link most Democrats with social and political radicalism. The GOP added a few members to the Senate, dropped about a dozen seats in the House, and lost no fewer than eleven governorships. The electoral results clearly revealed that the Democrats, though badly divided and demoralized, remained the majority party. Impressionistic evidence seemed to indicate that many voters had found Nixon's last-minute demagoguery distasteful; many moderates unfavorably compared the president's final, mud-slinging speeches to the low-key, almost too-folksy reply of Senator Edmund Muskie, the Democratic party's 1968 vice-presidential candidate and leading hopeful for 1972. The lesson of 1970 was not lost on the White House. Nixon's political strategists abandoned grand theories about "an emerging Republican majority" and began to plan a campaign which divorced the president, as much as possible, from the rest of the Republican ticket. Meanwhile, the president put the "old Nixon" back in mothballs. He left all the invective to a more subdued Agnew, organized more subtle campaign strategies for 1972, and accentuated his role as a "world statesman."

The 1970 election seemed to indicate that most Americans were tiring of the shouting and political discord of the late 1960s. Strident appeals no longer satisfied. Most blue-collar workers, for example, realized that economic problems—particularly inflation and unemployment—could prove much more dangerous than permissiveness and negativism. Many parents recognized that their children looked a lot like the long-haired hippies Agnew wanted to cast out with the garbage. On the other side of the overestimated generation gap, the days of the "Movement" were about over.

By 1970 the New Left political movement was in disarray. Seeking militant allies and fresh sources of inspiration, a few young radicals looked to prison inmates, particularly articulate blacks such as George Jackson, as leaders in a violent new assault against American institutions. This desperate strategy—an alliance with the most powerless group in American society, one heavily infiltrated by police informers and agent provocateurs—ultimately proved suicidal. Jackson, who became a celebrity after publication of some of his prison letters, was eventually killed (assassinated, claimed his admirers) during an attempted escape from San Quentin Prison in 1973. A small group of white radicals, who entered the New Left movement through their work with prisoners, met a similarly violent end. Calling themselves the Symbionese Liberation Army (SLA), a handful of young revolutionaries, led by an escaped black convict named Donald DeFreeze, briefly gained national attention in 1973 by gunning down the Oakland, California, superintendent of schools (a progressive black educator) and by

250

kidnapping Patricia Hearst, daughter of a prominent San Francisco newspaper publisher. The SLA converted their captive and evaded police and FBI pursuers for several months. Then in May 1974, six members of the group perished after a spectacular shootout with Los Angeles police, and in September 1975 Patty Hearst and her friends were finally apprehended. Long before the rise and fall of the SLA, however, most young people had lost interest in both radical and revolutionary politics.

By reducing American ground forces in Vietnam, promising an end to the draft, and helping to lower the voting age to eighteen, the Nixon administration removed three highly visible irritants. Although many of the other old "radical" issues remained—the war, for example, dragged on—they failed to ignite the old passions. Instead of rallying to the newest youth candidates, most college students decided to concentrate on their studies or to relax with rock music. If they wanted intellectual excitement, students of the early 1970s turned to science fiction and mysticism rather than to New Left politics or radical sociology: Robert Heinlein and John Brunner replaced Marcuse and Goodman; Carlos Castaneda attracted more readers than C. Wright Mills.

The counter-culture no longer seemed either an imminent threat or an instant panacea. In many respects, the cultural revolution had faded into the general mass culture. Permissive ideas about sex and drugs invaded all levels of American society. Middle-class Republicans from suburbia displayed their "liberation" by attending X-rated movies and reading Dr. Reuben's sex manuals. Even conservative columnist William F. Buckley admitted to smoking pot. Length of hair no longer provided a gauge of politics; even the hair of male Republicans began to stray over the collar and below the ears. The easy-going life style of the counter-culture fell prey to the hucksters on Madison Avenue, and the youth rebellion gave way to the mini-skirted "Dodge Rebellion." Long-haired young men and braless young women—undoubtedly the same models who had recently posed for *Gentlemen's Quarterly* and *Vogue*—hawked expensive stereo equipment, Pepsi-Cola, and even prefaded, prepatched Levis. "The youth cult has been taken over by Warner Brothers," Abbie Hoffman wryly complained. Many cultural radicals gave up altogether and retreated to rural communes. Others turned off to drugs and turned on to religion.

By November 1970, what *Rolling Stone* called the age of paranoia seemed to be over. Most Americans began to forget black power and cultural radicalism. They liked to recall the achievements: Neil Armstrong's landing on the moon in July of 1969 seemed grander in hindsight than it had in the present. Richard Nixon—shielded by button-down advisers like John Erlichman and H. R. Haldeman, two former Eagle Scouts who neither drank nor smoked—presided over political and economic affairs with a seemingly sure hand. When *Time* named Nixon "Man of the Year" two years running, the 1960s seemed really dead.

RETRENCHMENT AND DETENTE

Claiming that the 1970 elections provided a mandate for a return to traditional American values, Richard Nixon sought to reshape the national government accordingly. Moderate Republican George Romney was hounded out of HUD after he persisted in proposing expensive programs for inner cities. Nixon dropped his friend and adviser on domestic affairs, Robert Finch, another moderate Republican. Impatient with bureaucratic routine and angered by the administration's policy toward environmental issues, Secretary of Interior Walter Hickel angrily left the cabinet, protesting the Haldeman-Ehrlichman-Kissinger-Mitchell stranglehold on the president. Unquestionably loyal, this "Berlin Wall" isolated Nixon from obstreperous critics and reinforced his attitudes. Except for Kissinger, this closed circle of advisers barely knew the techniques of politics, certainly not the art of government.

Although the president, with the assistance of the autocratic Haldeman, tightly reined the White House staff, other branches of the national government proved less tractable. Appointment of four "Nixon judges"—Chief Justice Warren Burger and Justices Harry Blackmun, Lewis Powell, and William Rehnquist—helped check much of the Warren Court's liberal activism, particularly in cases involving obscenity laws and the rights of criminal defendants. But other decisions of the new Burger Court conflicted with the president's personal views: the Court struck down state statutes which imposed the death penalty, invalidated restrictive abortion laws, and ruled against the Nixon administration's claim of broad power to wiretap "domestic subversives." (The Court handed down the last decision two days after police discovered the Republicans' bugging devices in Democratic party headquarters.) The sprawling federal bureaucracy also failed to toe the Nixon line. J. Edgar Hoover, Nixon's old friend, resisted a plan to share some of the FBI's power with operatives from the White House and the CIA, and officials of the Internal Revenue Service generally parried the administration's attempt to use tax laws against their "enemies."

The Democratic-controlled Congress opposed most of the president's domestic ideas. In his 1971 State of the Union message, for example, Nixon trumpeted fears that the flow of power to Washington was robbing the people of their control over local affairs, and he pro-

posed a "second American Revolution." Curiously, much of his program channeled even more responsibility to the national government: a
national plan for health insurance, a centralized environmental protection agency, and a major cabinet-reorganization scheme. The center-
pieces of this "new federalism" were welfare reform and revenue
sharing. Congress responded lethargically. Nixon's program to change
the welfare system proposed a $2,400 minimum income for a family of
four, plus incentives for the "working poor." Right-wing critics opposed this family assistance program because they feared it would increase spending, and liberals rejected the suggested allowance as too
low. After nearly two years of debate, Congress did pass a moderate
revenue-sharing act which promised to return more than $30 billion to
states and cities between 1972 and 1977. White House spokesmen
talked of a new era in federal-state relations, but governors and mayors
soon realized that this sudden largess scarcely compensated for cuts in
other national programs. Many critics noted that much of the new
money would go to smaller cities and towns rather than to the crisis-
ridden urban areas.

Nixon's determination to cut federal spending, in hopes of easing
inflationary pressures, and his aloof manner soon provoked outright
hostility between White House and Congress. The president refused to
sign the 1971 tax bill unless legislators axed an amendment which substituted public financing for private contributions to presidential election campaigns. Unwilling to risk the consequences of a confrontation,
Congress acquiesced. In late 1971 Nixon vetoed a $6 billion public-
works bill and a $2 billion child-care measure, denouncing the former as
inflationary and the latter as a threat to the family structure. When congressional committees asked presidential advisers to testify about
impoundment—Nixon's refusal to spend funds already appropriated
by Congress—and about the United States' not-so-secret war in Cambodia, the president forbade their appearance, claiming executive
privilege. When Capitol Hill ignored the White House's suggestion of a
maximum federal budget of $250 billion during fiscal 1972, the president
vetoed a $25 billion project to fight pollution. Outraged, the legislators
enacted the measure anyway, easily securing the two-thirds majorities.
By the end of 1972 conflict between the legislative and executive
branches had stymied government affairs and embittered personal relationships.

Faced with a hostile Congress, Nixon isolated himself and operated more and more in those areas firmly under presidential control:
conduct of foreign affairs and management of the economy. He cultivated the image of a world statesman, but a settlement in Vietnam
seemed remote, and the slow minuet of detente with Russia and China

253

consumed months of careful planning. Nixon still hoped that monetary policies would smooth out the roller-coaster American economy, as his economists predicted. For the moment, though, he exploited the visibility of his office and played upon popular emotions. In an effort to win support from those who favored a hard line in Vietnam, he ordered William Calley, the army lieutenant convicted for twenty-two murders at My Lai, confined to his apartment, not jailed, and promised a "personal review" of the case. In June 1971 the president denounced "forced integration of the suburbs" through busing. But such grandstand plays, by themselves, could not rescue Nixon from a worsening economic situation and an unpopular war.

Nixonomics

By early 1971, events had ruined the administration's hopes that higher unemployment would halt the spiral of inflation. Political priorities prevented any tax increase, while military spending remained high. Interest rates skyrocketed, nearly ending residential construction and forcing barely solvent businesses such as Penn Central Railroad into bankruptcy. Industrial production declined and the jobless rate hovered around 6 percent. Yet prices galloped forward. Big business and big labor had almost destroyed competitive markets, layering higher wages and higher costs upon an economy slumping into recession. For almost a year security prices edged downward on the nation's stock exchanges. Pundits spoke of *Nixonomics:* recession *and* inflation.

Nixon decided that any inflationary prosperity, however soft, was better than an economic slowdown which might, as it had in 1960, jeopardize his presidential campaign. He told a startled group of journalists, "I am now a Keynesian," and took up that favorite tactic of liberal Democrats, deficit spending financed by government borrowing. This dramatic about-face prompted Howard K. Smith, a television commentator, to quip, "It's a little like a Christian crusader saying, 'All things considered, I think Mohammed was right!'" The president even resorted to uncharacteristic "jawboning" during the summer of 1971, pressuring Bethlehem Steel to roll back an announced price hike by 50 percent. But prices spurted ahead elsewhere, and pump-priming measures scarcely dented unemployment. Though many administration advisers advocated an "incomes policy"—an across-the-board freeze on wages, prices, and interest rates—Nixon shied away from "artificial controls which could only foul things up."

Worrisome foreign trade statistics soon changed the president's mind. For eighty years the United States had exported far more than it imported, but after World War II huge military expenditures and corpo-

*"Our dollars are buying more—the country is in great shape—he's inno-
cent—and this is a lovely steak dinner."*

A 1974 Herblock cartoon expressed many Americans' distrust of official government statements on the economy and Watergate matters.

rate overseas investment created deficits in the balance of payments.
The country paid some of this debt with gold; by 1972, for example,
America's prewar hoard of bullion had shrunk by half, to $10 billion.
For the rest, creditors readily accepted paper dollars or short-term
commercial obligations. Central banks in Europe and Japan used both
as reserves against their national currency, creating an immense source
of domestic capital. Rather than suffer an accounting loss on the value
of such reserves or contract private credit, many nations ingested huge
amounts of "Eurodollars," pleased with their stimulating economic effect. By 1970, however, inflation had crippled America's ability to sell its
high-priced goods abroad, so more and more paper flooded overseas.
Too much of a good thing bloated Europe's money markets, inevitably

jolting prices. United States Treasury officials quietly urged England, West Germany, and Japan to revalue their currencies upward to discourage American buying, but only the Germans complied. Tokyo banks refused even to restore the yen's convertibility, thus trapping foreign profits in Japan, which in turn aggravated the dollar crunch. Then, at the end of June 1971, the Commerce Department announced a trade deficit, the first since 1890. As fears arose about the nation's solvency, speculators attacked the United States dollar, dumping vast amounts on world currency exchanges to avoid the losses of a widely expected devaluation.

After a hurried meeting with his advisers at Camp David in August 1971, Nixon dramatically responded to the international monetary crisis and the larger problems—including the new trade deficit—which fueled it. To foil speculators, the United States ceased to value the dollar in terms of gold. Instead, American currency would "float" on the exchanges, supply and demand determining its worth. A 10 percent tariff surcharge significantly reduced American imports; Nixon later bargained its removal to obtain new world monetary agreements. The new arrangement ended the dollar's career as a medium of international exchange; instead, it became just another currency whose value fluctuated. While diplomacy eased foreign economic pressures, Nixon's advisers plotted a new course for the domestic economy. The goal was clear enough: cuts in government spending would ease inflation, and an increase in productivity would narrow the nation's trade deficit. As an interim measure, called Phase I, the president froze wages and prices for ninety days.

Three months later, on November 15, 1971, the White House replaced these temporary controls with a permanent program to combat inflation. Phase II grappled with federal deficits (it slashed $5 billion from foreign aid and the federal civil service), but focused far more on stimulating business. A new Cost-of-Living Council banned wage hikes of more than 5.5 percent and limited retail price increases to 2.5 percent. This theoretical advance in real wages, Nixon calculated, would placate workers. Meanwhile, a developmental tax credit prompted many businesspeople to modernize their plants. They were now able to write off capital expansion on corporate income taxes. To stimulate the crucial automobile industry, Congress repealed the 7 percent excise tax on American-made cars. Such measures ensured greater production at guaranteed profits and, together with the certainty that Nixon would not risk retrenchment in an election year, perked up the sluggish economy. Consumer spending increased and public confidence blossomed in the spring of 1972. Inflation continued, especially in the uncontrolled food and farm commodity markets, but at a slightly lower overall rate. Though nearly anathema to the president's earlier free market principles, Phase II had turned the corner on Nixonomics, at least for the moment.

Nixon's Foreign Policy: Detente with Communist Rivals

While a cosmetic prosperity encouraged Republican election strategists, Nixon and Kissinger recharted American foreign policy. The Nixon Doctrine had already sounded a retreat for the old policy of direct military intervention in Southeast Asia, and the president and Henry Kissinger took new initiatives in relations with the two leading communist states. America's national interest required some accommodation with the Soviet Union to prevent nuclear Armageddon and, given Western Europe's restiveness, perhaps to inaugurate a more certain coexistence. As long as the United States treated China as a diplomatic pariah, any "normalization of relations" (Kissinger's favorite phrase) remained impossible in the Far East. Detente with Russia and China might also shake North Vietnam's faith in its communist backers, maybe even open an honorable exit from Southeast Asia. If the possibilities of the diplomatic situation intrigued the statesman in Nixon, this resilient politician also understood the likely result of ending the cold war. The promise of peace, even more than prosperity at home, would ensure praise, and guarantee votes, from a generation of Americans tired of constant emergency.

Detente balanced difficult negotiations with public courtesies. For two years, the Soviet Union and the United States intermittently discussed nuclear arms control—proposals to regulate future growth, not to scrap existing military hardware. During 1969 both powers pledged not to build underwater installations and agreed to begin strategic arms limitation talks (SALT) in April 1970. Such negotiations required intense bargaining which considered intricate technical issues as well as broad questions of overall strategic balance. Yet after mid-1971, when the United States formally accepted the principle of nuclear parity, diplomats made rapid progress.

Reassured by the progress of SALT, the Nixon administration took up a more visible but even less familiar task, relations with China. Small courtesies started a chain reaction. Nixon spoke of "the People's Republic," not Red China, and told journalists of his desire to visit "that vast, unknown land." Nervous about their ancient enemy, Russia, and about Japan's surging economy, Chinese leaders reopened Sino-American talks through both countries' ambassadors in Warsaw. Profound differences over Nationalist China and America's future in Asia persisted, but so did diplomacy: both sides were determined to end an era even if they could not inaugurate a new one. Nixon eased trade restrictions against China in early 1971, and the Chinese reciprocated with an invitation for a ping-pong tournament. Then in July Kissinger made a secret trip to Peking to arrange a presidential visit for 1972. The announcement of Nixon's trip startled both liberals and conservatives in the United States and refashioned world politics. The United Nations admitted the People's Republic three months later, rejecting the United States' more moderate two-China proposal, designed to preserve membership for Chiang Kai-shek's regime on Taiwan. The prospect of Sino-American detente apparently pushed the Soviet Union into some technical concessions at SALT and into an invitation, eagerly accepted, for Nixon to visit Moscow in the spring of 1972.

On February 21, 1972, one of the United States' most celebrated anticommunists traveled to Peking to shake hands and bow gently with Mao Tse-tung, the world's archetypal anticapitalist. President and First Lady walked atop the Great Wall, mingled with communist dignitaries, and ate a twenty-two-course state dinner. But public goodwill, carefully televised, could not dissolve longstanding animosities. Four days of negotiations with Premier Chou En-lai primarily produced a list of postponements. The United States agreed that Taiwan's future was "an internal matter," but China pledged to settle with Chiang "peacefully." Nixon reminded Chinese leaders of America's friendship with Japan, and Chou broached the subject of "Tokyo's militarism." Mao voiced sympathy for "the people's struggle" in Indochina; Kissinger responded with references to "self-determination" and America's "eventual withdrawal." Though the new contacts would go on—especially scientific exchanges and token shipments of grain from the United States—movement toward compromise on fundamental differences remained glacially slow. The forms of friendship hid the absence of substance: a new mood, not a new era, defined Sino-American detente.

Nixon's other foreign trip in 1972, a May visit to Moscow, produced different results. An air of cordiality never emerged; television recorded Soviet rulers at work with Americans, not partying with them. If the somewhat chilled atmosphere never thawed, diplomats apparently did continue the trend away from cold war. Both sides avoided propaganda debates and negotiated. The two countries agreed to extensive technological cooperation in medical research, space exploration, and environmental protection. Some months later, technical experts polished off several important trade agreements. Most important, Nixon and Soviet leader Leonid Brezhnev also initialed two arms-control treaties, the first fruits of SALT.

These agreements reflected an even greater undertaking. The

United Press International

President Nixon and Chou En-lai: dinner diplomacy seemed to promise a new era in Sino-American relations.

world's most advanced, most powerful countries tacitly recognized that their responsibilities for world peace outweighed the imperatives of advantage in their quarter-century rivalry. Though still dubious of its opponent, each would now yield to his reasonable national interests. The Soviets ignored potential provocations in Indochina; the United States lived uneasily with Russia's growing influence in the Middle East. But no objective, each pantomimed to the other, was worth nuclear war. Domestic mellowing within the two countries furthered this new stance. Confident of their military strength, proud of their society's achievements, and aware of America's troubles in Vietnam, most of Russia's leaders no longer feared the United States. War-weary American officials seemed finally convinced that they could not export democracy everywhere. Perhaps the debacle in Vietnam, by reassuring Moscow and frightening Washington, made feasible a new era. Or was it the insistent prod of Henry Kissinger and the ambition of Richard Nixon, driven to secure a place in history? Whatever the reason, Russia and the United States began to collaborate, at least to prevent war between themselves.

Vietnam

Despite such triumphs, Vietnam still threatened the president's reputation and sapped America's strength. During 1971 Nixon continued negotiations in Paris while fighting in Southeast Asia. Again hopeful that an ARVN (South Vietnamese army) victory would energize Saigon's morale, President Thieu and his American ally attacked Laos. Under a massive shield of American air power, ARVN troops advanced rapidly. But when the North Vietnamese counterattacked, the inexperienced ARVN troops retreated in confusion. Invasion became rout. Terrified South Vietnamese dangled from helicopter skids, trying to escape; American advisers reported wholesale desertions. After the failure of this attempt to give Saigon more "breathing space," Nixon concentrated upon his other hope, Kissinger's intermittent peace talks.

After several months of secret diplomacy in Paris, Kissinger and North Vietnam's Le Duc Tho had made some progress, but their meetings failed to achieve a final formula for peace. Encouraged by their opponents' misadventures in Laos and Cambodia and already planning their own military offensive, leaders in Hanoi still insisted that Thieu and his henchmen must go. For its part, however, the Nixon administration saw Thieu's presidency as the symbol of South Vietnam's self-determination. Patient bargaining amid the luxuries of Parisian townhouses could not unravel the basic puzzle: if Thieu stayed on, he would subvert any "free" election between communist and anticommunist groups. Yet without Thieu and his political organization, the country would easily fall under communist control, for the NLF was its only other organized political force. No middle ground remained; years of war had either polarized the people of South Vietnam or numbed them.

Apparently stalemated at the bargaining table, both sides yet again reached for a military solution. In late March 1972, North Vietnam attacked along a broad front, aiming to occupy as much strategic territory as possible. Communist units drove frighteningly close to Saigon, capturing An Loc, a gateway city only thirty miles away. Thieu's listless troops fell back on all fronts, as American air power, by itself, failed to check the communist ground advance. Nixon resumed bombing raids against North Vietnam almost immediately after the attack began, but the communist offensive continued week after week. Many in the Pentagon again predicted the humiliation of defeat. Nixon angrily told the nation that the United States would not "become a pitiful, helpless giant," and on May 12 he ordered the navy to mine North Vietnam's harbors and escalated bombing raids against the North. Few military targets remained untouched, as Nixon's critics claimed that the new attacks risked civilian casualties.

The violent spring spurred diplomacy. When Russia calmly ignored Nixon's escalation, Hanoi must have realized that its chief benefactor would not support any military "final solution." With Nixon seemingly certain to win a second term as president, North Vietnam saw nothing to gain by delay. Painfully, Kissinger and Le Duc Tho fashioned another ceasefire, arranged for an international peacekeeping force, formulated a complex plan for free elections, and established a timetable for troop withdrawals and prisoner exchanges. On October 26, several weeks before the end of the 1972 presidential campaign, Kissinger announced that a short, final round of talks would settle minor issues. "Peace," he said, "is at hand."

THINGS FALL APART

The 1972 presidential campaign substituted short-sighted cynicism and self-congratulatory naiveté for more venerable political techniques. Ideology pervaded both parties. Republicans equated their victory with the national interest, justifying illegal actions as patriotic necessities. The Committee to Re-Elect the President (CREEP) told its recruits, "Winning in politics isn't everything, it's the only thing." Some reformers in the Democratic party, most of whom finally coalesced around Senator George McGovern, seemed more anxious to pursue splinter causes than practical politics. Working people, ethnic voters, moderates, and Southerners gradually drifted away from the old Democratic coalition, at least when they cast their ballots for president.

The Streamlined Republicans and the Discontented Democrats

Nixon loyalists choreographed a campaign of great technical polish. Phase II eased popular discontent about the economy, and a new treasury secretary, John Connally, talked reassuringly about the future. The president's advisers isolated their candidate, intentionally obscuring issues, never exposing him to unfriendly audiences. When antiwar spokespeople challenged Nixon to end the war, he dramatically answered them: "I have brought peace with honor." Throughout the tranquil hum of the 1972 Republican campaign, Nixon's coterie presented him as an individual aloof from petty political considerations. Most voters shrugged off press accounts of questionable campaign financing tactics with a resigned "everybody-does-it" attitude. Nor did many people worry about a mid-June break-in and wiretapping operation at the Democratic National Committee offices in the Watergate Apartments. After all, the president's press secretary had denounced the break-in as a "third-rate burglary attempt." Even revelations that employees of CREEP and former members of the White House staff were involved in the Watergate affair failed to sidetrack the Republican campaign. Instead, Nixon's much-publicized trips to Peking and Moscow made most citizens proud of their president's efforts toward international goodwill.

In vivid contrast to the Republicans' slick campaign, the Democrats' vote-getting efforts bogged down immediately during the bitter primary campaign. Rallying behind George McGovern of South Dakota, practitioners of the "new politics" expanded the techniques of Eugene McCarthy's "children's crusade" of 1968. Grass-roots volunteers canvassed voters directly, touting their candidate and seeking productive issues. McGovern and Alabama's George Wallace forced their party into new molds while its more traditional candidates, men like Edmund Muskie, Henry Jackson, and Hubert Humphrey, chased elusive compromise positions.

The Democratic presidential primaries eliminated one candidate after another without producing any consensus within the party. Although Senator Edmund Muskie of Maine dominated preprimary calculations, the New Hampshire primary left many Democrats wondering about his ability to handle high office. Angered by some personal attack apparently orchestrated by saboteurs from the Nixon campaign, Muskie publicly broke down in tears. He also carefully avoided clear-cut positions on most issues. Vietnam must end, though the United States must maintain its military strength and, by implication, its global overlordship. "Change," Muskie said of social issues, "must be slow to be permanent." Muskie won easily in New Hampshire, but an unexpectedly high number of Democratic voters supported George McGovern, a man who, unlike Muskie, did offer forthright proposals. America's war in Southeast Asia, McGovern believed, had tainted its society and shamed the nation throughout the world. Redemption lay in an immediate withdrawal of all troops and, the former World War II bomber pilot insisted, in cessation of air strikes. In a broader sense, McGovern opposed a global foreign policy and favored large cuts in military spending as a means of ending the arms race and preventing future Vietnams. McGovern's strong showing in New Hampshire—he won almost 40 percent of the vote—undercut Muskie's triumph and, most important, focused media attention on McGovern's unlikely candidacy.

More than a simple-minded antiwar activist, the former history professor hoped that his program for social justice could produce a new political coalition. Government subsidies would provide health care on the basis of need, not of ability to pay. A national floor under incomes, perhaps as much as $6,500 for a family of four, would guarantee all citizens a minimum standard of living. A variant of this plan would grant every American, regardless of age or wealth, an annual stipend of $1,000. This massive redistribution of income would narrow the gap between rich and poor while sustaining a new prosperity based upon consumer spending. McGovern planned to finance his programs by closing corporate tax loopholes, increasing levies on those with annual incomes of more than $15,000, and paring military budgets. He also favored amnesty for draft evaders and opposed harsh penalties for possession of marijuana. Such opinions reflected his humaneness, if not a great deal of political sagacity.

Another voice of protest, this one from Alabama, also attracted millions of Democrats during the spring of 1972. George Wallace appealed to three elements in the old Democratic coalition—blue-collar workers, ethnic voters, and Southerners—while ridiculing "exotic left" reformers. His tirades against "the asinine busin' of little children" symbolized more than calculated racism. Too long, Wallace argued, Washington had insisted upon sacrifices from "the average American" while ignoring his or her problems. Wallace called instead for a government "for the truck driver and the beautician." Relentlessly, he sloganized against "parasitic foundations which pay no taxes" and against "pointy-headed professors" and "lawyers who carry their lunches in briefcases." In the South and in states like Michigan and Indiana, with a large proportion of working-class people, his rhetoric won many votes—more than any other Democratic presidential candidate. Then on May 15, at a small shopping center in Laurel, Maryland, an assassin lunged out of the crowd, firing point-blank at Wallace. Once again, Americans watched a presidential hopeful crumple to the ground, attended by the stooped figure of a beautiful wife and the bewildered cries of a now useless campaign staff. Badly wounded, Wallace would survive, but he faced months of recuperation and a lifetime confined to a wheelchair.

After Wallace's candidacy ended, McGovern moved inexorably toward the nomination. An efficient grass-roots campaign garnered several hundred delegates in nonprimary states. During June, McGovern won preference ballots in Oregon, Rhode Island, and New York, then capped his drive with a victory in California. But the convention, where McGovern had hoped to institutionalize his hold over the Democratic party, not just his corner of it, soon fell into disarray. A quota system had produced fresh faces: 40 percent of the delegates were women, 26 percent black, 22 percent under thirty. Many old-line Democrats, such as Chicago's Mayor Richard Daley, who had been defeated by a slate of "reformers," were absent; a middle-aged labor leader complained that he saw too many beards, too much hair, and not enough cigars. With Muskie's collapse, such middle-of-the-road Democrats could offer only the capable but unglamorous "Scoop" Jackson, and the forces of the "new politics" nominated McGovern with two hundred votes to spare. Wallace and his blue-collar Confederate constituency could not cross an ideological divide for the sake of party unity. Many regular Democrats, like Mayor Daley, perfunctorily supported McGovern but thought he could not win. Television coverage of the convention helped convince many people that young activists, blacks, and feminists had radicalized the Democratic party.

McGovern hoped to focus upon his social welfare programs, but questions of "radical-liberal" influence on the party and of McGovern's competency, not larger issues, soon dominated election rhetoric. Critics gleefully pointed out that the South Dakota senator could not manage his campaign, let alone the country. National headquarters degenerated into anarchy, three men—Lawrence O'Brien, Gary Hart, and Frank Mankiewicz—each running an ill-defined sector. In a hasty, last-minute decision, McGovern had chosen as his running mate Senator Thomas Eagleton of Missouri, long a close friend of organized labor. Before accepting the job Eagleton had assured Mankiewicz that he had "no skeletons in the closet," but shortly after the convention newspaper columnists reported that McGovern's vice-presidential choice had three times undergone electric shock treatments for nervous exhaustion. At first, McGovern stood with his colleague—"I am 1000 percent behind Eagleton." Finally, pressure from other Democrats forced him to request Eagleton's resignation. Then for over a week an embarrassed presidential candidate searched for a replacement; ultimately his sixth choice, former Peace Corps Director R. Sargent Shriver, accepted on August 8, 1972. McGovern's credibility evaporated.

Meanwhile, Nixon's managers portrayed their hero as an efficient world statesman, contrasting his performance with McGovern's operation. Aware of the strong local appeal of many Democrats, Nixon abandoned many partisan colleagues, ensuring his personal victory at the party's expense. CREEP, and ultimately the White House, not the Republican National Committee, ran the president's campaign. Following Haldeman's advice, Nixon ignored most domestic issues, shunned press conferences, and stressed his accomplishments in foreign policy. Then, on October 26, Kissinger announced an imminent peace settlement in Vietnam.

When the polls opened on November 5, most voters found few reasons to vote against Nixon and fewer reasons to vote for McGovern. But the final count surprised even the most optimistic Republicans: Nixon's 60 percent of the popular tally surpassed the Harding and Roosevelt landslides and nearly equaled Lyndon Johnson's crushing victory in 1964. McGovern carried only Massachusetts and the District of Columbia, the president winning in forty-nine states for an electoral margin of 521 to 17. Nixon swept the South by huge margins, his conservative racial stance and McGovern's identification with black aspirations unhinging old loyalties to the Democratic party. Yet presidential coattails proved surprisingly short. Republicans gained only twelve seats in the House while losing a net of two in the Senate, where Democrats staged upset victories in Maine, Rhode Island, Delaware, and Iowa. If Nixon still faced an overwhelmingly Democratic Congress, his personal prestige peaked in those weeks after the election. *Time* again named him "Man of the Year," opinion polls showed him the most respected president since Roosevelt, and he would soon complete America's withdrawal from Vietnam.

A Final Triumph: Ending America's Adventure

Despite Kissinger's election-eve optimism, Vietnamese complexities yet again frustrated peacemakers. When Kissinger returned to Paris for a presumably final bargaining session, he confronted a reluctant Le Duc Tho. All sides still sought victory at the table: for the Americans, a noncommunist South Vietnam; for Hanoi and the Viet Cong, a radical Marxist government in Saigon; for Thieu, the perpetuation of his dictatorship. Such antithetical goals, as they had so often in the past, produced a fateful, familiar cycle of events. In mid-December, Nixon ordered an armada of B-52s to attack North Vietnam twenty-four hours a day "until they are ready to negotiate." Despite heavy losses, American bombers attacked North Vietnam's factories, ruined rice fields, and, too often, accidentally destroyed schools, hospitals, and other civilian facilities. Some Americans protested, but most seemed numbed by the renewal of violence. This final barrage convinced North Vietnam to return to the bargaining table in early January, and Nixon gradually reduced the bombing. The two sides now quickly compromised a makeshift ceasefire.

The Paris Accords, signed on January 27, 1973, ended formal hostilities between North Vietnam and the United States. Washington promised to withdraw its remaining 50,000 men, dismantle its military installations, and deactivate mines in North Vietnam's harbors. No foreign soldiers were to remain in Laos or Cambodia, but Hanoi's troops could stay "in place" within South Vietnam. North Vietnam agreed to release American prisoners-of-war and to cooperate in national elections in the South. A complicated, two-tiered bureaucracy—observers from Canada, Hungary, Poland, and Indonesia, and a second team from the four belligerents themselves—would police the ceasefire. Later, an international conference would guarantee a long-term peace, presumably by neutralizing all Indochina and imposing coalition governments in Laos and Cambodia. Thus the United States escaped its longest war, a conflict which had wrenched its people and distorted its economy, with terms nearly identical to those worked out twenty years before in Geneva. Yet the new Paris Accords did not bring peace, only American withdrawal. The civil war in Vietnam between communist rebels and Thieu's dictatorship dragged on, 48,000 soldiers dying during the first eighteen months of the "ceasefire." The radical Khmer Rouge guerrillas in Cambodia penned the pro-American regime of Lon Nol in its capital, Phnom Penh. In 1974 and again the following year American presidents still sought money to defend "representative government" in Southeast Asia.

The Watergate Affair

Like a classic Greek drama, the Watergate scandals rippled outward from almost accidental beginnings, engulfing the powerful in the consequences of their arrogance. Sometime during the middle of Nixon's first term, members of the White House staff began to use government power to pursue partisan, even personal, vendettas. Many of them justified such activities by pointing to the "lawlessness" of their opponents: antiwar demonstrators threatened "to stop the business of government," a radical fringe group bombed the Capitol building, other radicals publicly plotted "revolution," and liberals like Daniel Ellsberg purloined secret government documents for the press. Believing that the news media often romanticized such actions, some officials of the Nixon administration felt that they were only copying the dirty tricks of their enemies. Mostly young lawyers and former advertising men who lacked political experience, they ignored or did not understand the traditional rules of partisan politics. By 1972 many of the president's men claimed that the national interest required Nixon's re-election, justifying dubious practices and outright crimes as unpleasant but necessary steps to safeguard "national security" and the public welfare. Self-brainwashing eventually turned upon its perpetrators, discrediting them all, ousting most from office, jailing some. Successive revelations of misdeeds by the Nixon administration intensified the national hostility between Republicans and Democrats, between White House and Congress, and disillusioned the American people. In a time of rapid changes overseas and mounting economic crisis, the federal government became locked in an increasingly deadly constitutional struggle.

Despite repeated protestations that the president and the White House were innocent of wrongdoing in the Watergate incident, some newspaper reporters continued to investigate the clearly partisan crime. Amid snowballing media speculation, Nixon ordered a staff inquiry and told the public on August 29, 1972, that "what really hurts is if you try to cover up" a crime. In September a federal grand jury indicted James McCord, director of security for CREEP, and his four accomplices, plus two former White House officials, G. Gordon Liddy and E. Howard Hunt. Five of the defendants pleaded guilty, and jurors convicted two others of the break-in at Democratic headquarters. But Judge John Sirica, like many members of the press and the American public, expressed doubts that these judicial proceedings meant that the government had really solved the Watergate case. In mid-March 1973 McCord wrote to Sirica, charging that the White House had pressured the Watergate defendants into silence with offers of executive clemency and huge amounts of money. Not only had government officials approved the Watergate operation, the former CIA agent claimed; they had also conspired to cover up their involvement. McCord's letter prompted the Watergate grand jury and the Senate's special Watergate committee, chaired by Sam Ervin of North Carolina, to deepen their probes into suspicious activities by the White House.

Attempts by Nixon loyalists to contain the scandal outside the White House were clearly failing. Fearing that other officials would make him a scapegoat, John Dean, counsel to the president, began to bargain with federal prosecutors in early April. About the same time, Jeb Stuart Magruder, a former member of CREEP and the Nixon White House, admitted that he had lied in earlier appearances before the Watergate grand jury: The bugging of Democratic headquarters was not "a wild scheme concocted by Hunt" but a much-discussed plan which John Mitchell had approved directly. While the Watergate prosecutors, the press, and the Senate's new committee pursued evidence of such activities, another scandal broke. In late 1971 the "plumbers," a group of White House operatives authorized to plug security leaks, had burglarized the office of Daniel Ellsberg's psychiatrist. Apparently they were seeking material to discredit the man who released the Pentagon papers to the *New York Times* and *Washington Post*, an act which had infuriated the president and his aides. On April 26, at Ellsberg's trial for theft of government property, the prosecution admitted the illegal entry by the plumbers. The judge later declared this a violation of Ellsberg's civil rights and ordered a mistrial.

Shaken by the sudden reversal in his fortunes, Nixon jettisoned three of his top advisers and tried once more to seal off the Oval Office from the slime of Watergate. On April 30, 1973, he told a national television audience that he accepted the responsibility—but not the blame—for the actions of over-zealous subordinates and that he applauded the efforts of a "courageous judge" and a "vigorous free press." Absorbed in the business of running the country, he explained, he had failed to monitor campaign practices. He also announced the resignations of Erhlichman and Haldeman—"two of the finest public servants it has been my privilege to know"—and the forced departure of John Dean. Several weeks later, Nixon appointed a special Watergate prosecutor, Harvard law professor Archibald Cox, and the president's press secretary indicated that the prosecutor could have "complete independence" to investigate the Watergate affair. Nixon's new attorney general, Elliot Richardson, made similar assurances to the Senate during his confirmation hearings.

These moves provided only temporary comfort for the embattled president. His explanation that he knew nothing about the operations of CREEP or his White House staff made him appear, at best, incompetent. Even before the Senate hearings began, his credibility was plummeting. Bumper stickers joked, "Honk if you think he's guilty."

The Senate Watergate hearings opened slowly. As minor CREEP and administration officials testified, Senator Sam Ervin—with his old-fashioned morality, shock of white hair, and trembling jowls—became a national symbol of honor and rectitude. Finally the star witnesses, Jeb Magruder and John Dean, told their stories. Magruder suggested possible presidential involvement in efforts to conceal Watergate, and Dean directly linked Nixon with illegal activities. Speaking carefully and displaying a remarkable memory, Dean quoted the president as saying that it would be "no problem" to raise a $1 million hush-fund and that payments should be made to E. Howard Hunt. In addition, Dean implicated Ehrlichman, swearing that Nixon's chief domestic lieutenant had instructed him to "deep-six" evidence in the Potomac River. Throughout his lengthy testimony and cross-examination, the young lawyer revealed a White House staff and a president who were petty, vindictive, and unconcerned with legal niceties. Adding to Dean's account, other witnesses testified about Watergate and other misdeeds, the string of bizarre activities which John Mitchell called "the White House horrors."

Richard Nixon also had his defenders. Mitchell attempted to refute the charges leveled against him and the president by Dean and Magruder. Nixon, Mitchell assured the committee, had known nothing about the break-in or the cover-up. Ehrlichman and Haldeman claimed that neither they nor the president had done anything wrong. A combative, arrogant Ehrlichman defended the Ellsberg break-in and other questionable actions on familiar grounds of national security. Crew-cut Bob Haldeman, once the second most powerful man in Washington, softly denied everything. Such give-and-take—Dean's word versus

Senator Sam Ervin swears in John Dean at the Watergate hearings.

Ehrlichman's, Magruder's versus Haldeman's—might have led to public boredom; certainly by late summer the Senate committee was running out of energy and new information.

During the hearings, however, the committee staff stumbled upon a crucial discovery. On July 16 a former White House aide, Alexander Butterfield, reluctantly testified that sophisticated recording equipment had taped the majority of presidential conversations for the last two years. Presumably these reels could determine, once and for all, Nixon's role in the Watergate episode. The Senate committee, as well as Special Prosecutor Cox and the Watergate grand jury, requested crucial segments of the tapes, but the president argued that their disclosure would violate the confidentiality of the presidency and erode the separation of powers. A complicated legal battle ensued. Congress and Archibald Cox became increasingly angered by the White House's delaying tactics. Frustrated, Cox finally told a televised press conference that he would ask Judge Sirica to declare the president "in violation of a court ruling" for his failure to turn over immediately a set of tapes. Determined to oust the special prosecutor, Nixon fired Attorney General Richardson and his deputy, William Ruckelshaus, on October 20 when they refused to dismiss Cox. Later that evening, Solicitor-General Robert Bork fired

269

the prosecutor, soothing presidential rancor. The "Saturday Night Massacre" produced an outpouring of popular protest and made it appear that Nixon was trying to get Cox before Cox got Nixon.

A continuing chain of scandal enveloped Nixon and his administration. Only ten days before the Saturday Night Massacre, Spiro Agnew had resigned the vice-presidency to escape a jail term for evading income taxes on bribes he was receiving from Maryland building contractors. His blatant plea-bargaining—Agnew threatened a constitutional crisis unless promised leniency—saddened many citizens, while others remembered years of Agnewesque alliteration against judges who were "soft on criminals." The smooth working of the Twenty-Fifth Amendment soon installed his successor, House Minority Leader Gerald Ford. Popular with his fellow congressmen, Ford also enjoyed the reputation, perhaps undeserved, of an intellectual lightweight.

Almost daily revelations of embarrassing episodes quickly clouded even this success. When the White House finally handed over a few tapes, prosecutors discovered that recordings of some conversations "had never existed" and that others contained sizable gaps, erasures which technical experts later judged intentional. During the winter of 1973, newspapers reported that the president had become a millionaire while in the White House, partly because he had paid miniscule income taxes. Nixon later accepted the judgment of a congressional committee and a ruling of the Internal Revenue Service that he owed nearly $450,000 in back taxes. About the same time, congressional investigators began probing federal expenditures for extensive remodeling of his estates at Key Biscayne, Florida, and San Clemente, California. Final audits revealed that the government had spent millions of dollars, ostensibly for security reasons, on items such as ice machines and new shrubbery. Watergate disclosures also continued: the grand jury, now directed by a new special prosecutor, Texas attorney Leon Jaworski, indicted forty-one people for obstruction of justice and other crimes during the 1972 campaign. Convinced of Nixon's involvement, yet unwilling to confront the constitutional issue of a president's vulnerability to indictment, the jurors listed Nixon as an "unindicted co-conspirator."

Pressed by public skepticism and a growing pile of subpoenas and court orders for his tapes, in late April Nixon released edited transcripts—not the actual recordings—of crucial meetings concerning Watergate. Even Nixon's version (other transcriptions showed that the "Nixon tapes" had deleted a number of items which damaged the president's claims of innocence) revealed an expedient morality, couched in rough language, which bothered even many of the president's firm supporters. Far from exculpating Nixon, the new evidence

As the investigations into Watergate-related crimes proceeded, the storm of controversy around President Nixon grew.

seemed to implicate him in the cover-up and hinted at schemes for political revenge against "enemies" like the *Washington Post*. Many people thought Nixon unfit to govern. Nixon's transcripts revealed that John Ehrlichman had once said of L. Patrick Gray, acting FBI director, "Let him twist slowly, slowly in the wind." This cruel dismissal now became Nixon's epitaph during the long summer.

A President Is Forced to Resign

By then, Nixon's presidency was nearly finished. The Judiciary Committee of the House of Representatives, twenty-four Democrats and fourteen Republicans, was already hard at work on articles of impeachment. Nixon made a last, double-edged counterattack. His lawyer, James St. Clair, fought to prevent release of further tapes. Nixon himself spoke to carefully selected audiences, often in the deep South, hoping for a show of public support, but only a hard core of true believers still believed in his innocence. His statement, "Your president is not a crook," shocked more than it soothed. And when he argued that only criminal acts would justify impeachment, many thought it a tacit admission of serious wrongdoing.

During late July and early August of 1974 a tangle of events closed in, finally ending any doubts about the president's fate. The Judiciary Committee heard both its Democratic and Republican counsels urge Nixon's impeachment. He had, they concluded, obstructed justice in the Watergate cover-up and abused government power in attempts to compromise federal agencies. Five days later the Supreme Court ordered the White House to turn over sixty-four additional tapes. Chief Justice Burger, speaking for a unanimous court, rejected the claim of "executive privilege" in this case: "The generalized assertion of privilege must yield to the demonstrated, specific need for evidence in a pending criminal trial." That same day, July 24, the Judiciary Committee began its televised debate on impeachment.

Contrary to fears that Nixon's impeachment would "tear the country apart," people seemed strangely calm, relieved that constitutional process would soon end months of uncertainty. Serious, fair-minded discussion among committee members reinforced this mood. Most of the president's accusers appeared more saddened than vindictive. Though no "smoking pistol" of irrefutable presidential involvement in Watergate had yet surfaced, most Democrats and a few Republicans argued that a pattern of presidential behavior and a mountain of indirect proof implicated Nixon in obstruction of justice. He had repeatedly interfered in the FBI's investigations of Watergate and, so John Dean claimed, ordered payment of hush-money. What John Mitchell called "the White House horrors"—efforts at campaign sabotage and illegal operations by the plumbers—only reinforced the case for Nixon's removal. William Cohen, a Republican from Maine, compared the president's guilt to snow falling in the night: no one saw it happen, but the next morning it was there. Fighting the weight of persuasive evidence, Nixon's defenders demanded direct proof of specific criminal acts and claimed that mistakes of judgment could not become grounds for impeachment.

Finally, a "swing group" of conservative Southern Democrats and moderate Northern Republicans voted with the majority Democrats in late July, and the Committee formally charged the president with three impeachable offenses. For covering up the Watergate scandal, for misusing federal agencies, and for refusing to supply Congress with subpoenaed tapes, the articles said, there was no recourse but impeachment and removal from office. Only ten loyalists supported the president on these articles. Observers predicted the indictment would easily carry the House, but some still doubted whether the Senate could muster a two-thirds majority for conviction. Nixon's lawyer predicted a long fight in the upper chamber.

Then, suddenly, the pieces came together. In compliance with the Supreme Court order, Nixon released additional tapes on Monday, August 5. Though they "might damage my case," he still maintained that he had done nothing to justify his removal from office. But almost no one in Washington believed him any more. Among other things, the new transcripts revealed that Nixon had been deceiving his own attorney. After seeing the new evidence, the president's chief aide, Alexander Haig, began preparations for the accession of Vice-President Gerald Ford. The tape of a conversation on June 23, 1972—Nixon's first day back in Washington after the Watergate break-in—showed the president and Haldeman planning to cloak White House involvement in the crime. Here, after eighteen months of protestations of innocence, was the "smoking pistol." Nixon's defenders on the Judiciary Committee belatedly switched their votes, and leading Republican senators visited the White House, telling the president that his removal was a certainty. On August 8 Richard Nixon told the nation that he would resign, but he still confessed only "wrong judgment," not impeachable offenses. His calm, dignified speech dwelled on his hopes for world peace and his accomplishments in foreign affairs. He closed with a reference to "the man in the arena who dares greatly in order to achieve greatly."

But the private man, Richard Nixon himself, did not leave until the next morning, when he said goodby to the White House staff. During a speech filled with self-pity, a confused Nixon rambled through a variety of unconnected topics. Breaking down, he recalled his mother and his father. Despite his clear self-enrichment, he claimed that no one in his administration had profited from public service. He told his staff and friends, "Never hate those who oppose you, for you will end by destroying yourself," rueful advice he apparently wished he had heeded. As he left for his seaside estate in California, many thought Richard Nixon a lonely, driven man, somehow overwhelmed by the temptations of his office or betrayed by flaws in his character. Others disagreed, insisting that Nixon and his aides had started the nation down the road toward tyranny. But his successor, Gerald Ford, spoke more kindly. "May the man who brought peace to millions find peace within himself."

THE APPOINTED PRESIDENT

"I am acutely aware," Gerald Ford said after his hastily improvised inauguration, "that I have received the votes of none of you." Despite whispered slurs about his intellectual qualifications (Lyndon Johnson had once quipped that "Jerry Ford couldn't walk and chew gum at the same time"), the new chief executive found trust, even respect, from a country eager "to put Watergate behind." But the nation's first appointed president brought a change only of style, not of substance. Promising an open administration, Ford bemused Americans by fixing his own muffins for breakfast and by celebrating a fireside Christmas with his family at a Colorado ski resort. He enjoyed meeting people, some days even shaking hands with tourists waiting to visit the White House. Ford held as many press conferences and delivered as many speeches in 18 months as Nixon had in five years. Updating Franklin D. Roosevelt's example, he experimented with informal talks on television to explain complicated economic issues. Only Ford's sudden pardon of Richard Nixon clouded the new president's untainted image, but even this controversy over Nixon's legal accountability soon subsided. Ford smiled a lot; he mispronounced words—the phrase, "in my judg-a-ment," punctuated every speech. He seemed, in short, human and approachable.

Though refreshingly different from the brooding, suspicious Nixon in style, Ford continued his predecessor's economic and foreign policies. His appointment of Nelson Rockefeller, the centrist former governor of New York, to be vice-president indicated no change in Ford's essentially conservative course. Despite new faces, the deadlocked political patterns of the Nixon White House lingered on, dividing Congress from president, arousing popular distrust of government itself.

The Lurching Economy

The Watergate scandal had paralyzed the national government just when complex economic problems required new policies. Afraid of "addictive controls," in early 1973 Nixon replaced Phase II price ceilings with voluntary restraints. Predictably, consumer prices shot upward, and within six months Treasury Secretary George Schulz candidly admitted, "Phase III is a failure." So in midsummer Nixon again froze prices, this time for 60 days, while his advisers debated alternatives. Inflation-induced shortages in wheat, beef, and oil forced the White House to reinstate selective controls, primarily on retail consumer goods. Yet by April 1974, Nixon had again reversed course, canceling all Phase IV regulations.

Convinced that "artificial bureaucracies" could never substitute for the "free" marketplace, Nixon and then Ford relied on indirect panaceas. In February 1973, the United States again devalued the dollar, this time by some 10 percent, forcing other countries to float their currencies or face an inrush of American goods. Nixon's advisers hoped that devaluation would stimulate a commercial boom which would cut unemployment at home. To ease inflation, the cabinet—deprived of its liberals by midyear—cut government spending for social welfare programs and public works. By October 15 the president had vetoed nine major bills, even education and antipollution measures. He calmly announced that he would impound funds, rather than spend them, if Congress overrode his decisions. With prices at their highest levels in history, Republicans talked about "allowing supply and demand to allocate resources." Shocked at what they considered to be favoritism for the rich, Democrats struggled to pass alternate plans, but Congress became mired in thickets of complexity and politics. Growing personal hostilities, aggravated by Watergate, soon coalesced into a permanent adversary relationship between the two branches of American government. Meanwhile, inflation continued at record levels, nearly 10 percent annually, while unemployment hovered just under 6 percent, a recession rate.

During the first weeks of his presidency, Ford targeted inflation, rather than unemployment, as the nation's most serious economic problem. But no sooner had the White House organized a campaign against rising prices—Ford called upon Americans to "WIN" or "Whip Inflation Now"—than the country slid into its worst recession since the 1930s. Consumer demand dropped precipitously, especially in the crucial automobile industry where higher sticker prices and worries about the availability of gasoline frightened off potential buyers. Triggered by large lay-offs in Detroit, unemployment quickly spread. Slackening

275

demand closed more and more factories which, in turn, further reduced demand. Faced with a jobless rate averaging 12 or 13 percent and with falling production almost everywhere, the president reversed course in late 1974. Now focusing on jobs, he projected a budget deficit of some $60 billion and asked Congress for a tax cut, both heavily inflationary devices designed to increase retail spending and to create a demand for manufactured goods. After several months of politicking, Capitol Hill finally passed an act which rebated some taxes already paid in 1974, reduced the withholding rate, and provided tax credits for the purchasers of new homes. Government also forced down interest rates, though the prime level still hovered around 8 percent. Meanwhile, state unemployment insurance programs cushioned the effects of disappearing consumer demand. Taken together, these measures prompted a modest revival during the summer of 1975, though inflation also resumed, once again rising toward double-digit rates.

While economics bedeviled Americans, other issues also widened the gap between president and Congress which had opened during the Watergate scandals. Afraid that dependence on Arab oil might weaken American foreign policy, Ford wanted to raise the price of domestic gasoline by boosting federal taxes and ending all price controls on oil. The marketplace would "ration" gasoline and, in effect, force down consumption. Democrats in Congress countered that Ford's approach would only accelerate inflation and unfairly hurt poor people, while oil companies enjoyed windfall profits. Other factors complicated an easy resolution of these differences. During the 1974 elections, voters had returned many younger, more liberal congressmen to Capitol Hill. These freshmen legislators, together with some of their more experienced colleagues, recoiled at the business-as-usual politics of logrolling. Already by early 1975 they had ousted several powerful committee chairmen who had long blocked liberal legislation. Then too, many legislators saw an opportunity in the Watergate scandals to reassert their prerogatives. This fiesty, heavily Democratic Congress refused presidential leadership, instead outlining its own energy program. But Ford vetoed bills that would have maintained price controls and allocated funds for mass transit, while publicly denouncing government gasoline rationing as unworkable. Lacking coherent leadership—more than ten Democratic senators, for example, were maneuvering for their party's presidential nomination—Congress enacted laws to improve gasoline mileage in American cars and increased taxes on "gas guzzlers." Because of the unpopularity of almost any conservation device, as well as the rivalry between Congress and president, the energy crisis illustrated a growing sense of drift that troubled many Americans during the mid-seventies.

Detente

Economics bored Nixon; he once dismissed a complicated monetary dilemma with a curt, "I don't give a damn about the Italian lira!" Instead, he pursued laurels and, as Watergate unfolded, redemption as well in foreign affairs. Henry Kissinger became secretary of state in February 1973 and soon speeded the pace of negotiations with communist powers. Diplomacy by small courtesy continued. The United States lifted many trade and travel restrictions against China; Brezhnev visited Washington during June 1973; Nixon made another trip to the Soviet Union in mid-1974. Russia, America, and China avoided risking direct conflict, each respecting the reasonable national interests of the other two.

The implications of this "detente" emerged clearly in the Middle East during the fall of 1973. On the Jewish holy day of Yom Kippur, Egyptian and Syrian armies attacked Israel, apparently with Russia's tacit approval. With United States diplomatic support and vast donations from American Jews, the Israelis first weathered the assault, then drove deeply into Arab territories. By the middle of October, Israeli units had isolated Egypt's third army and were shelling suburbs around Damacus, Syria's capital. The Arabs embargoed shipments of crude oil to Western powers who backed Israel, principally the United States. Then escalation stopped. Moscow refused direct aid to its clients in the Middle East. Anxious to defuse Arab-Israeli hostilities, not just to maintain a local balance of power, Kissinger argued that the United States could best help Israel by negotiating with its enemies, not fighting them. After a month of dramatic shuttle diplomacy during May 1974, the secretary had achieved most of his objectives: a tenuous ceasefire, an end to the Arab oil embargo, the opening of talks for a permanent territorial settlement. Nixon's week-long trip to the Middle East during the summer forecast a shift in American policy, away from all-out support of Israel toward a more balanced effort at regional peacekeeping.

Yet detente required concessions from all sides—concessions which frequently could not be made. Despite behind-the-scenes maneuvering by both Russia and the United States, Tel Aviv demanded near-absolute guarantees for its future security, while Cairo insisted upon an Arab-dominated Palestine carved out of strategic Israeli territories. Egypt's Anwar Sadat, Nasser's successor, seemed ready to abandon his predecessor's ambitious dreams of uniting the Muslim world in favor of reviving his country's economy and easing its authoritarian politics. In Israel, although militants claimed that only armed force could ensure survival of the Jewish state, moderates believed that compromise would best achieve that end. Hoping to push Tel Aviv toward concessions, as well as to recoup American prestige among the Arabs, Kissinger tilted United States diplomacy toward neutrality, consistently working toward an overall peace accord. By fall of 1975 Kissinger had hammered out an agreement in which Israel restored captured land to Egypt in return for guarantees of future security and promises of more military aid from the United States.

Despite apparent impasse over Middle Eastern dilemmas, Russia and America steadily worked toward tolerance, if not amity, in other areas. The ubiquitous Kissinger periodically surfaced in Moscow to work out the next phase of SALT, and American businessmen sold large amounts of grain to the Soviet Union.

Perhaps because of the lessened tensions, Washington's quarter-century alliance with Western Europe weakened. Detente with the Soviet Union undermined the perceived threat which had sustained NATO. Regional issues preoccupied most Europeans; if somewhat chastened by Vietnam, the United States still reached for wider influence. Then too, military strategy divided the alliance. Some European statesmen saw the continued presence of American ground troops as a means to ensure American participation in any war with the Soviet Union, but Washington wanted its allies to take over more of their defense or to acquiesce in Russian-American plans for mutual troop withdrawals. Internal rivalries also frayed NATO. Their policy on monetary matters, the Middle East, and oil hopelessly at odds with Washington's, French diplomats barely spoke civilly to their American counterparts. Economic adversity and government instability raised doubts about Britain's future role in Europe. Though Kissinger heartily approved Chancellor Willy Brandt's efforts during 1973 to regularize West Germany's relations with its communist neighbors, this new *Ostpolitik* only added to the centrifugal pressures within NATO. And by 1975 a new leftist government in Portugal presented greater dilemmas: what could be the role of a left-leaning government in an organization directed against communism? Clearly, American diplomacy no longer dominated Western Europe.

Denouement in Southeast Asia

In practical terms, Southeast Asia tested Washington's retreat from postwar globalism. During 1973, the conflict between Viet Cong rebels and Saigon's dictatorship wound up again. The Vietnam ceasefire never really worked, and Lon Nol's pro-West regime in Cambodia continued to totter on the brink of collapse. Very much aware of congressional and public restraints on their action, Kissinger and Nixon at first shunned any escalation. Only during the spring of 1974, in the face of steady Viet Cong advances, did they hint at reviving military aid. The Viet Cong stepped up their propaganda campaign and infiltrated areas reserved to Saigon. President Thieu fought back, and by the summer intermittent war had again returned to most of South Vietnam. Hanoi's almost legendary general, Nyugen Giap, was organizing a coordinated assault by all his forces scheduled for the spring of 1975. Disintegration and demoralization in the South aided his plans. Thieu arrested opponents, banned opposition political parties, and closed down most newspapers. His corrupt rule alienated all but those who profited from it.

Then, during the spring of 1975, Thieu's regime collapsed. To consolidate his military position and possibly frighten the United States into sending more hardware, Thieu suddenly withdrew his armies from the three northernmost provinces of South Vietnam. But the planned retreat turned into a disorganized rout when Giap's troops took the opportunity to attack. Unwilling to fight for Thieu's self-serving clique and deprived of American air support, the disspirited ARVN troops raced southward, pillaging their villages as they went. The North Vietnamese and Viet Cong followed, scarcely having to fight, while hundreds of thousands of civilian refugees crowded highways. Only at the gateway to Saigon itself, the provincial capital of Xuan Loc, did the South Vietnamese make a stand, but the communists overwhelmed the city in less than a week. On May 1, the North Vietnamese and Viet Cong entered Saigon while the last American officials were escaping from the United States embassy by helicopter. Lon Nol's regime in Cambodia had already succumbed to communist Khmer Rouge rebels. The communists had won the long Second Indochina War.

Most Americans accepted this not unanticipated result, though several weeks of face-saving maneuvers followed. Military airlifts flew over 100,000 South Vietnamese, mostly those closely identified with the United States, to new homes in America. Some two thousand American families adopted war orphans. Meanwhile, Kissinger and Ford blocked the diplomatic and psychological consequences of the communist victory. Quietly reassuring allies in Western Europe, the secretary of state denied that his country would yield to "neo-isolationists" at home. The administration also successfully countered congressional efforts to reduce the numbers of American soldiers stationed overseas and to pare military spending. To regain an image of diplomatic initiative, Kissinger again gave his attention to Middle Eastern affairs, still hoping that a tilt toward neutrality might scare Israel into compromise and bolster the prestige of moderate leaders in the Arab world. Ford used less subtle tactics. During a press conference he startled reporters with talk that the

United States "did not rule out a first strike with nuclear weapons," apparently a veiled warning to North Korean leaders who were talking of "liberating" South Korea. Then in late May 1975, the new Khmer Rouge regime in Cambodia seized an American merchant vessel, the *Mayaguez*, and imprisoned its crew for allegedly carrying contraband within Cambodia's territorial waters. The bizarre incident puzzled many experts, who attributed the implausible attack to overzealous local commanders rather than to Cambodia's new leaders. But Ford, determined to flex American muscles and recoup his sagging popularity at home, dispatched a naval task force and some two thousand Marines to rescue the thirty-one-man crew. Critics denounced such "gunboat diplomacy," but most Americans supported their president. Clearly, although the communist victory in Vietnam may have marked the limits of United States power, America's worldwide reach would not quickly disappear.

AMERICA AT THE BICENTENNIAL

Though new dawns glowed in American foreign policy—particularly the beginning of detente—old evenings still lingered in domestic life. Watergate had wearied most citizens, increasingly convinced of widespread corruption yet equally certain that the guilty, such as Nixon and Agnew, would escape punishment. Cynicism discredited politicians generally. One prestigious poll showed that over three-fourths of the voters possessed little confidence in either the executive or Congress. Recession and inflation discouraged everyone, including those economists whose formulas for recovery so often misfired. "Stagflation"—economic stagnation accompanied by inflation— threatened the materialist roots of a generation accustomed to an ever-higher standard of living. Shortages provoked fears of greater troubles in the future, especially after the energy crisis did more to immobilize government than to activate it. A prominent political economist, Robert Heilbroner, wrote pessimistically of the human prospect, "No matter what we do, within one hundred years civilization as we know it will cease." Such uncharacteristic pessimism emerged elsewhere in American society. Most cures for the energy crisis, such as strip mining, shocked environmentalists. Racial animosities continued, aggravated by economic doldrums. Affluent suburbs fought to maintain their American dream while some large cities struggled to maintain even the appearance of stability; by mid-1975, New York City faced the real possibility of total financial collapse. More and more, affairs seemed beyond human control.

Yet, as the nation approached its bicentennial, not everything about American life seemed mired in confusion or resignation. Congressional investigations exposed CIA plots to assassinate foreign leaders like Fidel Castro and to overthrow legal but anti-American governments such as Salvador Allende's Marxist experiment in Chile. Though cynics dismissed such probes as whitewashes, others believed that arrogant bureaucrats would not so readily abuse their powers in the future and credited the system with an ability to reform itself. Space technology soared on as America's Apollo spacecraft linked with its Russian counterpart, the Soyuz, during the summer of 1975. A handshake between astronaut and cosmonaut symbolized the two superpowers' aspirations for adventure and for peace. The future, as always, was what people would make of it.

BIBLIOGRAPHY

The most readily available Watergate documents are in *The Senate Watergate Report* (2 vols., 1974); for complete documentation consult the multi-volume hearings of the House Committee on the Judiciary. Theodore White has published an early account of Nixon's downfall, *Breach of Faith* (1975), and Jimmy Breslin has penned a brief yet still informative study, *How the Good Guys Finally Won* (1975). Many participants in the "White House horrors" have been preparing their memoirs and accounts. Jeb Stuart Magruder, *An American Life* (1974), was the first to appear. From another vantage point, Carl Bernstein and Robert Woodward reveal how they helped unravel the mysteries of Watergate in *All the President's Men* (1974).

A former Nixon aide, William Safire, has published a lengthy account of the pre-Watergate years, *Before the Fall* (1975). An earlier, more critical version appears in Rowland Evans and Robert Novak, *Nixon in the White House* (1971). And John Osborne, political columnist for the *New Republic*, has published a series of volumes entitled *The Nixon Watch* (1970–73). Though written long before Watergate, Garry Wills, *Nixon Agonistes* (1970), remains an enlightening study. Bruce Mazlich's psychological profile, *In Search of Nixon* (1972), is less satisfying.

On the 1972 election consult Theodore White's far-too-uncritical chronicle, *The Making of a President, 1972,* and Joseph M. Ray, ed., *The Coattailless Landslide* (1974). Press coverage of the 1972 campaign is dissected in Timothy Crouse, *The Boys on the Bus* (1973), and American Institute for Political Communication, *The Presidential Campaign of 1972* (1974). Alan Gartner et al., eds., *What Nixon is Doing to Us* (1973), contains a series of critical essays. Jules Whitcover and Richard M. Cohen, *A Heartbeat Away* (1974), details the last days of Spiro Agnew.

The best survey of the changes Nixon and Henry Kissinger brought to the conduct of American foreign policy is Henry Brandon, *The Retreat of American Power* (1973), a thoughtful book which incorporates the slow ending of the war in Vietnam and Nixon's overtures toward the communist bloc into a coherent explanation that dominance was no longer possible. See also Robert E. Osgood et al., *Retreat from Empire? The First Nixon Administration* (1973), for nine thoughtful essays covering the geographical spectrum of American interests. Though too often self-righteous in tone, see the leftist critique of Nixon's policy toward China and the Soviet Union in the essays edited by Lloyd C. Gardner, *The Great Nixon Turnaround* (1973). Frank Van der Linden, *Nixon's Quest for Peace* (1972), prematurely heralds a new era of friendship. The best books on Henry Kissinger are Stephen R. Graubard, *Kissinger: Portrait of a Mind* (1973); and David Landau, *Kissinger: The Uses of Power* (1972), both concerned more with the intellectual basis of his diplomacy than with traditional biography.

Index